Global Social Policy & Governance

Global Social Policy & Governance

Bob Deacon

SAGE Publications
Los Angeles • London • New Delhi • Singapore

First published 2007

SAGE Publications Ltd
1 Oliver's Yard
55 City Road
London EC1Y 1SP

SAGE Publications Inc.
2455 Teller Road
Thousand Oaks, California 91320

SAGE Publications India Pvt Ltd
B 1/1 Mohan Cooperative Industrial Area
Mathura Road, New Delhi 110 044
India

SAGE Publications Asia-Pacific Pte Ltd
33 Pekin Street #02-01
Far East Square
Singapore 048763

British Library Cataloguing in Publication data

A catalogue record for this book is available
from the British Library

ISBN 978-1-4129-0761-3
ISBN 978-1-4129-0762-0 (pbk)

Library of Congress Control Number: 2006931639

Typeset by C&M Digitals (P) Ltd., Chennai, India
Printed on paper from sustainable resources
Printed and bound in Great Britain by The Cromwell Press Ltd, Trowbridge, Wiltshire

For
Vappu Taipale
for having the vision to support global social policy analysis

Contents

Figures and Tables

Figure

Tables

Acknowledgements

In addition to thanking the many international civil servants I have conversed with and my Finnish GASPP colleagues (Meri Koivusalo, Eeva Ollila, Minna Ilva), I want to express a special thanks to the following for their continued belief in the value of what I have been writing and for the many ideas stolen over glasses of wine and pints of beer: Gerry Lavery, Santosh Mehrotra, Guy Standing, Paul Stubbs, Timo Voipio and Nicola Yeates. For emotional and nurturing support I want to thank my wife Lynda, the six (I hasten to add grown-up) children we have between us, and my father-in-law and dog-carer Reg, who refreshingly doesn't agree with much that I have to say! Thanks to my students at Sheffield upon whom I have tried out half-baked ideas. Thanks also to Alexandra, one of my PhD students, for reading every word and commenting. And thanks go to two anonymous referees for helpful suggestions, and to Zoë Elliott and Anna Luker at SAGE for being patient.

Holly House
Skipwith
20 July 2006

Table 1.2 is from Gough, I. and Woods, G. (eds) (2004) *Insecurity and Welfare Regimes in Asia, Africa and Latin America*. Cambridge: Cambridge University Press.

Table 5.1 is from Stubbs, P. (2003) 'International Non-State Actors and Social Development Policy', *Global Social Policy*, 3(3): 319–48.

Table 6.1 is from Oxfam (2005) 'Gleneagles: What Really Happened at the G8 Summit'. Briefing Notes.

Table 6.2 is adapted from Atkinson, A. (ed.) (2005) *New Sources of Development Finance*. Oxford: Oxford University Press. By permission of Oxford University Press.

The Structure of the Book

Chapter 1 defines both social policy and globalisation and considers the ramifications of globalisation on the making and study of social policy at national and global level. **Chapter 2** reviews the social policies of the World Bank. **Chapter 3** does the same for the IMF, the WTO and the OECD. **Chapter 4** does the same for the UN including its social agencies, the ILO, WHO, UNESCO, UNDP, UNDESA, and UNICEF. **Chapter 5** examines the social policies being argued for by international non-state actors including global think tanks, knowledge network, global business and global civil society. **Chapter 6** turns specifically to global social policy understood as supranational social policy. Emerging mechanisms of global redistribution, global social regulation and global social rights articulation are reviewed. **Chapter 7** examines the effectiveness and legitimacy of the global social governance institutions and process responsible for evolving and implementing global social policies. Several global social governance reform propositions are examined in detail. Finally, **Chapter 8** considers the implications of all that has gone before for the analysis of social policy in a global context and for the political strategies required for ensuring greater social justice within and between states.

There is a close link between the structure of this book and the structure of the 'Global Social Policy Digest' that is published every four months in the journal *Global Social Policy*. A pre-publication draft version of this Digest appears at www.gaspp.org from which live links to web-based sources used are available. I can't stress enough the importance of following up most chapters by reading the later policy developments monitored in the Digest, which I also edit. Indeed, at the time of writing (Summer 2006), exciting developments are taking place, none of which will have come to fruition by the time I send this to the publishers. Among these are the High Level Panel sitting to propose reforms to streamline the UN, the drafting by UNDESA of a set of social policy guidance notes for countries, and the imminent collapse of the Doha WTO round which would be celebrated by many in the Global South. The linkages are:

Chapter 2, 3, 4, 5: Digest section 'International actors and social policy'
Chapter 3 WTO section: Digest section 'Trade and social policy'
Chapter 6: Digest section 'Global social policies: redistribution, regulation and rights'
Chapter 7: Digest section 'Global social governance'

Web addresses at the end of each chapter were correct at the time of publication. Any updates will be made when the book is reprinted.

Abbreviations and Acronyms

ADB	Asian Development Bank
AIDC	Alternative Information and Development Centre
AIDS	Aquired Immune Deficiency Syndrome
APEC	Asian Pacific Economic Cooperation
ASEAN	Association of South East Asian Nations
ASEM	Asia Europe Meetings
AU	African Union
BIAC	Business and Industry Advisory Council (OECD)
CAN	Community of Andean Nations
CCMs	Country Coordinating Mechanisms
CDF	Comprehensive Development Framework
CEDAW	Committee on the Elimination of Discrimination against Women
CERD	Committee on the Elimination of all Forms of Racial Discrimination
CERI	Centre for Educational Research and Innovation
CESCR	Committee on Economic Social and Cultural Rights
CLASCO	Latin American Council of Social Services
CODESRIA	West African Council of Social Sciences
CRC	Convention on the Rights of the Child
CROP	Comparative Research Programme on Poverty
CSD	Commission for Social Development
CSI	Coalition of Service Industries (in USA)
CSR	Corporate Social Responsibility
CUT	Central Trade Union Federation (of Brazil)
DAWN	Development Alternatives with Women for a New Era
DFID	Department for International Development
ECLAC	Economic Commission for Latin America and Caribbean
ECOSOC	United Nations Economic and Social Council
EDRC	Economic Development Review Committee
EFA	Education For All
EFA-FTI	EFA Fast Track Initiative
ESCAP	Economic and Social Commission for Asia and the Pacific
ESSD	Environmentally and Socially Sustainable Development
ETI	Ethical Trading Initiative
EU	European Union
FDI	Foreign Direct Investment

FPSI	Finance, Private Sector and Infrastructure
FTAA	Free Trade Area of the Americas
FTO	Fair Trade Organisation
G7/G8	Group of seven/eight industrial nations (Canada, France, Italy Germany, Japan, UK and USA, G8 is G7 plus Russia)
G20(N)	Group of twenty developed nations
G20(S)	Group of twenty developing countries
G77	Group of 'seventy seven' developing countries
GAPS	General Agreement on Public Services
GASPP	Globalism and Social Policy Programme
GATS	General Agreement on Trade in Services
GATT	General Agreement on Tariffs and Trade
GAVI	Global Alliance for Vaccination and Immunisation
GCC	Global Corporate Citizenship
GDP	Gross Domestic Product
GDN	Global Development Networks
GINS	Global Issues Networks
GCIM	Global Commission on International Migration
GNI	Gross National Income
GNP	Gross National Product
GPPN	Global Public Policy Networks
GSM	Global Social Movements
HD	Human Development Network
HDI	Human Development Index
HDR	Human Development Report
HIPC	Heavily Indebted Poor Countries
HRC	Human Rights Committee (now Council)
IADB	Inter American Development Bank
IBASE	Brazilian Institute of Social and Economic Analysis
IBRD	International Bank for Reconstruction and Development
ICC	International Chamber of Commerce
ICCs	International Consulting Companies
ICCPR	International Covenant on Civil and political Rights
ICEDAW	International Convention on the Elimination of all forms of Discrimination Against Women
ICERD	International Convention on the Elimination of all forms of Racial Discrimination
ICESCR	International Covenant on Economic Social and Cultural Rights
ICFTU	International Confederation of Free Trade Unions
ICU	International Clearing Union
IDA	International Development Association
IDB	Inter-American Development Bank
IDPF	International Drug Purchasing Facility
IFC	International Finance Corporation
IFF	International Finance Facility
IFFIm	International Finance Facility for Immunisation
ILO	International Labour Organisation

ILOSES	ILO's Social and Economic Security Programme
IMF	International Monetary Fund
IMO	International Organisation on Migration
INGO	International Non-Governmental Organisation
ISO	International Standards Organisation
KNETs	Knowledge Networks
MDGs	Millennium Development Goals
MEI	Multilateral Economic Institutions
MERCOSUR	Mercado Comun del Cono Sur (Common Market of the Southern Cone)
MOST	Management of Social Transformation Programme (of UNESCO)
NGO	Non-Governmental Organisation
NHRIs	National Human Rights Institutions
NHS	National Health Service
OCS	Operational Core Services
ODA	Official Development Assistance
ODC	Overseas Development Co-operation
OECD	Organisation for Economic Co-operation and Development
OECD:DAC	OECD's Development Assistance Committee
OHCHR	Office of the High Commissioner for Human Rights
OMC	Open Method of Coordination
PAYG	Pay-As-You-Go
PHARE	Poland and Hungary Aid in Reconstructing the Economy
PPPs	Public Private Partnerships
PREM	Poverty Reduction and Economic Management
PRGF	Poverty Reduction and Growth Facility
PRSP	Poverty Reduction Strategy Papers
PSI	Poverty Strategies Initiative
SA8000	Social Accountability 8000
SAARC	South Asia Association for Regional Cooperation
SADC	Southern African Development Cooperation
SAI	Social Accountability International
SAPRIN	Structural Adjustment Participatory Review Initiative
SARN	South Asian Research Network
SARS	Severe Acute Respiratory Syndrome
SDD	Social Development Department (of the World Bank)
SDRs	Special Drawing Rights
SPS	Agreement on the application of sanitary and phytosanitary measures of the GATT
SPS	Social Protection Section (of World Bank)
SPSP	Social Protection Strategy Paper
SRM	Social Risk Management
TBT	Technical Barriers to Trade
TFESSD	Trust Fund for Environmentally and Socially Sustainable Development
TNC	Transnational Corporation
TNI	Transnational Institute
TRIPS	Trade Related Intellectual Property Rights

TUAC	Trade Union Advisory Committee (to OECD)
TWN	Third World Network
UDHR	Universal Declaration of Human Rights
UKDFID	United Kingdom's Department for International Development
UN	United Nations
UNCED	United Nations Conference on Environment and Development
UNCTAD	United Nations Conference on Trade and Development
UNDESA	United Nations Department of Economic and Social Affairs
UNDP	United Nations Development Programme
UNDPTCDC	UNDP's Programme for Technical Co-operation between Developing Countries
UNEP	United Nations Environment Programme
UNESCO	United Nations Education, Scientific and Cultural Organisation
UNHCR	United Nations High Commission for Refugees
UNHDR	United Nations Human Development Report
UNICEF	United Nations Children's Fund
UNIDO	United Nations International Development Office
UNRISD	United Nations Research Institute for Social Development
UNUCRIS	United Nations University Centre for Regional Integration Studies
USAID	United States Agency for International Development
WDR	World Development Report
WEF	World Economic Forum
WFTU	World Federation of Trade Unions
WHA	World Health Assembly
WHO	World Health Organization
WSF	World Social Forum
WTO	World Trade Organisation

Introduction

This book is about global social policy. Global social policy consists of two things: first, it is the social policy prescriptions for national social policy being articulated by global actors such as international organisations; second, it is the emerging supranational social policies and mechanisms of global redistribution, global social regulation and global social rights. This book is also about the global social governance of these two elements of global social policy.

It is a **textbook** for students of social policy, social development, international relations and globalisation among others. It reviews in one volume the extent to which international actors of many kinds are now involved in the formulation of social policies for countries, and in the creation of an embryonic system of supranational social policy and governance both at regional and global level. It is also an **argument** for an alternative to neo-liberal globalisation, for a reformed globalisation that is capable of addressing the social dimension of globalisation. It is an argument for a more systematic approach to global **redistribution**, global social **regulation** and global social **rights**. But it is, I hope, no simple restatement of the 'European' case for global social reformism against the 'USA'-supported neo-liberal case for global market freedom. The book tries to come to terms also with the voice of the Global South in the current debates about whether to and how to reform the institutions of global social governance. One result of this is its defence of the idea of supranational regional social policy. The book is also a report of a **research** programme. Since 1997 I have had the good fortune to direct the Globalism and Social Policy Programme (GASPP) that has been funded mostly by the Finns to do two things: review evidence about the impact of globalisation upon national social policy and welfare states, and to begin to articulate an alternative to neo-liberal globalisation. Seven international GASPP seminars were organised between 1997 and 2004 that helped develop the thinking of the GASPP team. Within the GASPP programme a series of sub-projects have been undertaken by myself and colleagues focusing upon the role of INGOs in international social policy, the emergence of public–private partnerships in international health policy, the external policy of the European Union, the role of consulting companies in international policy diffusion, the innovations taking place in global social governance, the impact of trade measures on social policy, the social dimension of regionalism and more besides. It is the collective research effort that informs aspects of this book. The book is also a reflection upon what I have learned about these questions as a result of being a **participant** in about 40 conferences, workshops, seminars and consulting projects during the past ten years, addressing aspects of global social policy and its governance organised by the World Bank, ILO, WHO, UNICEF, UNDP, UNESCO, UNDESA, UNRISD and the EU. Without this engagement with and conversations with international social policy-makers the book could not have been written. In one sense this book is a tribute to all of those hidden from view, international civil servants and intellectuals within and around these organisations who have, in my view, been largely responsible (within the broader political context set by the anti-globalisation movements) for turning the global social policy ideas tide away from the domination in the 1980s and 1990s of targeted poverty alleviation towards the renewed defence of universal access to high-quality public services.

This book is not primarily about how globalisation has impacted on particular countries. It is not about the extent to which some welfare states have survived and some have been changed by global neo-liberal **economic** pressures. There are now many books on this topic, an indication of a few is given at the end of the first chapter. This book is rather about the global **politics** of welfare as articulated at the supranational level. Of course, this global political process impacts down on particular countries and some indications of this is given in the book. Another book would be needed to review the country-specific **operational** activities and impacts on specific countries of the World Bank, the UNDP, the ILO and INGOs.

The International and Global Dimensions of Social Policy

This chapter

- Provides a number of ways of thinking about social policy
- Provides a number of ways of thinking about globalisation
- Reviews five ways in which globalisation influences social policy
- Reviews the ways of thinking about social policy in the light of globalisation's impact
- Offers an explanatory framework for national and global social policy change in the context of globalisation.

This book is about social policy and globalisation and the ways in which the contemporary processes of globalisation impact upon social policy. Social policy is here understood as both a scholarly activity and the actual practice of governments and other agencies that affect the social welfare of populations. An important argument of this book is that neither the scholarly activity of social policy analysis nor the actual practice of social policy-making can avoid taking account of the current globalisation of economic, social and political life. This is true in two quite distinct senses. In terms of the social policies of individual countries, global processes impact upon the content of country policies. Equally important, the globalisation of economic social and political life brings into existence something that is recognisable as supra-national social policy either at the regional level or at the global level. Social policy within one country can no longer be **understood** or **made** without reference to the global context within which the country finds itself. Many social problems that social policies are called upon to address have global dimensions, such that they now require **supranational policy responses**. One of the arguments of the book is that since about 1980 we have witnessed the **globalisation of social policy** and the **socialisation of global politics**. By the last phrase is meant the idea that agendas of the G8 are increasingly filled with global poverty or health issues.

Social policy

Social policy as a field of study and analysis is often regarded as the poor relation of other social sciences such as economics, sociology and political science. It is dismissed as a practical subject concerned only with questions of social security benefits or the administration of health care systems. Some of those who profess the subject would insist to the contrary, that by combining the insights of economics, sociology and political science and other social sciences to address **the** question of how the social wellbeing of the world's people's is being met, it occupies a superior position in terms of the usefulness of its analytical frameworks and its normative concerns with issues of social justice and human needs.

Social policy as sector policy

The subject area or field of study of social policy may be defined in a number of ways that compliment each other. At one level it is about policies and practices to do with health services, social security or social protection, education and shelter or housing. While the field of study defined in this sectoral policy way was developed in the context of more advanced welfare states, it is increasingly being applied to developing countries (Hall and Midgley, 2004; Mkandawire, 2005). When applied in such contexts, the focus needs to be modified to bring utilities (water and electricity) into the frame and to embrace the wide range of informal ways in which less developed societies ensure the wellbeing of their populations (Gough and Woods, 2004). It is one of the arguments of this book that whereas social policy used to be regarded as the study of developed welfare states and development studies as the study of emerging welfare states, this separation did damage to both the **understanding** within development studies of how welfare states developed and to the **actual social policies** in the context of development that have too often had merely a pro-poor focus, to the detriment of issues of equity and universalism.

Social policy as redistribution, regulation and rights

Another approach to defining the subject area is to say that social policy within one country may be understood as those mechanisms, policies and procedures used by governments, working with other actors, to alter the distributive and social outcomes of economic activity. **Redistribution** mechanisms alter, usually in a way that makes more equal the distributive outcomes of economic activity. **Regulatory** activity frames and limits the activities of business and other private actors, normally so that they take more account of the social consequences of their activities. The articulation and legislation of **rights** leads to some more or less effective mechanisms to ensure that citizens might access their rights. Social policy within one country is made up, then, of social redistribution, social regulation and the promulgation of social rights. Social policy within the world's most advanced regional co-operation (the EU) also consists of supranational mechanisms of redistribution across borders, regulation across borders and a statement of rights that operates across borders.

Social policy as social issues

Yet another approach to defining the subject area of social policy is to list the kinds of issues social policy analysts address when examining a country's welfare arrangements. In other words, social policy as a subject area is what social policy scholars do. A standard social policy text (Alcock et al., 2003) lists among the concepts of concern to social policy analysts: 'social needs and social problems', 'equality rights and social justice', 'efficiency, equity and choice', 'altruism, reciprocity and obligation' and 'division, difference and exclusion'. These are elaborated below.

- **Social justice:** What is meant by this concept, and how have or might governments and other actors secure it for their populations? Possible trade-offs between economic efficiency and equity appear here. Mechanisms of rationing or targeting are included.
- **Social citizenship:** Whereas other social sciences are concerned with civil and political aspects of citizenship, social policy analysts focus upon the social rights of citizens. What social rights might members of a territorial space reasonably expect their governments to ensure access to?
- **Universality and diversity:** How might social justice and access to social citizenship rights be secured for all in ways that also respect diversity and difference? Issues of multicultural **forms** of service provision arise, as do policies to combat discrimination and ensure equality of opportunity and agency.
- **Autonomy and guarantees:** To what extent do social polices facilitate the autonomous articulation of social needs by individuals and groups and enable them to exercise choice and influence over provision? How can such an approach be reconciled with guaranteed provision from above?
- **Agency of provision:** Should the state, market, organisations of civil society, the family and kin provide for the welfare needs of the population, and in what proportion?
- **Who cares:** Should the activity of caring be a private matter (more often than not done by women for men, children and dependants) or a public matter within which the state plays a role and the issue of the gender division of care becomes a public policy issue? More broadly, social policy analysts are concerned with issues of altruism and obligation. For whom is one responsible?

Social policy as a welfare regime theory

Social policy analysts have, within the context of these approaches to the subject, developed two strands of literature that might usefully be briefly reviewed. One concerns the mapping and evaluation of the diverse ways in which countries do provide for the welfare of their citizens and residents, and the other offers explanations of social policy development and welfare state difference. Most attempts to classify (OECD) welfare states into typologies start with Esping-Andersen's (1990) classic three-fold typology of liberal, corporatist and social democratic regimes. These are distinguished in terms of their organising principles, the funding basis of provision, and the impacts of their policies on inequalities. Liberal welfare states such as the USA emphasise means-tested allocations to the poor and a greater role for the market.

Table 1.1   Welfare regimes in the developed world

Type of welfare state	Organising principle	Decommodification index	Impact upon inequality
Liberal	Market	Low	Low
Corporatist	Workplace	Semi: notional insurance	Reflects inequalities at work
Social Democratic	Citizenship	High: free at point of use	High

Note: See text about productivist welfare states of East Asia

Corporatist welfare states such as Germany and France are based much more on the Bismarckian work-based insurance model with benefits reflecting earned entitlements through length of service. In contrast, social democratic welfare states such as Sweden place the emphasis on state provision for citizens financed out of universal taxation. The differences may be captured as in Table 1.1.

To this must be added the fouth world of 'productivist' welfare described by Holliday (2000). He and others (Goodman et al., 1998; Ramesh and Asher, 2000: Rieger and Leibfried, 2003) argued that low welfare expenditure states in East Asia ensured the meeting of welfare needs through a process of state-lead economic planning and highly regulated private provision such as compulsory savings. Here social rights to be met by the state were not a central part of the social policy discourse, rather a concern to encourage family and firm responsibility.

Other analysts have drawn attention to the degree of woman-friendliness of welfare states and asked if the diverse regimes meet differently the welfare needs of carers. One typology (Siarrof, 1994 in Sainsbury, 1994) distinguishes between:

1   Protestant social democratic welfare states (Sweden) within which the state substitutes for private care and women find employment in the public service so created.
2   Christian democratic welfare states (France) that support women in their caring functions at home but do not make it so easy for women to enter the work force on equal terms with men.
3   Protestant liberal welfare states (the USA) which offer limited support for caring work and some help towards equitable access to employment, but much of this depends on private provision of services in the marketplace.
4   Late female mobilisation welfare states (Greece, Japan) where the issues of access to work and/or support for caring functions have only just entered the policy agenda.

These diverse welfare regimes have also been commented on in terms of their ethnic minority friendliness. Particular attention is focused here on the insider–outsider aspect of the ethnic citizenship basis of the German and Japanese welfare system, compared with the formal equal opportunities policies and multi-lingual education opportunities provided for in some Scandinavian countries. (For an overview of this comparative social policy literature, see Kennet, 2001, Ch. 3.)

Goodin et al. (1999) have provided the definitive evaluation of the three worlds of welfare in a longitudinal study of three exemplar countries: The Netherlands (social democratic), Germany (corporatist) and the USA (liberal). They examined empirically over time the performance of the three countries on several criteria including the level of poverty, the degree of social exclusion, the efficiency of the economy, and the capacity it offered citizens to make life choices. These authors concluded that on **all** criteria social democracy was superior to corporatism, which in turn was superior to liberalism. It is this empirical conclusion combined with people's perception of the success of such regimes that has led to such a heated controversy about the perceived threats to social democracy of the global neo-liberal project.

Social policy and explanations of welfare state development

Early work in social policy to account for welfare state development was not readily able to explain diversity. Neither the 'moralistic' or 'social conscience' approach of Titmuss (1974), nor the 'materialist' or 'logic of industrialisation' approach of Rimlinger (1971) and Wilensky and Lebeaux (1958) were suited to this task. Accounts that **have** offered plausible explanations of diversity among welfare states include the 'pluralist' or 'politics matters' approach of Heidenheimer et al. (1991), the 'Marxist' or 'class struggle' approach of Gough (1979) and the 'power resource' (or 'democratic class struggle') approach of Korpi (1983). From these last two approaches we have learned that social democratic welfare states are associated with a high degree of working-class mobilisation and political representation, and that liberal welfare states are associated with an absence of these factors. The fashioning of cross-class coalitions and solidarities were also an important part of the universal welfare state story. The middle class were brought into (or bought off by) the Scandinavian welfare state settlement by ensuring high-quality universal services that met their needs too. In a rather different way, the conservative regimes of Germany and France met the needs of a middle class through wage-related benefits that to some extent privileged them. These types of explanation were then developed further by Williams (1989, 2001, 2005) to account not only for the class-related dimensions of welfare states but also for the gendered and ethnic-friendly character of welfare states. With the concept of 'discourses of work, family, nation', she argued that particular welfare state settlements were an outcome not only of class but also of gender and ethnic conflicts, degrees of mobilisation around each of these, and the associated discourses around work (who should get it and how should it be rewarded?), family (who cares for whom and with what support?) and nation (who is an insider and who an outsider regarding welfare entitlements?) deployed in these conflicts.

The chapter now turns to a consideration of the globalisation process. Having done that, we shall be able to return to these several ways in which we described the subject area of social policy and ask:

- How does globalisation affect social policy understood as **sector provision of services like health and social protection?**
- How does globalisation alter the way social policy analysts address issues of **redistribution, regulation and rights?**
- How do the **issues of social justice, citizenship rights, universality and diversity, agency of provision and caring responsibilities** alter within a global context?

- Does globalisation encourage developed welfare states and developing countries to adopt and prefer one or other of the **diverse welfare state models** that we reviewed?
- How might globalisation modify the **explanations we offer for social policy development** and what does it do to class, gender and ethnic welfare struggles?

Globalisation

Here are two definitions of globalisation: 'Globalisation may be thought of initially as the widening, deepening and speeding up of world-wide interconnectedness in all aspects of contemporary life' (Held et al., 1999); and 'globalization [involves] tendencies to a world-wide reach, impact, or connectedness of social phenomena or to a world-encompassing awareness among social actors' (Therborn, 2000).

When social scientists talk about globalisation they are talking about a process within which there is a shrinking of time and space. Social phenomena in one part of the world are more closely connected to social phenomena in other parts of the world. This kind of definition that sees cross-border connections as the key to understanding globalisation has to be distinguished from debates for or against globalisation. Usually these debates and conflicts are about particular international polices and practices – typically economic ones which may be associated with the wider process of globalisation but are not a **necessary** feature of it. These disputes are usually about the **form** that globalisation is taking or the **politics** of globalisation, rather than the fact of time and space shrinkage. Indeed, this book engages in a debate about the neo-liberal form that globalisation is taking and the kinds of global and national social policies being argued for by global actors, but it does not dispute that there is a shrinking of time and space and that globalisation is in that sense uncontestable and irreversible.

Most commentators agree that globalisation embraces a number of dimensions including the economic, political, productive, social and cultural. Among the aspects of globalisation which reflect this range of dimensions are:

- increased flows of foreign capital based on currency trading;
- significantly increased foreign direct investment in parts of the world;
- increased world trade with associated policies to reduce barriers to trade;
- increased share of production associated with transnational corporations;
- interconnectedness of production globally due to changes in technology;
- increased movement of people for labour purposes, both legal and illegal;
- the global reach of forms of communication, including television and the Internet; and
- the globalisation or 'MacDonaldisation' of cultural life.

These processes and other associated phenomena have in turn led to the emergence of a global civil society sharing a common political space. However, while economic activity has become more global and we have seen the birth of a global civil society, global political institutions tend to lag behind these developments. They are to a large extent stuck in an earlier historic epoch of inter-governmental agreements. Indeed, the reform of global political institutions and processes to better govern global social policy is an important theme of this book and will be discussed in Chapter 7.

Held and McGrew (2002a) elaborated a typology of political positions held with regard to globalisation:

- neoliberals (who welcome the economics of free-market globalisation);
- liberal internationalists (who still see the world as essentially made up of states collaborating with each other through the UN system);
- institutional reformers (who consider that aspects of globalisation lead to the need to strengthen and reform aspects of international governance);
- global transfomers (who see globalisation as an epoch-changing process and seek a socially responsible globalisation with strengthened global social governance);
- statists/protectionists (who regard globalisation as a threat and seek to protect through trade barriers their country's social development); and
- radicals of two kinds, Marxists and localists (who want to replace international capitalist globalisation with either a post-capitalist world order or to re-nurture local production in a sustainable way).

The political position taken in this book lies somewhat uncomfortably between the institutional reformer and global transformer position, laced with a deal of radicalism of both kinds.

Globalisation's impact upon social policy

The argument to be developed in this book is that this new globalisation impacts upon the subject area and practice of social policy in the following ways:

- **Sets welfare states in competition with each other**: This raised the spectre (Mishra, 1999), but not necessarily the reality (Swank, 2002), of a race to the welfare bottom whereby states reduced their welfare commitments for fear of losing capital investment. It raises the question as to what type of welfare state or social policy best suits international competitiveness without undermining social solidarity (Scharpf and Schimdt, 2000; Sykes et al., 2001). Evidence is now accumulating which suggests that in the Global North equitable approaches to social policy may be sustainable (Swank, 2002; Castles, 2005), whereas they may not, in conditions of neoliberal globalisation, be so easily replicable within the Global South (Chapter 8).
- **Brings new players into the making of social policy**: International organisations (IOs) such as the IMF, World Bank, WTO and UN agencies such as WHO, ILO and so on have become more involved in prescribing country policy. This has generated a global discourse about desirable national social policy. The within-country politics of welfare has taken on a global dimension with a struggle of ideas being waged within and between international organisations as to desirable national social policy. The battle for pension policy in post-communist countries between the World Bank and the ILO is a classic example (Deacon, 1997; Holzmann et al., 2003; see also Chapters 2, 3 and 4).
- **Raises the issues with which social policy is concerned, those of redistribution, regulation and rights, to a supranational level that has both a regional (EU, ASEAN, MERCOSUR, SADC and so on) and global dimension**: The struggle between

liberal and social democratic approaches to economic and social policy takes on a global and regional dimension. New global social movements enter the picture too and contribute from below to a **global politics of welfare** (O'Brein et al., 2000; Yeates, 2001; Scholte Schnabel, 2002; Munck, 2005; Chapter 5). Whether neo-liberal globalisation could and should give way to a social reformist globalisation within which global redistribution, regulatory and rights policies and mechanisms can be developed is addressed in Chapter 6. These changes raise a debate about the need for reformed global social governance mechanisms that is addressed in Chapter 7.

- **Creates a global private market in social provision:** Increased free trade has created the possibility of mainly American and European private health care and hospital providers, education providers, social care agencies and social insurance companies operating on a global scale and benefiting from an international middle-class market in private social provision. The implication of this development for sustaining cross-class solidarities within one country in the context of development is discussed in Chapter 3. Research on this issue will be examined there (Sexton, 2001; Mackintosh and Koivusalo, 2005; Chavez, 2006; Holden, 2006).

- **Encourages a global movement of peoples that challenges territorial-based structures and assumptions of welfare obligation and entitlement:** Recent debate about migration within an expanded EU has lead to restrictions on the welfare entitlements of recent migrants and the emergence of the idea of a two-tier welfare state despite the evidence that European welfare states may need migrant labour (Jordan and Duvell, 2003; Thomas, 2005). Here otherwise socially just social democratic welfare states have been found wanting from the point of view of the new migrant, whereas more liberal welfare states are found to be more receptive to the welfare needs of migrants (albeit within a context of 'lower' liberal welfare state entitlements). The impact of migration upon welfare provision in developing countries is equally profound, both in terms of the loss of skilled welfare state labour (doctors and nurses) and in terms of reliance on foreign remittances. International care chains have emerged within this context (Ehrenreich and Hochschild, 2002; Yeates, 2004). Thus migration challenges territorial borders of solidarities, and it will be argued that on the one hand it presages global solidarities and global citizenship, while on the other hand it reconstitutes solidarities around family, religion and ethnicity. These issues are picked up in Chapter 5, where we discuss them in the context of global social movements.

These are the broad ways in which it is argued that globalisation impacts upon social policy as a subject area and as a practice of governments and allied actors. In terms of the five ways we defined the subject area of social policy earlier, we can therefore suggest the following.

In terms of social policy understood as **sectoral policy** (health, education, social protection), two things stand out. One is the role of international organisations (Chapters 2, 3 and 4) in influencing national social policy through loans or conditional aid or technical assistance. We shall see that at present the world has in effect two global ministries of health, two global ministries of education and two global ministries of social protection. During the period of the creation and influence of the UN agencies in the 1950s and 1960s and into the 1970s, it was clear that global advice on sector policy came from the WHO, the UNESCO and ILO. Once the World Bank, in the 1980s and 1990s, included social sector issues in its lending policy and practice, it began to operate in effect in competition with the UN social agencies. Its policy prescriptions for developing country health, education and social protection policy were often at odds with the advice given by UN agencies. Furthermore, it became better endowed than the UN agencies and had more clout both in financial terms and in terms of the **perceived** quality of its professional staff. The other is the increased scope that the globalisation of markets offers private providers of hospitals, pension funds and aspects of education provision. The welfare mix between government provision and private provision is shifting in favour of the later in the context of globalisation.

In terms of social policy understood as polices and processes of **redistribution, regulation and rights**, a number of things stand out. The first is that because of the perceived impact of global economic competition on a country's ability to tax in order to spend, the extent to which countries are able to redistribute has been brought into question. Similarly, because of a fear of capital flight, a country's ability to impose social regulations on business has been brought into question too. Guaranteeing social rights becomes rather more difficult in this context. If it is true that to some extent capital has escaped national rules by its capacity to move abroad, then the political task becomes one of reinventing those rules at a regional and global level. What becomes necessary if the global economy is to have a social purpose are global taxes and global social regulations geared to the realisation of a set of global social rights (Chapter 6).

In terms of social policy understood as a concern with **issues of social justice, citizenship rights, universality and diversity, agency of provision and caring responsibilities**, a number of assertions can be made here which will be followed up in subsequent chapters. Social justice questions in a global era take on an international dimension. How can a continued concern with addressing issues of social justice within one country (the traditional preoccupation of social policy analyst) be reconciled with a new concern to ensure social justice across borders? This has both philosophical and political dimensions. The Rawlsian conception of justice often used in social policy literature applies to within-border issues of justice in a capitalist society. Here a degree of inequity is justified so long as the resulting impact upon economic growth raises the level of income of the poorest. Attempts have been made to reformulate this principle between states (O'Neill, 1991; Pogge, 2002). A hugely contested area in globalisation studies is whether the existing form of neoliberal globalisation, while permitting inequity within and between countries, actually does raise the standard of living of the world's poor (Dollar and Kray, 2001; Milanovic, 2003). In political terms, the question becomes one of whether an alliance between the poor of the Global South can be forged with the better-off poor of the Global North that improves the lot of the former without unacceptably undermining the lot of the later. This becomes expressed concretely in the conflicts around global labour standards and other policy questions (Chapters 3, 4 and 5).

Thinking about the concept of **citizenship rights** in a globalising world only serves to highlight the double-sidedness of the concept. On the one hand citizenship within the context of democratic developed capitalist societies is about securing rights and entitlements for all within a defined territorial space. On the other hand it is about excluding from the benefits of citizenship those outside this entity. In the last years of the last century we have seen a simultaneous deepening and strengthening of citizenship rights and entitlements within some countries and a tightening of restrictions

Table 1.2 **The global welfare mix**

	Domestic	**Supranational**
State	Domestic government	International organisations
Market	Domestic market	Global market, TNCs
Community	Domestic NGOs	International NGOs
Household	Households	International household strategies

Source: Gough and Woods, (2004: 30).

on migrants seeking access to those very same citizenship rights. Overlaying this development has been the emergence of supranational citizenship rights within the most advance world region, Europe, and at the same time within Europe a strengthening of polices of exclusion towards the outsiders. These developments serve to call into question a conception of citizenship based upon territory. Conceptualisations of dual citizenship rights for migrant workers and even global citizenship entitlements for all enter the discourse of social policy analysis and even the practice of international governance. These issues are explored fully in Chapter 6.

Within one country the question of **universalism and diversity** for social policy analysts and social policy-makers is often posed as how to facilitate the universal meeting of human needs in ways that respect cultural diversity. In so far as globalisation has increased the pressures for and practices of cross-border migration, this only serves to make this policy question more urgent within any one country. Questions of belonging and identity arise. Calls on the part of host countries for a more assertive commitment to their country of adoption by new migrants vie with the increased possibilities for retaining an identity of origin in a world of easy communication. At the same time, as we shall see in Chapters 5 and 8, similar debates and policy choices arise at a global level. The UN did declare a set of universal human rights and evolved a convention of economic, social and cultural rights. However, these rights have been questioned by countries influenced by fundamentalist religious values. Is it possible to sustain a universal set of rights, including social rights that have purchase world-wide, in a global order where it is perceived by some in the Global South that such 'universal rights' are promulgated by very self-interested and hypocritical northern governments?

Which **agency** should provide for the welfare needs of a population (state, market, civil society organisation, family) takes on an extra dimension of complexity in an interconnected world, particularly in those countries now attempting to develop their welfare states in the context of a global economy. Gough and Woods (2004) capture this particularly well in their exposition (summarised in the Table 1.2) of the ways in which all of these possible agencies now take on an international dimension. Not only might national governments be a welfare provider, but so might international organisations. Not only might national private companies provide private schools, but so might global education providers. Not only might local NGOs contribute to the welfare mix, but so might international NGOs such as Oxfam. Not only might care be provided by a close relative, but so might substitute care be made possible by the remittances sent back to families from abroad.

This links to the final set of issues with which social policy scholars and makers are concerned, that of **caring obligations and responsibilities**. Social policy analysts have demonstrated the gender and racial divisions of caring (Williams, 1989; Sainsbury, 1996; Daly and Rake, 2003). Women care for men and children. Black people serve whites. In general, women do more of the care for men and dependents when this care is provided in the home. Even in those countries where some aspects of care are institutionalised, women occupy the majority of the caring roles. Class and ethnic differences become important in these cases, though. Black and minority migrant workers undertake a greater share of the lower-skilled caring jobs in public institutions. It is one of the arguments of this book that globalisation widens in quite complex ways the gender, class and ethnic divisions of care while it at the same time may have facilitated a release from family-based caring responsibilities for some women both in the richest countries and the poorest. In the USA, for example, white middle-class women and men have their caring duties undertaken by black or Hispanic migrant workers. But at the same time, the World Bank has accepted the idea that investing in the education of women is a good way of speeding the demographic transition to smaller families and hence a reduced burden of care. However, economic globalisation has at the same time pulled women into sweatshops and into the international sex trade.

In terms of social policy's identification of a number of **diverse worlds of welfare**, globalisation poses the question as to whether it is likely to impel countries towards any one of these models. Sykes et al. (2001) noted that while some scholars (Mishra, 1999) had argued that neoliberal globalisation would drive countries to adopt liberal or residual social polices, others suggested that developed countries were immune from such global economic pressures. Sykes concluded that for Europe, global economic pressures did have some impact on a country's social policy, but the nature of this impact was dependent upon the type of institutional welfare state already in existence. Liberal welfare states became more liberal. Social democratic welfares states were, given the political will, largely sustainable. Conservative corporatist welfare states were most challenged but also most resistant to change. I (Deacon, 1997, 2000a) have argued that, focusing on East European post-communist societies, the **politics** of globalisation rather than the **economics** of globalisation have shaped country thinking about social policy, especially as these countries are open to the influence of the World Bank and other international actors. Kwon (2001) has demonstrated that in at least one East Asian productivist welfare state the impact of globalisation has been to compel it in the direction of more universal state provision. Taylor (2000) has also shown how some middle-income countries have increased public welfare spending in the context of globalisation. However, it remains true that certainly for most middle- and lower-income countries the period of the Washington Consensus saw the destruction of the embryonic state welfare services of much of Latin America, Africa and South Asia in favour of targeted and residual policies.

The final question that we suggested should be addressed was how might globalisation modify the **explanations we offer for social policy development** and what it does to class, gender and ethnic welfare struggles? The answers to this question are deferred until we consider a prior question addressed below.

Studying and understanding social policy in a global context

Social policy as scholarly activity has drawn on political economy, the sociology of class, gender and ethnicity, and institutional political science to develop fairly robust theories for explaining welfare state development and welfare state diversity. Do these theories need to be modified to account for (a) national social policy change in the context of globalisation, and (b) can these theories can be adapted to offer plausible accounts of the emergence and character of a supranational or global social policy? We need to take an excursion into other fields of scholarly endeavour to determine which is of use to us.

The account used in this book to offer explanations of the ways national social policy changes in the context of globalisation and the way in which a supranational global social policy has emerged draws upon insights from development studies, international relations and international organisation theory, policy transfer and diffusion literature, global social movement studies, concepts of hegemonic struggle as well as some new work around the ethnography of global policy. Within this complex intellectual framework certain conceptualisations will emerge as being of particular use. Among these are the concepts of **welfare regime theory** (as distinct from welfare state regime theory) (Gough and Woods, 2004), **complex multi-lateralism** (O'Brien et al., 2000), global **policy advocacy coalitions** (Orenstein, 2004, 2005) **global knowledge networks** (Stone and Maxwell, 2005) and the **politics of scale** (Clarke, 2004b, 2005; Gould, 2005; Stubbs, 2005).

Development studies literature has not until recently used the language of social policy (Hall and Midgely, 2004; Dani, 2005). It has been concerned either with the broader concept of development that includes and necessarily privileges the economic underpinnings of development or, especially in an African context, with overseas aid policy and interventions in particular sectors like poverty alleviation, reproductive health care and basic education. Gough and Woods (2004: 32) have, however, provided an admirable basis upon which to sustain a dialogue between the concerns of social policy analysts and those of the development studies specialist. They argue and demonstrate that the **welfare regime theory** of Esping-Andersen (1990) and those who followed him should be renamed 'welfare-state regime theory', applying as it does at best to developed OECD countries. The countries of the world as a whole fall, according to Gough and Woods (2004), into three meta-welfare regimes. These are the welfare state regimes of the OECD world, informal security regimes within which peasant economies co-exist with peripheral capitalism and within which there is a less distinct policy mode, and insecurity regimes within which predatory capitalism operates in the context of more or less collapsed states.

Crucial from the point of view of an argument in this book is the way in which the social policy regimes of some particular countries are described in the Gough and Woods (2004) volume as hybrid-sharing characteristics of welfare state regimes and informal security regimes. Thus Barrientos (2004) suggests that Latin America as a whole might have been best characterised before the neoliberal reforms of the 1990s as **conservative-informal** regimes because the small formal sectors of the economy operated with work-based, wage-related welfare entitlements imported from Europe. After the reforms, many countries gave way to market-based private provision with a residual safety net for the poor. This regime is then characterised as a **liberal-informal** regime. It will be argued in the next chapter that the World Bank and other global actors were able to push for these reforms and undermine the partial conservative welfare states of much of Latin America. They could do this because, whereas in the context of Europe a conservative welfare state represented a form of more or less universal welfare state entitlement serving the cause of equity and social justice, in the context of Latin America, where only a small sector of the economy and population were served by this kind of social policy, it served precisely the opposite ends, privileging some and excluding the majority. A similar account could be given of the 'premature' or 'partial' state welfare policies of much of post-colonial Africa and South Asia. Here new elites attempted to conserve and develop, often in impoverished circumstances, the urban hospital and the urban university as well as the civil service pension fund bequeathed by colonialists. To attack these 'bastions of privilege' in the name of the rural poor was an easy populist thing for the World Bank and other external actors to do. As we shall see, the problem was that in the name of criticising these enclave welfare regimes, the very idea of universal state welfare provision was rubbished and lost for two decades in development studies discourse and practice.

Political scientists writing about international relations in the context of globalisation are divided in their analysis between the two extremes of realists and cosmopolitan democrats. For realists still live in a world of sovereign states; they use the principal–agent theory to show how international organisation policies are nothing but the products of inter-state bargaining. For cosmopolitan democrats, the management of the world is transforming in the direction of a system of global governance, with an emerging system of global regulations that are influenced by other global process and actors (Held et al., 1999). Between the extremes of the state-centric realists and the cosmopolitan dreamers, most international relations theorists give much attention to the ways in which a large number of non-state and often private actors have entered the space we shall call the **contested terrain of emerging global governance**. Josselin and Wallace (2001) include transnational corporations, global knowledge elites or networks, organised criminal syndicates, the Catholic Church and global Islamic movements, international trade unions and private armies in their review. To these should be added International Non-Governmental Organisations (INGOs). It is not just that these actors enter the global political space and argue, but they also take on in a private capacity international regulatory activity not yet undertaken by the underdeveloped system of formal global governance. Thus firms evolve private international regimes of self-regulation in many spheres (Hall and Biersteker, 2002). Global or at least transnational social movements from below have become a major force in the global politics of globalisation (Porta et al., 1999; Kaldor, 2003; Scholte, 2005). Issues like world poverty, global taxation, international labour standards, and access to pharmaceuticals in poorer countries can no longer be discussed at meetings of the G8 or the WTO without there being a major presence on the streets of international campaigning groups on all of these issues. The World Social Forum (WSF) attempts to provide a global organising space for these activities to match the organising space provided to international business by the World Economic Forum (WEF).

One study that focused upon the ways in which global social movements interacted with and influenced the policies of multilateral economic institutions (O'Brein et al., 2000) is particularly instructive. Its examination of the relations between the World Bank and the women's movement, the WTO and labour, the World Bank, WTO and the environmental social movement drew important conclusions:

> Our study has stressed the link between forms of international institution and social movements in which the state is just one area of contact and struggle (albeit an important one). The MEI–GSM relationship can be direct and need not be mediated by the state. Social forces with and across state borders are a factor in determining the nature of international order and organisation. (P. 234)

These authors coin the term 'complex multi-lateralism' to capture this reality within which the realist's concern with state–state interaction sits side by side with a new set of trans-national power dynamics within which international organisations and the social movements they are confronted by have a degree of policy autonomy at a global level. It is this framework that we will find particularly useful in explaining some aspects of the ways international organisations influence state social policy, but also GSMs influence international organisation social policy.

This conclusion that there might be a terrain of contestation about global social policy and that not only states but also international organisations and GSMs are actors in it will be returned to time and time again. For now it is useful to note how this view leads us to challenge an otherwise important recent contribution to the literature at the interface of development studies and international relations. Boas and McNeill's study of the policies of several international organisations including the World Bank, the WTO and the OECD, concludes rather pessimistically that:

> Powerful states (notably the USA), powerful organisations (such as the IMF) and even powerful disciplines (economics) exercise their power largely by 'framing': which serves to limit the power of potentially radical ideas to achieve change. (2004: 1)

While there is truth in this, it will be suggested in the course of this text that a more nuanced and more accurate conclusion might be that powerful states (notably the USA), powerful organisations (such as the IMF) and even powerful disciplines (economics) contend with other powerful states (notably the EU, China, Brazil), other powerful organisations (such as the ILO) and other disciplines (such as social and political science) to engage in a war of position regarding the content of global policy. This alternative conclusion echoes John Clarke's recent attempt to capture the sense in which we live in and against a neoliberal global order:

> … the work of constructing a neo-liberal hegemony is intensive, deploys different strategies, and encounters blockages and refusals. It has to engage other political-cultural projects – attempting to subordinate, accommodate, incorporate or displace them. To obscure such intense political-cultural work confirms the neo-liberal illusion of inevitability. If, on the contrary, we draw attention to the grinding and uneven struggle to make the world conform – and recognize the limitations and failures of this project – questions of conflict, contestation, and the 'unfinished' become rather more significant. Living in a neo-liberal world is not necessarily the same as being neo-liberal. Attention to the different sorts of *living with, in and against* neo-liberal domination is a necessary antidote to 'big picture' projections of its universalism. (2004b: 102)

This bridges nicely to the concept of **global policy advocacy coalitions** used by Orenstein (2004, 2005) to analyse the development and world-wide selling of the global pension policy preferred by the World Bank since 1990. The details of this story will be told in the next chapter. What is important here is the identification of private and formal international actors (such as those we listed earlier) and an account of the ways in which global policy is first put on the agenda and then campaigned for. Earlier work on the role of epistemic communities noted that:

> How decision makers define state interests and formulate policies to deal with complex and technical issues can be a function of the manner in which the issues are represented by specialists to whom they turn for advice in the face of uncertainty … epistemic

> communities (networks of knowledge based experts) play a part in ... helping states identify their interests, forming the issues for collective debate, proposing specific polices, and identifying salient points for negotiation. (Haas, 1992: 3)

The same can be said of the ways in which international networks of knowledge-based experts play a part in helping international organisations shape the issues for collective debate. Indeed, since 1992 the world has witnessed a proliferation of kinds of international knowledge-based experts or knowledge networks (KNETS) (Stone and Maxwell, 2005). Whether understood as 'epistemic communities' who share a codified form of 'scientific' knowledege about an issue (such as pensions), or as 'discourse coalitions and communities' who use symbols language and narrative as a source of power, or as 'embedded knowledge networks' who possess authority because of their track record for problem solving, KNETS are now an integral part of the emerging forms of global governance. As Stone, modifying Held, puts it, 'KNETS do not simply "crystallize around different sites and forms of power"(Held, 2000: 19), the network is a site and form of power' (2005: 100). In a globalised world devoid of any effective global democratic processes, these KNETS substitute for other forms of policy making. Stone notes that:

> Global or regional networks are ... not subject to the usual reporting and account-ability requirements of public bodies in liberal democracies. The public – even the well informed and politically literate of OECD countries – are still largely unaware of the roles, reach and influence of global networks ... Combined with the technocratic character of many such networks, the public is excluded and political responsibility is undermined. (2005: 103)

In the case of the global pension policy story told by Orenstein (2005) the agenda setting was very much in the hands of a global knowlege network based upon economists schooled in the Chicago school of neo-liberal economics. This network had a global reach in terms of its links to Milton Friedman, Friedrich von Hayek and others (Valdes, 1995). It then became centred upon work in the World Bank initiated by Larry Summers, the then chief economist, which was eventually published in 1994 as *Averting the Old Age Crisis*. A transnational advocacy coalition was then developed to further the adoption of these reforms. This coalition included the World Bank, USAID, the Inter-American Development Bank (IDB) and other actors (Orenstein, 2005: 193).

This work in international relations on how global policy becomes shaped by knowledge networks and then argued for by global advocacy coalitions is somewhat different in emphasis from other scholarly work based upon world society theory. Adopting a more sociological approach to the subject, Meyer et al. (1997) argue that global society rests on and reinforces universalistic definitions with which science gains more authority. They argues that many features of the nation state derive from world-wide models constructed and propogated through global cultural and associational processes. The approach within world society theory is to start not from the nation state as a basis for sociological analysis, but rather from an already existing global society that transcends borders. Cross-border professional associations act to spead policy ideas and practices wherever there are members. Education policy and practice, health care procedures and practices become the same everywhere in conformity with professional standards. While clearly this has some explanantory value with regard to how policies in one country become transposed to another country, it lacks a sense of contest and conflict about policy options. It has echoes of functionalist sociology of the Talcott Parsons' theory, whereby every social phenomenon is understood as serving a higher societal function. Conflicts of interest and conflicts of policies are missing. A glance at the policy transfer and policy diffussion literature (Dolowitz and Marsh, 1996) reveals accounts of policy transfers across borders where it is clear that 'choices' are being made by some countries to borrow the policy of another, either because it is being coerced into doing so by powerful global actors or because it is in conformity with its particular ideological goals, or better fits to sets of national cultural assumptions. In other words, national social policy choices reflect globalised policy options and contestations about these.

Finally, in this review of aspects of the literature which might inform our understanding of how global social policy is made and implemented, we turn to the **politics of scale**. This is referring to the idea that it is not adequate to attempt to capture the complexity of policy-making in a globalised world by thinking in terms only of layers of government or governance. An account of policy-making which talked only in terms of the taken-for-granted levels of sub-national, national, regional and global is seen as lacking an important aspect of policy-making in a globalised world. What is important here is that policy-making is not only taking place at different taken-for-granted levels of governance, but that **key policy players are transcending each level at any one moment**. The policy-making process is multi-sited and multi-layered as well as multi-actored, all at one time. Within this context also, individuals as change agents and policy translators can act in the spaces between levels and organisations (Stubbs, 2006). The World Bank is **in** Tanzania. Care international, a mega-INGO, is **in** Tanzania. The consultation process between the Bank and the Tanzanian civil society about social policy involves local NGOs informed by international consultants. To understand something of the complexity of social policy-making **for** Tanzania, one needs to examine actors and activities at the Bank, in the government, in INGOs, in international consulting companies and in donor government international development sections. The 'global' is in the local, and the 'local' in the global captures a little of this politics of scale. Within this context the national policy-making process can become distorted, so that those who are better able to travel between these scales are better able to influence policy. Indeed, Gould has argued that 'transnational private agencies [find] themselves brokering and, to some extent, supplanting local civil society representation in policy consultation' (2005: 142).

This process opens up the possibilities for individuals and individual companies to operate wearing shifting identities. In this sense, the insights provided by Janine Wedel, based on her case study of American aid to Russia in the early 1990s, offers a number of highly pertinent middle-range concepts in order to study these processes. While she prefers the metaphor of aid as a 'transmission belt', her focus is on 'the interface between donors and the recipients' in terms of 'what happens when differing systems interact' (Wedel, 2004: 154–5). She addresses the importance, in these encounters, of multiplex networks (2004: 165), where players know each other, and interact, in a variety of capacities, with multiple identities (which she terms 'trans-identities'), and in a variety of roles. Her tale is one of shifting and multiple agency, promoted in part by what she terms 'flex organisations', which have a 'chameleon-like, multipurpose character', with actors within them 'able to play the boundaries' between national and international; public and private; formal and informal; market and bureaucratic; state and non-state; even legal and illegal (2004: 167).* At the extreme, this leads to the possibility of individuals playing a large role in global policy-making. Jeffrey Sachs, a villain of the piece in the Wedel story of Russian privatisation, becomes reincarnated as the author of the report of the WHO's Commission on Macro-Economics and Health, and subsequently head of the UN task force on the MDGs project (see Chapter 4).

This review of the wider development studies and international relations literature has argued that certain concepts and approaches from them are of value in trying to make sense of global social policy. These include **welfare regime theory, complex multi-lateralism, global policy advocacy coalitions, global knowledge networks and the politics of scale**. The later approach in particular enables us to understand global social policy-making as multi-sited and multi-actored. However, this emphasis on individual actors as change agents and policy advocacy coalitions has led us a long way from the political economy or class-struggle basis of explanations of welfare state development within one country which we examined earlier. In the light of the foregoing, can we find any way of scaling up the explanations we offered earlier of welfare state change within one country using notions of class, gender and ethnic struggles, mobilisations and discourse to account for elements of the making of global social policy?

Returning then to the final question that we left unanswered in the section on globalisation's impact upon social policy, how might globalisation modify the **explanations we offer for social policy development?** Obviously we have to factor in the new international actors and hence the new multi-actored and multi-located policy-making processes that we have already identified. But what of the broad analytical frameworks bequeathed to us by comparative social policy analysis? First, in terms of the moral reform approach to social policy change, a case could be mounted that in so far as there has been a shift within the last decades from a fundamentalist neo-liberalism to something which is concerned to attend to the worst social consequences of economic globalisation, this might be explained in part by a growth in a moral concern for the poor of the developing world. It is certainly true that religious organisations have been at the forefront of global campaigns for debt relief and poverty alleviation. Equally, the logic of industrialisation thesis might be invoked to explain some aspects of social policy shifts in the context of an industrialising developing world. Certainly politics still matter, as reflected in the contest of ideas about welfare between and within international organisations such as the World Bank and the ILO.

However, as we argued in the section on theories of welfare state development, this contest of ideas about global and national social policy needs to be understood in part as a product of material stuggles between social classes and gender and ethnic groups. Class struggles can and do take on cross-border dimensions; the social movements of women have become globalised; within-ethnicity forms of organisation have taken on an international dimension too. It is one of the contentions of this book that the analytical framework provided by Williams (1989) of a racially structured, patriachal capitalism, which was used by Ginsburg (1992, 2004) to understand why the social policies of Germany, Sweden, the USA and the UK were so different, can be adapted to contribute to our understanding both of national social policy within a global context and of emerging global social policy.

---

* I am indebted to Paul Stubbs for this summary; it is to be found in Stubbs (2005).

In terms of national social policy in a global context, it is generally agreed that one consequence of the neo-liberal globalisation project has been to strengthen the power of capital over that of labour. Capital is free to move across borders, labour is more restricted. Constructing cross-border trade union solidarities in defence of national welfare provision is not easy. As a consequence, the share of income going to profits rather than wages has increased (Wade, 2004). This is not to say that there has been a full-blown undermining of national welfare state provision in developed countries as a consequence of trade union weakening. This has happened, but only in some places (for example, Germany) in small measure. In other middle-income countries, in contrast, an increased presence of trade unionism has led to universal welfare gains (for example, South Korea).

Any summary assessment of the impact of globalisation upon the capacity of women to organise within countries to defend their gendered welfare interests must be more nuanced. While women **as workers** may have suffered some of the same effects of globalisation upon their capacity to defend and improve pay and working conditions, organisations of women **as women** have been strengthened by globalisation's easing of transnational networking. As we shall see in Chapter 5, UN conferences such as the Fourth World Conference on Women in Beijing facilitated the growth of a global women's movement that empowered women in many developing countries in particular to confront issues of patriachry and women-unfriendly development policies for the first time. Since then there has been 'much to celebrate' in progress towards gender equality (UNRISD, 2005).

In terms of within-ethnicity forms of organisation, the story is less well documented. There is some suggestion that while neoliberal globalisation is spreading a global western culture, at the same time local and ethnic identities have become more important. Cross-border movements of people may have led in part, paradoxically, to an increased identification with and networking with one's country of origin. Postwar diasporas have become an important factor in the policy-making of some countries. Reaction in some developed welfare states has been to restrict welfare benefit access to new migrants. On the other hand, it has been suggested (Chau, 2004) that globalisation's push towards markets and democracy everywhere has has the effect of stimulating oppressed ethnic majorities to wrest power and resources from hitherto market-dominating ethnic minorities (for example, Indonesians against Chinese). Globalisation has therefore increased the importance of inter-ethnic stuggles in shaping national social policy.

How can the framework of capitalism, patriarchy and a racially structured imperialism with its concomitant global social divisions of class, gender and ethnicity and associated struggles over work, family and nation be applied to the shaping of a supranational global social policy? How are the new global actors that have been identified as playing a role in shaping global social policy influenced by these global conflicts of interest? Who is winning at the global level? Capital or labour? Patriarchy or women? Whites or people of colour? In what ways do global social policies embody these clashes of interest? Figure 1.1 attempts to capture schematically how the analytical framework might be transposed onto the global playing field.

First, in terms of class struggle this has a global dimension. At one level the entire range of international organisations, the policies they formulate and the intellectuals working within and around them might be understood, according to Sklair (2002: 99) or Soederberg (2006), as the fraction of the global capitalist class, the 'globalised

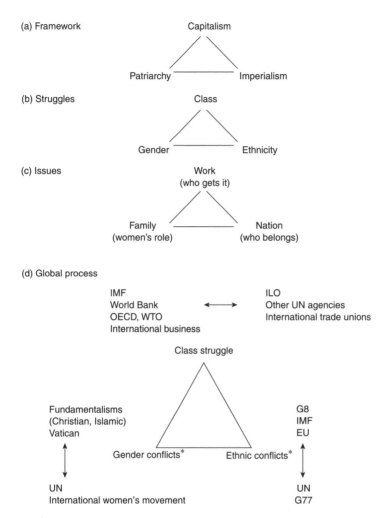

(a) Framework

Capitalism

Patriarchy ——————— Imperialism

(b) Struggles

Class

Gender ——————— Ethnicity

(c) Issues

Work
(who gets it)

Family   Nation
(women's role)   (who belongs)

(d) Global process

IMF   ILO
World Bank   ←——→   Other UN agencies
OECD, WTO   International trade unions
International business

Class struggle

Fundamentalisms   G8
(Christian, Islamic)   IMF
Vatican   EU

Gender conflicts*   Ethnic conflicts*

UN   UN
International women's movement   G77

*These conflicts are reflected in the disputes between UN Human rights
convertions on the one hand and fundamentalist or ethnic/national responses of
some countries and actors, and broadly speaking between the white G8 and the
black South (G77).

Figure 1.1   Global conflicts of interest and global social policy

professional' seeking to legitimate and shore up a globalised *capitalism* to prevent it
becoming a globalised *socialism*. For me, on the other hand, what is important is
whether the 'globalised professionals' are formulating a global neoliberal social
policy or something which we might recognise as a global social-democratic social
policy, so that the global economy serves a global social purpose. In this context, then,
I interpret the contest between the more neoliberal ideas and policies of the World
Bank and the more social democratic policies of the ILO as one reflection of a global
class struggle. As we will see in Chapter 5, global business is well positioned to influence global policy, and global trade unionism rather less so (Farnsworth, 2005).
Moves to bring global business into partnership with the UN through such devices as
the Global Compact (Chapter 4) are variously interpeted as the UN selling out to

global business or as a means of imposing a global social responsibility upon business. Equally important in terms of the impact of globalisation upon the relative balance of class forces at the transnational level, is the ways in which global interconnectedness appears to be detaching the middle class of developing countries from a focus upon the national state-building or developmental project into a searching after their own interests within a global marketplace (Cohen, 2004; Gould, 2005).

In terms of the global gender struggle, we have already referred to the ways in which some parts of the UN system have enabled a global women's movement to organise and influence across borders. The UN declarations of human rights does give space to gender equity and rights issues. The contest here is not so much between the women-friendly policies of many of the UN social agencies and the patriarchial sentiments and policies of the World Bank or WTO, but rather that there is still contestation about these policies within the UN debating and policy-making chambers. A number of governments, notably the USA and some Islamic countries, and also the Vatican (which has state status at the UN), are now questioning some of the previously taken-for-granted assumptions about the desirability of these women-friendly policies. Within the World Bank, however, as Sen (2004, 2006) has shown, the arguments about the positive developmental effects of putting women at the centre of development by, for example, ensuring equal opportunity for girl education and by micro-credit for women, are now accepted as mainstream.

The question of ethnicity and struggles on the part of the largely non-white Global South to undo the huge global inequities left over from the imperial epoch within which the whites were the beneficiaries lies at the heart of the battle for global economic and social policies. Whether and how the global division of labour laid down in the period of empires can be altered, whether and how there can be restitution for past (and indeed continuing) exploitation of the South by the North, whether and how the debts incurred by the South to the North can be written off, whether and how a systematic policy of global transfers of resources from the Global North to the Global South to fund education health and social protection might be made to work, are *the* crunch issues. Here the World Bank and the IMF are clearly owned by and still acting for the Global North. The UN and WTO (which does have a majority membership from the South) are forums for the continuing playing out of these issues. In the past two decades the Global South has found a new voice and strength in these meeting places. Almost every global social policy issue becomes one of heated controversy between the EU block, the USA and the G77 or some alliance of the developing countries such as the new G20(s) led by Brazil, China and South Africa. At issue are such matters as the price of essential drugs and the funding of primary education.

Class, gender and ethnic conflicts cut across each other within one country. So it is in the global arena. Indeed, it will be argued in this book that there is now a major fault line in the global discourse about desirable national and global economic and social policies between, on the one hand, a northern-centred debate between a USA-influenced desire for global neoliberal policies and a European-influenced desire for global social democratic policies, and on the other hand a southern-centred debate about getting out from under *any* northern-imposed agenda for global economic and social policy. The intellectual struggle engaged in by northern social reformists in the global arena is cut across by the intellectual struggle engaged in by southern de-globalisers. Finding a way out of this impasse is one of the key challenges for those of us who are keen to work for a more socially just world with more socially just global social policies. This is the subject of this book, but in particular the issue which will be returned to in the last chapter.

Further Reading

On globalisation: Scholte, J. (2005) *Globalization: A Critical Introduction*. Basingstoke: Palgrave, and Held, D. and McGrew, A. (2002) *Globalization/Anti-Globalization*. Cambridge: Polity.

On globalisation and social policy: Yeates, N. (2001) *Globalization and Social Policy*. London: Sage.

On globalisation and welfare states: Glatzer, M. and Rueschemeyer, D. (2005) *Globalization and the Future of the Welfare State*. Pittsburgh, PA: University of Pittsburgh Press.

On social policy in a development context: Mkandawire, T. (ed.) (2004) *Social Policy in a Development Context*. Basingstoke: Palgrave.

On comparative social policy: Kennet, P. (2004) *A Handbook of Comparative Social Policy*. Cheltenham: Edward Elgar.

Global Social Policy journal.

Related Websites

www.gaspp.org
www.globalwelfare.net

2

The Social Policy of the World Bank

This chapter

- Provides an introduction to and brief overview of the role of international organisations in influencing national social policy
- Describes the World Bank's social policy advice to countries under five headings: poverty alleviation, pension policy, social development policy, and provision of health and education services

Overview of Chapters 2, 3 and 4

International organisations influence national policy through a variety of channels:

- research, agenda setting and the development of knowledge frameworks;
- policy-based lending and project conditionality; and
- establishing global codes, rules and norms.

The purpose of this and the next two chapters is to examine critically the social policy advice given to countries by the World Bank, IMF, OECD,UN, ILO, WHO and other international organisations. Here these organisations are regarded partly as depositories of principles and norms which confer on their secretariats a degree of political autonomy. They are involved in their own right on the international stage. That is not to say that the policies of these organisations are not derived in part from major state interests. Often the hegemonic state plays a dominant role in shaping the policies of international organisations (Boas and McNeill, 2004). At issue, therefore, is whether the social policy advice of the international organisations reflects a more universalistic or social democratic approach, or a more residual and selective liberal approach to social policy. Have we seen a global consensus appearing within and between international organisations that is strongly influencing countries in an era of globalisation towards one or other welfare model, or is the story rather one of contestation and dispute?

The World Bank, IMF and UN agencies have a long history of claiming to help countries at a lower level of economic development to better meet the welfare needs of their populations. This 'advice' by the Bank and IMF has in many cases been linked to what came to be known in the 1980s and early 1990s as *structural adjustment*, whereby the countries were made, as a condition attached to loans, to cut what was regarded as excessive public spending to balance their books and enable the development of their private economies, often through a strategy of export-led growth. This 'advice', which came to be known as the Washington Consensus, ended an earlier period within which some countries had protected their own industries through a strategy of import substitution. In general terms, the dominant international advice by the dominant international agency has therefore favoured a residual or targeted approach to social spending more reminiscent of the USA model than of the European approach. Within the ILO and some other UN agencies, on the other hand, were to be found supporters of the view that social expenditures were a means of securing social cohesion and an important social investment in human capital. The ILO in particular supported a conservative corporatist type of social protection. The OECD favoured the notion that certain state welfare expenditures should be regarded as a necessary investment. No international organisation, save possibly UNICEF, could be said to defend the redistributive approach to social policy characteristic of the Scandinavian countries.

In an earlier study of the role played by such international organisations in shaping post-communist social policy, my colleagues and I concluded that the:

> opportunity created by the collapse of communism for the global actors to shape the future of social policy has been grasped enthusiastically by the dominant liberal tendency in the World Bank. In alliance with social development NGOs who are being given a part to play especially in zones of instability, a social safety net future is being constructed. This NGO support combined with the political support of many southern and some East European governments is challenging powerfully those defenders of universalist and social security based welfare states to be found in the EU, the ILO and in smaller number in the Bank. (Deacon, 1997: 197)

As we shall see in this and the next two chapters, these conclusions still broadly stand, although there continues to be interesting shifts of the position of particular players within this debate. The IMF has taken the social dimension of globalisation more seriously, considering whether some degree of equity is beneficial to economic growth. The World Bank has on the one hand articulated more clearly its risk management approach to social protection in the context of globalisation, but on the other showed leanings towards giving greater support for public sector spending. The OECD now warns that globalisation may lead to the need for more, not less, social expenditure. The ILO has begun to show signs of making concessions to the Bank's views on social security, while at the same time developing important new ideas on 'universalism from below'. More recently the role of the WTO with its views on the desirability of fostering a global market in health and social service provision, is assuming a prominence it did not have.

The World Bank: from targeted poverty alleviation, through pension privatisation and public service effectiveness to empowering people?

A book would be needed to tell the full story of the World Bank's influence on social policy. This is partly because its social policy content and influence have changed over the years, partly because it is a complex organisation in itself, with several sectors tasked with formulating aspects of social policy, and partly because policy formulation sections are separate from the operational side of the Bank. Bank policy may be distorted or even ignored in operations in countries on the ground. At the highest level of organisational division there are three parts of the World Bank Group that are of interest to us: the International Bank for Reconstruction and Development (IBRD), which lends money for projects usually on condition that certain policies are followed, the International Development Association (IDA), which lends at low-interest rates to low-income countries, and the section of the Bank often overlooked by social policy analysts, the International Finance Corporation (IFC), which stimulates private sector development. Those who write about the World Bank usually include the IBRD and IDA in this definition, reserving the term 'World Bank Group' for the full range of organisations.

At a lower level of organisation inside the World Bank (IBRD and IDA), the sectors of interest to us changed significantly in 1996. Before then there existed the three departments: Environment, Education and Social Policy, and Development Economics. Most of the social policy questions were addressed by the Education and Social Policy department, which focused on labour-intensive growth, investment in education and health, and pension reform backed up by a then ill-defined safety net for the poor. However, a small group of 'heretics', known then as the 'thematic social policy group' in the Environment Department, preferred a more anthropological approach to understanding poverty and addressed the social and political frameworks necessary for poverty alleviation.

In 1996 a major reform gave rise to five 'networks' named:

1 Finance, Private Sector and Infrastructure (FPSI);
2 Environmentally and Socially Sustainable Development (ESSD);
3 Poverty Reduction and Economic Management (PREM);
4 Operational Core Services (OCS); and
5 Human Development Network (HD).

PREM continues to be a major focus of Bank work on poverty, especially in poorer countries, and contains within it a number of specialist sections including the Gender Group. Most of the Bank's explicit formulation of social policy is generated from three families within the HD Network. These are:

• Health Nutrition and Population;
• Education; and
• Social Protection.

Each of these families has generated a sector strategy that forms one element of the accounts below of different aspects of Bank social policy. However, there continues to exist in new organisational form the anthropologically orientated 'social policy heretics' of the Social Development Section in ESSD (Davis, 2004). They formulated the 'Social Development Operational Plan: Empowering People by Transforming Institutions' in 2005 (World Bank, 2005d) that is reviewed later. Of considerable importance, at least in terms of the public face of the Bank, are the annual *World Development Reports (WDR)*. These are written after much internal and lately external formal consultation processes. Of particular importance to us are the WDR 1990 on Poverty (World Bank, 1990), the WDR 2000/2001 on Poverty (World Bank 2001a) the WDR 2004 Making Services Work for Poor People (World Bank, 2003c) and ®WDR 2006 on Inequality (World Bank, 2005a). In addition to all of this is the World Bank Institute, which is often the agency used to sell bank policy via workshops involving country Ministerial staff.

Poverty alleviation: from safety nets as an attack on social security to a new focus on equity?

The election of Margaret Thatcher in Britain and Ronald Reagan in the United States marked a trend towards the Right among several major OECD states that was to impact upon social policy thinking within the World Bank. Equally important was the onset of the debt crisis after 1982. The crisis started in Latin America, but was evident in Turkey, the Philippines and many African countries as well. Rising interest rates, the second oil shock, and the slowdown in the global economy in the early 1980s reversed the large flow of private lending that had gone to developing countries in the 1970s.

This scarcity of private capital flows increased the leverage of the IMF and World Bank over developing country policy. A new orthodoxy emerged, dubbed the 'Washington Consensus' after the city where sat the IMF and the World Bank and the US government. This new approach argued that the debt crisis had been the result of the 1950s and 1960s inward-oriented, statist development strategies. The problems of the developing countries were not shortage of capital, but policies that concentrated resources in the public sector, distorted incentives to the private sector and limited trade and foreign investment. A crucial innovation of the debt crisis period was the rapid growth of 'structural adjustment' or 'programme' lending. Such lending was extended not in support of particular projects, but in support of policy reform. These reforms included macroeconomic policy adjustments – fiscal, monetary and exchange rate policy – and a variety of other measures as well, from privatisation to trade liberalisation and financial sector reform. Over the 1980s, the scope of policy conditionality widened dramatically, and encompassed a number of social policy issues. This emphasis on policy conditionality continued well into the 1990s as the World Bank became deeply involved in policy lending to Eastern Europe, the newly independent republics of the former Soviet Union, China and Vietnam.

It was the perceived negative impact of this period of structural adjustment on the prospects for the poor and for the sustainability of social services in developing countries that led to the beginnings of a major intellectual challenge to such structural adjustment lending. This began with the criticism by Cornia et al. (1987) in the

UNICEF report on *Adjustment with a Human Face*. Partly in consequence, the World Bank's report on *Poverty* in 1990 (World Bank, 1990) began the period where the Bank was to declare that its *prime* goal was that of poverty alleviation. In 1991 the policy paper *Assistance Strategies to Reduce Poverty* was published. This was followed in 1992 by the *Poverty Reduction Handbook*. By 1993 the Bank was able to claim in its annual report that the share of adjustment lending that addressed social issues climbed from 5 per cent in fiscal 1984–86 to 50 per cent in fiscal 1990–92. That the Bank became heavily involved in policy-based lending to try to reduce poverty in poor countries, and indeed in post-communist Eastern Europe after 1989, is not in dispute. At issue is the *content* of that anti-poverty policy. The Bank wanted to continue with its preferred approach of limiting public expenditure on what it regarded as at best premature or at worst undesirable public sector social protection systems while supporting the poor. At issue was what to do with the poor who could be helped without jeopardising the economic requirements and constraints of adjustment. Faced with this problem, the World Bank, the IMF and other external donors encouraged governments to protect the poor but urged them to stand firm against the demands of the labour unions and urban popular classes.

In essence, a *social safety net approach* to poverty alleviation was being constructed that had echoes of US residual or liberal social policy. As Carol Graham, who was then a visiting fellow at the Bank in the Vice Presidency for Human Resources, put it on the dust jacket of *Safety Nets, Politics and the Poor* (1994):

> Rather than focus their efforts on organised interest groups – such as public sector unions – which have a great deal to lose in the process of reform, governments might better concentrate their efforts on poor groups that have rarely, if ever, received benefits from the state. The poor, meanwhile, may gain a new stake in the ongoing process of economic and public sector reform through organising to solicit the state for safety net benefits.

Against organised labour, against European corporatist social security structures, and for the very poor; that was the political strategy of the dominant anti-poverty thinking in the Bank. An alliance was to be struck between the Bank and INGOs such as Oxfam who have an interest in being involved in attempts to reach the poorest of the poor. One element of this focus on the poor became the social funds that were championed by the Bank. These were established with donor money as semi-autonomous budgets set up to bypass government social security departments and to address directly the needs of the poor. They were also designed to 'stimulate participatory development initiatives by proving small-scale financing to local NGOs, community groups, small firms and entrepreneurs' (Fumo et al., 2000: 9). Women with entrepreneurial skills have often been beneficiaries of these (Subbarao and Bonnergee, 1997). However, they were subsequently criticised (Fumo et al., 2000: 25; Hall and Midgeley, 2004: 274) on four counts: they often did not reach the poor but instead proactive NGOs; they were not mainstreamed into government anti-poverty policy; they became substitutes for government expenditure so that if a social fund was active in health provision the equivalent government budget line might be cut; and they were not linked to funding sources that were sustainable in the long term.

Although there were some criticisms of this safety-net paradigm, the focus of much INGO and scholarly criticism was to become the *process* of policy conditionality as such rather than, in this case, the safety-net policy *content*. However, in 1997 the

Bank did establish with much publicity the Structural Adjustment Participatory Review Initiative (SAPRIN) with INGO and local NGO involvement that focused on structural adjustment policies in several countries. The report *Policy Roots of Economic Crisis and Poverty* was not published till 2002 (World Bank, 2002a). It concluded that structural adjustment policies 'have contributed to the further impoverishment of and marginalisation of local populations while increasing economic inequality' (World Bank, 2002a). The fact that the report was published long after the Bank had changed its approach, at least formally, from policy conditionality to process conditionality enabled the President of the Bank, James Wolfensohn, to dismiss the report as not addressing the new situation (Bretton Woods Project, 2002).

Earlier criticism of structural adjustment policies had by 1999 led the Bank away from *policy conditionality* to *process conditionality*. The poor, or at least NGOs and other civil society groups acting for them, were to be given a greater say in the formulation by governments of their anti-poverty strategies. This coincided with the beginnings of the policies (for example, HIPIC) that had by now been put in place to begin to unburden poor countries of the debts they had incurred during the period of the 1980s and 1990s (see Chapter 6 for more on debt relief). At the same time the Banks' Comprehensive Development Framework (CDF), launched in 1999, stressed the importance of non-economic development objectives such as nutrition, health and education status. It seemed at that point to commentators like Kanbur, who was to become involved quite soon in a failed attempt to help formulate Bank anti-poverty policy (see below), that the negative lessons of the 'trickle down' years and the negative impacts of structural adjustment had been appreciated. A new era in which concerns with equity and security would be the starting point for growth-promoting polices was optimistically envisaged (Kanbur and Vine, 2000: 102).

In this context, the Poverty Reduction Strategy Paper (PRSP) procedure was launched in 1999. These were to be *country-owned* policy documents prepared in consultation with civil society, and their completion became a condition for debt relief under HIPIC or for accessing soft loans from the IDA's 'Poverty Reduction and Support Credit'. Over 60 of these PRSPs are in the pipeline at the time of writing, and many have been completed. Criticisms of this process have included the fact that the consultation process has often involved local branches of INGOs rather than more genuine representatives of civil society and often bypassed parliamentary scrutiny (Gould, 2005). It is also argued that they are not formulated at a time or in a manner that can really influence government budgets. Moreover, it has been argued by Charles Gore (2004) of UNCTAD that the actual policies arising under this process are little different from those imposed in an earlier period by the Bank. This is because the authors know they have still to be approved by the Bank, and that they suspect that unorthodox policy options would not go down well and, furthermore, these orthodoxies had, despite Kanbur's optimism, not really changed. Also this reflects the hegemony over policy ideas that the Bank has managed to construct over the past decades through workshops for civil servants held under the auspices of the World Bank Institute.

Finally in this section it is instructive to examine the debate over the content of the Bank's 2000/2001 World Development Report (WDR) on Poverty. The Norwegian-based Comparative Research Programme on Poverty (CROP, 2000) provided an excellent analysis of the WDR 2000–2001. Several contributions to the volume signal the extent to which the Bank's authors had departed from a narrow view of poverty as income-based, requiring merely economic growth combined with trickle-down policies to solve the problem that was evident in the 1990 report. In this report instead are sections addressing the social capital of the poor and how it might be enhanced. An explicit acknowledgement is made in the report of the contribution of Amartya Sen in *Development as Freedom* (1999) within which poverty is seen in part as a matter of capabilities. The capabilities of the poor can only be enhanced by addressing their deprivation in terms of education and health and also by addressing issues of the voices of the poor. Moreover, in the chapter on 'Making State Institutions Pro-Poor', an institutional perspective on government action to reduce poverty is introduced, within which civil society's contribution to democratic institutions is regarded as an important contribution to poverty eradication.

Particularly instructive within this volume is the contribution of Einar Braathan (2000), who provides a discourse analysis of the report. He suggests that the fact that the Bank opened the drafting of this report to a web-based discussion involving contributions from a global array of actors was a conscious attempt to secure both *legitimacy* for the report and to secure a *hegemony* over the way in which poverty would in future be addressed by most of this global intellectual and policy community. Examining the report as a discursive act authorised by the World Bank in search of hegemony, the key question becomes which pre-existing or alternative ideas about poverty and its reduction does it embrace, and which ones does it sideline? Braathan examines the report for the extent of its acceptance or rejection of four possible approaches to the issue: that of 'social paternalism', 'social liberalism', 'social corporatism' and 'social radicalism'. While social paternalism was the key feature of the 1990 report, the 2000–2001 report moves away from this focus except, of course, in so far as the Bank still believes that the Global North can help those in the Global South improve their lot. The 2000–2001 report, he argues, is rather more identified with a mixture of the social liberal approach and the social corporatism approach. Chapters focused on expanding the opportunities for the poor by, for example, expanding poor people's assets are indicative of the first of these. Chapters such as those concerned with making state institutions more responsive to the poor are indicative of the second of these. This is, of course, in keeping with the argument presented earlier, that the Bank since 1990 wanted to align itself with the poor against the entrenched interests of those not poor who were benefiting from state social security systems. Social radicalism on the other hand, 'the legacy of European socialist and social democratic labour movements is not paid due attention to' (Braathan, 2000: 35). Even though the self-organisation of the poor is addressed within the report it is within the context of building their social capital rather than challenging the class basis of state power. *The Bank wanted the poor to reach up to the powerful to address their needs rather than across to other social groups to create a stronger social movement for radical social change.*

It was indeed the unwillingness of the Bank to go beyond this social corporatism approach that lay behind its failure in 2000–2001 to succeed entirely in its search for hegemonic influence. The lead author of the WDR consultation draft, Professor Ravi Kanbur, resigned after the Bank board signalled that it wanted changes to the first draft. In the first draft 'empowerment' of the poor was a strong theme that embraced a discussion of poor people's social and political rights. It was also first of three pillars of empowerment, security and opportunity. The final version after Kanbur's resignation reversed the order, putting opportunity first. Other changes between the first and final draft were also indicative of this shift in emphasis. In the relegated empowerment section, the chapter on state institutions changed from making them 'pro-poor' to 'more responsive to poor people', and the section on security replaced the concept of 'protecting the poor' with that of 'helping the poor manage risk', presumably because the first concept is associated with a European approach to collective social protection, whereas the later is more in keeping with a US individualised approach to social insurance. Controversy surrounds the extent to which the US Treasury were instrumental in seeking and securing changes of emphasis in the 2000/2001 WDR on Poverty (Wade, 2002; Broad, 2006). Wade suggests that during the period when comments on the earlier draft were solicited, the 'US treasury called for more emphasis on the need for faster economic growth, freer markets as the route to higher economic growth, less talk of widening income distribution being bad for growth' (2002: 225–6) The then US Treasury Secretary, Larry Summers, who had previously worked successfully (Wade, 2002) for the resignation of the Bank's Chief Economist, Joseph Stiglitz, for being critical of aspects of the Washington Consensus (see, for example, Stiglitz, 1998) weighed in publicly with a speech in which he argued that discussing poverty reduction without emphasising economic growth and open markets was like Hamlet without the prince.

The conditions within which the WDR 2006 on *Equity and Development* (World Bank, 2005a) was drafted were somewhat different. Summers had moved on to run Harvard (until sacked!) and John Snow, secretary to the US Treasury appeared less ideologically driven on these issues. The Bank was in the throws of changing its President. Whatever the reason, the earlier draft of the WDR produced in March 2005 appears to have retained its main arguments and structure after approval by the Bank's executive board in June 2005. The September published version remained largely faithful to the earlier drafts. This is significant because the report marks an important step in Bank-think on issues of equity and in particular on the institutional reforms needed to secure greater equity. The self-proclaimed main message of the report was 'Equity is complementary, in some fundamental respects, to the pursuit of long-run prosperity. Institutions and policies that promote a level playing field, where all members of society have similar chances to become socially and economically productive, contribute to sustainable growth and development' (2005a: 2). The comparative analysis presented in the report led to the conclusion that equity was in some sense good for growth for two main reasons: market failure to invest in all human capital and 'distributive conflicts' that 'reduce returns to investment'. The report goes on to argue, 'These adverse effects of unequal opportunities and political inequality on development are all the more damaging because economic, political and social inequalities tend to reproduce themselves over time and across generations' (2005a: 2). Somewhat striking is the summary paragraph, reproduced here in full:

> The central argument is that unequal power leads to the formation of institutions that perpetuate inequalities in power, status and wealth – and that these same institutions are typically also bad for the investment, innovation and risk-taking that underpin long term growth. Good economic institutions are equitable in a fundamental way: to prosper a society must create incentives for the vast majority of the population to invest and innovate. But such an equitable set of economic institutions can emerge only when the distribution of power is not highly unequal, and where there are constraints on the exercise of power by office-holders. (World Bank, 2005a: 8)

In terms of country-specific policy recommendations in the social policy field, the report calls for more equal opportunities for children and youth and mentions with approval income transfers conditional on school attendance (World Bank, 2005a: 12) and the 'public assurance of provisioning' in immunisation, water and sanitation, and information on hygiene and child care'. More radically, it asserts 'insurance markets for large scale health problems are beset with failure' and calls for 'public provisioning or regulation that provides some insurance for all' (World Bank, 2005a: 12).

The report's analysis of the *politics* of the redistribution needed to secure equality of opportunity would not look out of place in a social democratic primer to how to make countries fairer. Reviewing the history of now rich OECD countries, it notes that 'Finland ... shows how state, market and society can jointly generate equitable development outcomes' (World Bank, 2005a: 121). Most important, reflecting the WDR 2004 that focused on making services work for poor people, the WDR 2006 recognises that good quality public services are those used by all groups. 'Voice and accountability can strengthen the tax effort, as the services provided become a reflection of the desires of the broader electorate rather than a priveleged few' (World Bank, 2005a: 176). If followed through in country programmes, this would mark a departure from the Bank's obsession with targeting the poor. The report also goes on to call for action at the global level to address international inequality. We will discuss this in Chapter 6.

Social protection and pension policy: from intergenerational solidarity to individualising risk management

While the debate about poverty, particularly in poorer countries, involves primarily the PREM group within the Bank, debate about social protection policies needed to provide income support for the poor is led by the Social Protection family within the Human Development Network. Robert Holzmann, who was recruited to the Bank in the late 1990s, now presides over Bank social protection policy, including the Bank pension policy. To understand the importance of the role of the Bank in attempting with some success to shape national pension policy throughout the world, and in providing a conceptual framework for thinking about social protection issues more generally, the story needs to begin a little earlier. We will start with pensions and return to conceptual issues around social protection.

Before the 1980s, the spread of pension policies around the world was associated in large measure with the work and influence of the ILO in setting down 'international norms of social protection, generation of reform templates, provision of consultants and consulting advice and the use of high level regional meetings to popularise its ideas and approaches' (Orenstein, 2003: 180). Up until the 1980s, pension schemes around the world, following ILO advice, took the form of variations upon either the Bismarkian approach, which involved intergenerational solidarities whereby pensions were paid out of the 'insurance' contributions of those still at work, or the Beveridge approach, whereby state pensions were funded from taxation. The term pay-as-you-go (PAYG) was associated with the former but was often used to describe both. What happened to break the hegemony of this idea about pensions? What part did the Bank play in it?

The bombing and killing in his palace of the social democratic President of Chile Salvadore Allende with the support of the US government laid the ground for everything that followed. Under the subsequent hated dictatorship of Augustus Pinochet, Chile embarked in 1981 on a radical break with this tradition. It switched to a pension system operated by the private sector based upon a defined contribution formula whereby an individual's pension would depend solely upon the worth of an individual's contribution invested in a private fund. What gave this change worldwide importance was the subsequent collapse in 1989 of the 'communist project' in Eastern Europe and the former Soviet Union. A new tranche of countries wanting to embrace capitalism came to turn to the World Bank for loans. It was not long before the Bank formulated its pension policy based on the Chilean experience and began to make loans to Eastern Europe and elsewhere conditional upon the partial privatisation of PAYG pension schemes. The story of the Bank's adoption of its multi-pillar pension policy within which a key role was to be played by the second tier of a compulsory individualised private pension contribution was not without its complications. In order for the Bank to be able to increase its activities in Eastern Europe, it was obliged to recruit to the *operational* division for Eastern Europe a number of European-based social security experts who were, as it turned out, more in sympathy with the PAYG tradition (Deacon, 1997: 68–9,133–8). Indeed, by 1994 the Bank was in the unusual position of seeing published at the same time two differently orientated texts. One of these, published by the Development Economics section (World Bank, 1994b) edited by Estelle James, proposed that transition countries severely reduce public pension provision to a subsistence level, possibly with a means-tested flat rate minimum; the first tier. Compulsory would be the second individualised private second tier. A third voluntary private top-up tier would also be encouraged. This report became the flag-ship *Averting the Old Age Crisis* (World Bank, 1994b). The other publication pro-duced from the operations division for Eastern Europe (Barr, 1994) set out pension policy options much more in keeping with the existing practice in Western Europe. The common ground was the need to raise the pension age and the provision of a minimum benefit. The difference was in the scope provided in the Barr version for continuing a state PAYG wage-related scheme. Within the Barr version, a private tier would compliment and not replace this state commitment.

The dispute between the California Girls (Estelle James, Louise Fox and others who were associated with *Averting the Old Age Crisis*) and the Brighton Boys (the town where Nic Barr's book was written) did not end there. One small victory for the BBs was that Barr got to edit the chapter on social policy for the World Development Report on Transition Countries (World Bank, 1996). Barr re-crafted his words in his book to show some concession to the US liberal position but was able to state:

> A typical pension system in Europe and North America has a state pay-as-you-go pension covering more than subsistence, complemented by a variety of regulated privately managed pension funds … the approach accords a significant role to solidarity and shares risks broadly … the precise balance (between this and a Chilean individual funded sys-tem) depends on a country's objectives and constraints. (World Bank, 1996: 83)

This appearance of a transatlantic consensus on PAYG was, of course, made possible by the fact that the US social security scheme was anything but a privatised Chilean pension scheme. Interestingly, as Bush tries at the time of writing to push the USA social security scheme in a privatised direction, Estelle James, writing in the *Washington Post* (13 February 2005), notes that if the USA were to follow the

Chilean model it would incur (as did Eastern European countries that took her advice) huge transition costs to cover existing pension obligations while building up the new funds. She suggests, 'If the government borrowed money to cover the transition this would offset the increase in personal savings, interest rates would rise, and the opportunity to increase national savings and the GDP would be missed'. She continues, 'One of the lessons of Chile is that when the welfare of a nation's retirees is at stake, the government's obligations remain crucial and lasting'. Another example of the USA telling the rest of the world not to do what it does but do as its Bank's employees tell it to do!

This history of controversy regarding Bank pension policy can't be found, however, in the documents written by the Head of Social Protection family, Robert Holzmann, which is perhaps surprising as he hails from Europe. Writing in one of his early Bank position papers he asserted, 'we still conclude that the multi-pillar approach to pension reform is the correct one' (Holzmann, 1999). Indeed, under Holzmann's intellectual leadership the Bank and its associated Institute have continued to invest considerable resources in convincing government civil servants of the wisdom of adopting the multi-pillar approach to pension reform. The Pension Reform Primer Service was initiated, which provided comprehensive information on the design and implementation of reforms with country case studies. The World Bank Institute established an annual workshop together with the Harvard Institute for International Development beginning in 1997, targeted at client countries, with a core course on pensions, regional workshops and other training activities. Considerable effort also went in to dialoguing with the ILO and the OECD to counter challenges to the Bank approach that had been articulated by ILO staff (Beattie and McGillivray, 1995). We shall examine these criticisms in more detail in the section on the ILO and pension policy in Chapter 4.

Criticism of the Bank pension policy was also expressed by the then Chief Economist of the Bank, Joseph Stiglitz, who examined ten myths associated with individual private compulsory pension schemes and debunked them, concluding in a paper delivered in September 1999 to a Bank conference on New Ideas About Old Age Security that 'the arguments most frequently used to promote individual retirement accounts are often not substantiated in either theory or practice' (Orszag and Stiglitz, 1999: 2). These myths were:

- individual accounts raise national savings;
- rates of return are higher under individual accounts;
- declining rates of return under PAYG schemes reflect fundamental problems;
- investment of public funds in equities has no macroeconomic effect;
- labour market incentives are better under individual accounts;
- defined benefit plans necessarily provide more of an incentive to retire early;
- competition ensures low administrative costs under individual accounts;
- corrupt and inefficient governments provide a rationale for individual accounts;
- bailout politics are worse under public defined benefit plans; and
- investment of public trust funds is always squandered and mismanaged.

Stiglitz had no opportunity to develop the implications of these ideas for Bank policy as he was forced to resign from the Bank two months later in November 1999 by Lawrence Summers, the secretary at the US Treasury. Summers had made it clear to

Wolfensohn, the then Bank President, that the US support for Wolfensohn's second term of office was conditional on sacking Stiglitz (Wade, 2002). Not that the pension issue was the main bone of contention, this was rather the more generalised criticism that Stiglitz was beginning to articulate of the whole of Bank–IMF strategy with regard to neo-liberal macroeconomic management and the Washington Consensus (Stiglitz, 1998). Stiglitz indeed went on to found the Centre for Policy Alternatives at Columbia University and became an influence upon those working within the UN to shift global economic and global policies (see Chapters 4, 7 and 8).

With Stiglitz gone, Holzmann was free to pursue the agenda he inherited from the California Girls. Orenstein (2003, 2005) has charted the degree to which the Bank has subsequently been influential in securing pension reforms that embody a privatised individualised compulsory tier. While it was the case that the first global wave of pension policy formation between the end of the nineteenth century and the 1970s reflected the policies of the ILO and the European tradition, the next wave from the 1980s till now has reflected in large measure the policies of the Bank. 'The World Bank, rather than the ILO is dominant in the spread of multi-pillar reform, reflecting shifts in global discourse on social and economic policy' (Orenstein, 2003: 181). The World Bank's country operations became publicly accessible from 1994, so it is possible to track the direct influence of bank interventions in particular countries. From 1994 to 2004, 51 countries received assistance from the Bank in reforming their pension policy. Of these 51, 14 were poor countries where the Bank provided technical assistance initally to develop capacity prior to preparing a reform agenda at a later stage. Of the 37 others, 20 have subsequently initiated reforms that include the establishment of a system of mandatory individual savings accounts (Orenstein, 2005). They are located mainly in Latin America and Eastern Europe. That is not to say that the Bank had it all its own way. Particularly in Eastern Europe, there were head-to-head fights between the Bank's advisors and those of the ILO (Deacon, 1997; Holzmann et al., 2003). In the Ukraine, for example, try as it might, even after locating itself in the abandoned offices of the Central Committee of the Communist Party, the Bank could not find a local counterpart to play with, and the ILO and UNDP held the ground in an alliance with the Ministry of Labour and Social Protection (Deacon, 1997: 122). Whereas in Poland, the Bank found a willing reforming partner and opposition was weaker, and individual accounts have been introduced (Holzmann et al., 2003).

The question for the Bank pension reform advocates is having succeeded to an extent in Latin America and Eastern Europe, can they take the struggle to the European heartland? Here, as Holzmann et al. concede, 'reform progress has been highly variable' (2003: 11). They conclude by pinning their hopes on the new 'open method of co-ordination' established by the European Commission that requires countries to compare their social policies against certain benchmarks and best practice indicators. 'Perhaps the entry of the "Eastern European Accession" countries after 2004 will energize member countries because they will become more aware of reform alternatives' (Holzmann et al., 2003: 12). They might be helped in this continuing campaign to win the hearts and minds of pension policy-makers within Europe by the impact of the steady intellectual drip-feed across the Atlantic of technical concepts that underpin the reform paradigm. The intergenerational contract between today's contributors and today's pensioners embodied in the PAYG system that only required *today's* government to raise sufficient revenue to cover *today's* pensions came under challenge in the context of ageing populations by the invention by USA–World Bank economists of the technique of intergenerational accounting. This method calculates the anticipated cost of *all future pension obligations* against the anticipated tax incomes on the basis of today's tax rates to derive an implicit public pension debt. The assumption built into the accounting system is that future generations will not pay higher taxes than those of today. The refusal of the model to accept the logic that future generations might be better off and might reasonably expect to be taxed higher for a longer retirement period (Ervik, 2005: 32) leads to the calculation of seemingly unsustainable pension deficits. The case for individuals saving today for their own pension tomorrow is given a boost by these shock-horror stories. Ervik argues that the close intellectual and personal links between the Norwegian pension economists and those in the USA explain the use of these accounting techniques by the Commission established in 2001 to examine pension policy in Norway. In 2005 the Commission reported that the future debt liability for pensions was 286 per cent of GDP. 'These figures dwarf all others ... and contribute to an image of unbearable future burdens ... [which] urges politicians to take prompt action' (Ervik, 2005: 45). The Norwegian model of intergenerational solidarity becomes questioned in the process.

The pension reform story driven by the Bank is then another case of the power that epistemic communities have secured in a global context, working with certain scientific paradigms, to reframe the terms of public discourse and political debate. 'In narrowing the focus on global ideas to seemingly technical accounting concepts there is a real danger of exaggerating their importance and losing sight of other relevant factors' (Ervik, 2005: 47).

The same point can be made about the broader conceptual framework developed under Holzmann's auspices to analyse social protection issues more widely. The Social Protection Sector was established in 1996 and framed its Social Protection Strategy Paper (SPSP) based upon an initial conceptualisation by Holzmann and Jorgensen (1999). The SPSP, approved in 2000, is based upon the concept of risk management (SRM). Departing from the language of the ILO with its discourse of social solidarity, social security, social inclusion and social justice, the idea of risk management brought to the table the discourse of markets and insurance which seemed fitting for a the neo-liberal era of globalised uncertainty, insecurity and flexibility. Norton and colleagues commented that 'the SPSS was clearly influenced by the experience of reacting to the post-1997 Asian financial crisis ... [and] focuses upon how policy can help the poor to manage risk in the interests of human capital development' (2001: 38). The analytical and policy prescription framework distinguishes between *risk reduction* such as economic policy to stabilise the economy, *risk mitigation* such as income diversity and insurance, and *risk coping* such as selling assets, reducing consumption or engaging in socially undesirable activities. It is interesting to note, however, that at a recent 2006 inter-agency 'show and tell' seminar convened by the ILO, the representatives of the Bank's social protection section announced that the mission of the social protection sector had recently been adjusted to take more account of both the World Commission on the Social Dimension of Globalisation, and especially its concern to create decent work, and the World Bank's own Development Report, which was concerned to secure more equitable outcomes in a globalizing world. So the new mission asserts that it 'will assist countries to alleviate poverty and promote equitable and sustainable growth through ... the *creation of good jobs* through better labour markets regulations ... [and] provide minimum levels of subsistence and help to *correct market-based distributive outcomes*' (GSP Digest 2006a: 241–2)

Social development: transforming institutions and empowering people?

As will now be evident, it is not possible to give a definitive answer as to what is Bank social policy. The work, arguments and emphasis of those in the Poverty Reduction of Economic Management Department (PREM), the Social Protection Sections (SPS) and the Social Development Department (SDD) even within the IBRD do not always concur, not to mention the work of those in the separate IFC. Nonetheless, it has been demonstrated so far that the Bank's view about the social policy that countries should adopt in the social protection and poverty alleviation field is one that prefers selectivity over universalism, prefers targeted poverty alleviation measures such as social funds over contributory social security schemes, and prefers a large role for private individualised savings accounts. In terms of welfare regime types, the Bank's pronouncements can be described as either a social liberalism or a social corporatism, but a corporatism that only extends to the incorporation of the poor. Nowhere have we found evidence of the Bank using the language and analytical frameworks of European social democracy or the democratic class struggle.

Does this apply also in the case of the work of the Social Development Department (SDD)? Are the words 'Empowering People by Transforming Institutions' chosen as a title for its 2005 operational document setting out how the Bank should incorporate social development more centrally into Bank operations indicative of something even more radical? Explaining the logic behind the thinking of the SDD at a workshop in Helsinki in 2004 organised under the auspices of the Bank's Trust Fund for Environmentally and Socially Sustainable Development, Steen Jorgensen, who directs the Department and has masterminded the operational guidelines, explained that first the Bank was concerned with infrastructure development in the 1950s, then with finance issue in the 1970s, then human capital formation in the 1980s, followed by environmental assets in the 1990s. Only in the last few years had the bank addressed the issue of social capital and social assets within which, argued Jorgensen, issues of governance, social networks and equity issues play a part. If the Bank wanted to ensure a return on its previous attempts to encourage countries to invest in human capital, then it needed to ensure cohesive societies which welcomed the contribution of all. How far, then, does the thinking of his team merely reflect the same ideas as in the WDR 2000–2001 in which institutions are to be made more pro-poor, or how far does the notion of a struggle for power between entrenched interests and the poor in alliances with other social groups enter the analytical framework?

It might be unfair to scrutinise a document drafted for acceptance by the World Bank board for signs of radical thinking. Certainly this particular SDD document does not stray beyond an approach that Braathan (2000) had summed up as social corporatism. Thus we find in its account of the strategic priorities for the Bank: 'development policy lending will support government efforts to improve inclusion, cohesion and accountability using countries' own systems' and 'building government capacity for more effective stakeholder participation' (World Bank, 2005d: vii, 2). It continues, 'cohesive societies enable women and men to work together to address common needs, overcome constraints and consider diverse interests. They resolve differences in a civil, non-confrontational way, promoting peace and security' (2005d: 3). Little here of the historical experience of *social struggle* that lead to such cohesive societies in Europe over decades.

The analysis presented by Anis Dani, social policy advisor within the SDD at a closed workshop of donor social development advisors on 14 February 2005, which was not under the scrutiny of the Bank's board, might have been expected to adopt a more challenging stance. Dani (2005) usefully reviews the different meanings of social policy in a developed and developing context, and following Gough and Woods (2004), argues the case that in the context of development the concept of social policy needs to be broadened to include public policies orientated to social welfare goals which operate through a wide variety of policy instruments and is formulated by a wide range of actors including those at transnational level. Social policy then becomes redefined 'as a series of public policies designed to promote social development, undertaken by a variety of actors through a range of instruments' (Dani, 2005: 9). The radical step then taken is to incorporate the notion from Rao and Walton (2004) of 'equality of agency' and not just opportunity as one of the desirable goals of social policy/development. Social development includes the process of increasing 'the capacity of social groups to exercise agency, transform their relationship with other groups and participate in the development processes' (Dani 2005: 9). Challenging the limitations of equality of opportunity as policy goal, Dani continues 'Its limitation is that it tends to ignore the pervasiveness of group-based inequalities, such as those based on ethnicity, race, gender or caste' (2005: 10). He might have added class. His paper interestingly goes on to examine directly the global institutional environment that might enable or frustrate this more radical goal of social development. Here the slow progress that the international community has made in creating an enabling environment for social development is reviewed (see more on this topic in Chapter 6). The failure so far of most northern countries to achieve policy coherence between their trade, agricultural, environmental, immigration policies and the global objectives of development is noted. Perhaps we are seeing at least within the SDD of the Bank the articulation of the need for a more radical politics of social policy and social development not only at country but also at transnational level. Indeed, as was suggested above, one reading of the WDR on *Equity and Development* (World Bank, 2005a) is that concerns with the institutional and political barriers to equity are now centre stage even in the Bank. To handle the implications of this it will need to recruit many more social and political scientists.

Anis Dani and the SDD group subsequently organised in December 2006 a major conference in Tanzania on New Frontiers of Social Policy: Developments in A Globalizing World, and a new seminar series running in Washington. The conference and work programme address issues of (a) inequality, livelihoods and inclusion, (b) institutions, voice and accountability as well as (c) cultural diversity and social integration. The conference built upon the concerns with institutional and political and social structural obstacles to equitable development revealed in the WDR 2006 on 'Equity and Development' (World Bank, 2005a). Panels at the conference addressed 'Donor impact on domestic accountability', the 'Implementation of the WDR06' and the 'Role of international organisations in global social policy'. Among the speakers were Ian Gough, Geoff Woods, Ravi Kanbur, Jomo Kwame Sundaram and Sergei Zelenev of UNDESA, and interestingly Paul Stubbs, Nicola Yeates and myself of GASPP! An Arusha statement was agreed by participants that stated, among other things, that 'targeting public services at the poor alone is not always the most effective way of empowering and building their capabilities' (GSP Digest, 2006b: 121).

The 'radicalism' of the SDD might be explained in part by the fact that some funds for work in this area are provided by the very large Trust Fund for Environmentally and Sustainable Development (TFESSD) set up in 1999 with Norwegian funds and joined in 2002 by the Finns. Around 438 million dollars have been provided by Norway since 1999 and 3 million by Finland since 2004. Trust funds are in part a means for some of the Bank's stakeholders to influence thinking by injecting money that might often be spent on employing those nationals inside the Bank. At a review of the TFESSD in June 2004, Desmond McNeill, head of the reference group that liases between the fund and the Bank, concluded that work undertaken under the auspices of the Fund had shifted thinking on certain issues. Injecting non-economists had encouraged economist working with PREM in the Bank to think about governance issues. How far these new ideas translated into actual country-based projects was less clear. Some evidence, then, that even within the Bank a contest goes on between the liberal-inclined USA and, in this case, some social-democratically inclined Scandinavian countries to shape the contribution of the Bank to the global social policy and social development discourse. Whether this tendency will prevail is another matter. Past contests between radical and more orthodox tendencies within the Bank do not auger well. The debate between Milanovic (2003) and Dollar and Kraay (2001) pointing respectively to the negative and positive consequences of globalisation was 'won' by Dollar because of the Bank's External Affairs Department promoting only one side of the debate (Broad, 2006). This raises the question as to whether this trust fund money would be better spent not in the Bank but on strengthening the UN agencies such as the UN Research Institute for Social Development (UNRISD) who already were more sympathetic to Nordic thinking.

Improving or privatising public services? (health and education)

So far our focus has been social protection and social security. Turning to the provision of social services such as health and education or utilities such as water, the same story can be traced. The Bank-led structural adjustment policies of the 1970s, 1980s and early 1900s encouraged, indeed forced a retreat on behalf of developing countries from their attempt to continue to invest in high-quality hospitals and universities. Government expenditure should only, according to the Bank's orthodoxy at that time, be focused on the needs of the poor. This trend was continued in the 1990s in the former communist countries when the Bank warned against excessive public expenditure and encouraged its reduction.

The related issue here apart from the Bank's wish to reduce the scale of public expenditures is that of the choice between *universalism* and *selectivity*. Is the role of the state to target service provision only on the poor, or is there a defensible case for universal provision to all social groups? Townsend (2004), Tendler (2004) and Deacon (1997) drew attention to the domination within global social policy discourse during the 1990s, shaped in large measure by the Bank, of the concept of safety nets. Among the reasons that might be offered for the decline of the idea of universalism was the one suggested earlier that in the name of meeting the needs of the poorest of the poor the 'premature' or 'partial' welfare states of Latin America, South Asia and Africa (that the ILO had been so influential in building) were challenged as serving only the interests of a small privileged workforce and elite state employees. A new alliance was to be struck between the Bank and the poor. The analysis of the privileged and exclusionary nature of these provisions made by the Bank was accurate. However, by destroying the public state services for this middle class in the name of the poor, the politics of solidarity, which requires the middle class to have an interest in public provision that they fund, was to be made more difficult. The beneficiary index measures of the Bank showing how tertiary education spending and urban hospital provision benefited the elite contributed in no small measure to this development. *The Bank's technical experts, who were very able to measure who received public services, were ill-informed about the political economy of welfare state building which requires cross-class alliances in defence of public expenditure.* Once again American exceptionalism (in this case in terms of its residual welfare state) was sold as the desirable norm through the technical tools used by economists, rather than the analytical frameworks used by political scientists.

Are there signs of a rethink on the part of the Bank? One reading of the WDR 2004 (World Bank, 2003c) that was focused on making services work for poor people suggests that there might be some rethinking going on. There is a tension within the text and probably among the authors between those who stay with the line that much public spending by developing countries benefits the rich and is therefore to be refocused on the poor (for example, World Bank, 2003c: 4, fig. 2), and those who would appear now to have accepted and argue the point that 'cross-class alliances' between the poor and non-poor are needed to pressure governments to 'strengthen public sector foundations for service delivery' (World Bank, 2003c: 180, fig. 10.1). Most striking is the assertion that 'In most instances making services work for poor people means making services work for everybody – while ensuring poor people have access to those services. Required is a coalition that includes poor people and significant elements of the non-poor. There is unlikely to be progress without substantial "middle class buy-in" to proposed reforms' (World Bank, 2003c: 60). This section of the report goes on to quote approvingly the words of Wilbur Cohen, US Secretary of Health, Education and Welfare under President Lyndon Johnson in the 1960s when he said, 'Programmes for poor people are poor programmes'. Remarkable! The report itself is extra-ordinarily complicated in its recommendations and prescriptions and concludes with a rejection of the one-size-fits-all approach that the Bank used to be accused of when it tried to sell Chile to the world. Instead it adopts an eight-sizes-fit-all model. Which model is to be applied depends on the capacity of government, its openness to influence by the poor, the degree of homogeneity of the country and so on. At least two of the models involve a strong emphasis on governments being the major provider at either national or local level. Progress in this direction in the Bank's World Development Report may in part be due to the fact that a lead author was a Finnish economist. As we saw, Finland, together with other Nordic countries, has been undertaking a considerable amount of quiet influence by the placement of experts within World Bank and some Regional Development Banks.

It is conceivable that this also reflects the fact that whereas the Bank has been led in its pension policy by very ideologically driven proponents of privatisation such as Robert Holzmann, Estelle James or Michael Rutowski, both at the level of the Social Protection Section and at the country operational level this may not have been true to the same extent in the other two families – Health, Nutrition and Population, and

Education – that make up the rest of the human development network. We turn to an examination of the trends in Bank thinking and interventions in health service policy to examine this proposition.

In 1996 the internal Bank reorganisation gave birth to the Health, Nutrition and Population family alongside the Social Protection and Education families, all under the umbrella of the human development (HD) network. Before then, however, David De Ferranti, who was to become in 1996 the head of the umbrella HD network, seems to have been instrumental in generating papers and arguments that led to the Bank encouraging countries to raise user charges for services and to privatise partially some health services (Lee, 2003: 100–13). One of these was the seminal paper *Paying for Health Services in Developing Countries* (World Bank, 1987). Other health economists joined the Bank at this time (1987–93), their work culminating in the *World Development Report: Investing in Health* (World Bank, 1993) that 'threw down a gauntlet in that it delved directly into the issues of priority setting and public-versus-private financing of health care … many public health professionals were alarmed at the apparent undermining of the fundamental principle of universal access to basic health care' (Lee, 2003: 109). The report advocated cost recovery, pre-payment insurance and opening the market to private providers.

That is not to say there were no alternative voices within the Bank during this period of the ascendancy of health economists. Lee (2003: 113) suggests that disputes continued between the public health professionals, who were then organised in the Population Health and Nutrition Division (to be distinguished from the Health Nutrition and Population Sector established in 1996), and the health economists, often in the policy research department or country and regional operational divisions. She notes that since the mid 1990s there has been an apparent softening of the World Bank's position towards the Health Service Financing agenda. Certainly under Richard Feacham's directorship the newly created Health, Nutrition and Population Sector Strategy (World Bank, 1997) conveys much sympathy for the public health professional's viewpoint. The sector strategy reaffirms quite unequivocally:

> In most developed countries, and many middle-income countries, governments have become central to social policy and healthcare. This involvement is justified on both theoretical and practical grounds to improve: (a) *equity*, by securing access by the whole population to health, nutrition and reproductive services; and (b) *efficiency*, by correcting for market failure, especially when there are significant externalities (public goods) or serious information asymmetries (health insurance). (World Bank, 1997: 5)

This section continues with a direct challenge to those who would support private health insurance because 'insurance plans … often exclude those who need health insurance the most' (World Bank, 1997: 5), and a direct challenge to private health providers because 'private consumers are also at the mercy of medical providers who will charge what the market will bear' (1997: 5). It concludes, 'private health insurance is not a viable option for risk pooling at the national level in low or middle income countries' (1997: 8). Instead 'strong, direct government intervention is needed in most countries to finance public health activities and essential health, nutrition and reproductive services as well as to provide protection against the impoverishing effects of catastrophic illness' (1997: 8). If poor countries are unable to raise sufficient revenues then international donors would need to pay for public health interventions with large externalities.

At the time of writing, a revised sector strategy was in preparation and the stewardship of the sector was in the hands of acting Director Robert Hecht. Some indication of its thinking can be gleaned from the book by Roberts et al., *Getting Health Reform Right* (2003), that it is promoting as the text for its flagship course on Health Sector Reform and Sustainable Financing. Its current (2003–2005) work programme seemed to be influenced by the need to relate it to the MDGs and to the PRSPs. Unsurprisingly therefore, the work programme covered sustainable finance for child and maternal health services, pro-poor health financing both in the public and private sector, work on pharmaceuticals and government *stewardship*. On health-related user fees, the Bank asserted prominently on its web pages on 8 June 2005 that it did not support user fees for basic health services. Where abolishing fees is not practicable, the Bank says it works with countries to subsidise the premiums paid by the poor.(Gottret and Schieber, 2006). However, while discouraging user fees, the sector does appear to be undertaking an important promotional activity through a seminar series – Public Policy and the Private Sector – that seeks to secure more effective partnerships between the public and private sectors. This course, which includes sections on private sector assessment, vouchers, contracting with non-state entities, was in 2004 and 2005 running in Tanzania, Moscow, Brazil, Singapore and Washington.

This suggests that the softening in the Bank's approach to the private sector in health that was detected in the late 1990s and early 2000s is perhaps not being sustained. It is pertinent at this point to bring back into the picture the work of the often neglected International Finance Corporation (IFC), which is part of the wider World Bank Group. While the IBRD and the IDA, commonly known as the World Bank and its associated WDR 2004, might be giving some emphasis to issues of equity and to the importance of cross-class alliances in defence of effective services for the poor, this other arm of the World Bank Group is doing anything but. In terms of Wade's (2001, 2002) distinction between the civil society agenda and the finance agenda of the Bank, the work of the IFC is firmly part of the later agenda. The IFC exists to promote the flow of private sector capital to developing countries. It acts as a kind of channel for venture capital to encourage industrial development. In 2001 the IFC established its own Health and Education Department under the direction of Guy Ellena to begin encouraging such investments in these sectors and to loan funds for such purposes (Lethbridge, 2002, 2004, 2005: Mehrotra and Delmonica, 2005). This development is to be understood within the context of the IFC's production of its *Private Sector Development Strategy* (World Bank 2002b) in 2002 that was based upon an initiative launched for consultation in 2001. This final report planned to increase support to the private sector in the provision of health and education services. The report envisaged a closer co-operation between the IFC and the soft-loan IDA. It aims at an IFC-driven private sector participation in up to 40 per cent of IDA operations (Mehrotra and Delmonica, 2005). A further link is established between the Poverty Reduction Strategy Papers (PRSPs) that poor countries need to complete before accessing debt relief or the poverty reduction and growth facility. The PRSP *Sourcebook* of the Bank advocates 'establishing policies that encourage competitive and efficient service sectors, such as allowing entry where possible and encouraging foreign direct investment' (Mehrotra and Delmonica, 2005: 165).

Within this policy context the IFC is now promoting private sector investment in aspects of health service provision in a large number of countries in South and East

Asia, Africa, the Middle East, Latin America and the transition countries. Some of these investments are in aspects of the infrastructure or technology of health service provision such as information and communication technology, diagnostic technology and services where there is little dispute about the merits of such private sector involvement. However, much of it is in holding companies that directly encourage new forms of private delivery or in health insurance companies. Among recent loans are ones of US$22 million to ORESA Ventures that then created Medicover (Central and Eastern Europe) that provides health insurance to companies and individuals in Central and Eastern Europe (Lethbridge, 2005). This IFC initiative is gaining ground within the World Bank Group. In February 2005 it hosted a major conference in Washington on 'Investing in Private Healthcare in Emerging Markets'. Unsurprisingly, among the 16 announced speakers (www.ifc.org) nine were representing US or Latin American or UK companies with an interest in such investments including Netcare, Price WaterHouse Coopers, Acibadem HealthCare Group, Apollo Hospitals Ltd. Lending a gloss of academic legitimacy to this event were two UK scholars: Professor Julian Le Grand of LSE and Professor Alan Maynard of the University of York.

In terms of education policy, the Bank's 'Education Strategy Paper' was formulated in 1999 and is being revised for publication at the time of writing in 2006. Whereas the social protection strategy and policy has been driven and developed by market ideologues, the health strategy and policy has been marked by some moments of significant controversy over the role of the market, the education strategy and policy appears to be less beset with such problems. Its strategy paper is an even-handed professional assessment of the purpose and state of education in the context of a globalising world. It sets out an inclusive range of objectives of education policy ranging from its contribution to human capital development, the improvement of health and nutrition, to its contribution to social capital development, social cohesion and equity. At the outset it asserts, 'In education, government still plays a leading role – and most likely will – especially in the financing of primary and secondary education' (World Bank, 1999: 2). However, it does concede that 'other entities are also involved and likely will become increasingly so in the decades ahead. For example, the private sector, through its training of workers already provides a large part of the effective learning that many people retain' (1992: 2). The strategy is concerned with inequality in educational access and quality, and argues that inequality must be reduced, and points out that 'Public spending can be a strong instrument for equity – expanding opportunities – and raising living standards for all but especially for the poorest. Overall spending on education in developing countries has been found to be progressive – in that the benefits received by the poorest groups are greater relative to their incomes than those received by richer groups' (1999: 15). Only then does it focus upon the beneficiary index more normally used by the Bank to point out that 'Despite this, subsidies to education are not always well targeted. The richest households gain by far the largest share of the subsidies. While primary education spending is targeted to the poorest groups, spending on secondary and tertiary is not' (1999: 17).

This analysis explains the different emphasis of the Bank in its policies for primary education and for tertiary (and to some extent secondary) education. In primary education it fully supports the goal of the Education for All policy adopted by countries in 1990 and subsequently worked for by UNESCO (see Chapter 4) and other international agencies. Within that it has put a commendable effort into education investment at primary level for girls, pointing out that schooling for girls, reduces infant mortality rates, decreases fertility rates and increases economic growth. In support of this policy and of the educational goals of the MDGs, it established in 2002 with donor partners and other agencies the Education for All (EFA) Fast Track Initiative (FTI). This is provided with administrative support by the Bank but is chaired by a rotating G8 donor and non-G8 donor. It aims to achieve sustained increases in aid for education. It is encouraging countries either as part of the PRSP process or, if they are not involved in that process independently, to produce costed educational sector plans with a budget for donor contributions. In order to bridge the funding gap, the FTI established in 2003 the FTI Catalytic Fund as a multi-donor trust fund. The management and adequacy of this fund will be reviewed as an example of a global social redistribution activity in Chapter 6. Suffice to say at this point that at April 2004 the EFA-FTI Catalytic Fund had attracted only US$236 million from four donors, which 'is not enough even for the immediate needs of the first countries to join the FTI' (UNESCO, 2004: 34). Government plans are reviewed by the FTI Secretariat in conjunction with UNESCO. An annual FTI meeting takes place in the margins of the annual UNESCO High Level Group, monitoring the achievement of the EFA initiative.

This campaign to ensure education for all has forced a rethink in the Bank on the question of cost recovery or user fees in the primary education sector. In the series of *Education Notes* produced by the Bank, a recent one addressed this issue and begins boldly, 'The World Bank does not support user fees for primary education. Such fees are an important factor keeping the poorest children out of schools in many countries, reducing momentum towards EFA. Fees for textbooks and other materials can also block access to learning for many more children. For this reason, World Bank programs increasingly support efforts to ensure that, as fees are eliminated, other sources of finance are available' (World Bank, 2004c: 1). The note goes on to point out that the FTI's Catalytic Fund presents an extraordinary opportunity to provide temporary financing to EFA countries working towards the elimination of fees.

In terms of tertiary education and to some extent secondary education, the Bank takes a different view on the role of the government. Here the Education Strategy Document argues that 'private financing and provision can expand the number of student places, especially at secondary and tertiary level' (World Bank, 1999: 34). In this context, just as with Health Policy, the IFC is brought into play as a facilitator of investment in that sector. Investment conferences are held to speed this process. Unfortunately – but it has to be conceded that this was written before the WDR on Making Services Work for the Poor (see above) – the strategy paper at this point falls back on the questionable assumption that by allowing the better-off to go private, the state will be able to focus its help on the poor without addressing the concomitant quality issue which arises.

In sum the answer to the question as to whether World Bank policy is about improving or privatising public services for the poor is, it depends on where you look. The Bank faces different ways and addresses different constituencies in its public pronouncements. The emphasis is also sector-specific: privatisation is, according to all in the Bank, good for pensions; it is also probably acceptable for tertiary education, but questioned by some even if supported by the IFC for health. The intellectual struggle inside the Bank continues, but it does seem as if in operational terms those who favour privatisation have recently made the running in the health and pensions sector, and those who favour free public provision hold the ring in primary education.

Further Reading

On international organisations: Boas, M. and McNeill, D. (2003) *Multilateral Institutions: A Critical Introduction*. London: Pluto.

On the World Bank: Gilbert, C.L. and Vines, D. (1997) *World Bank: Structure and Policies*. Cambridge: Cambridge University Press. Stone, D. and Wright, C. (eds) (forthcoming) *The World Bank's Decade of Reform and Reaction*. London: Routledge.

From the World Bank: *WDR 2001/2, 2004 and 2006*.

On the Bank and poverty alleviation: Kanbur, R. and Vines. D. (2000) 'The World Bank and Poverty Reduction: Past, Present, Future' in Gilbert, C.L. and Vines, I. (eds), *The World Bank: Structure and Policies*. Cambridge: Cambridge University Press. On the Bank and pensions: Orenstein, M. (2005) 'The new pension reform as global policy', *Global Social Policy*, 5, 2.

The journal *Global Social Policy*, GSP Digest, The section on 'International Actors and Social Policy' (www.gaspp.org).

Related Websites

www.worldbankorg
www.ifc.org
www.brettonwoodsproject.org
www.globalpolicy.org
www.wdev. eu

3

The Social Policy of the IMF, the WTO and the OECD

This chapter

- Describes the social policy approach adopted by the IMF
- Reviews the implications for social policy of the WTO regarding standards, services and intellectual property rights
- Assesses the social policy advice of the OECD in terms of labour market, pension and health

The IMF: from structural adjustment to the poverty reduction and growth facility

Whereas the explicit involvement of the World Bank in the global debate concerning the best way to alleviate poverty is evident, the role of the IMF in this global discourse was until relatively recently muted by comparison. Indeed, it was only in 1999 with the replacement of the long-standing and controversial structural adjustment facility (created in 1986) with the Poverty Reduction and Growth Facility that poverty reduction became an **explicit** IMF objective.

That having been said, there did emerge through the work of Kopits (1994), Tanzi (1992, 1993), Ahmad and Scheider (1993), Chand and Shome (1995), Bruno (1992), Hardy (1991) and others, some attempt at public accountability to professional social policy colleagues by the fiscal affairs and human resource technical specialists inside the IMF. By the time of the Copenhagen World Summit on Social Development in 1995, the Fund had even produced a glossy brochure on the social dimensions of its policy dialogue (IMF, 1995). The impact of the IMF structural adjustment programmes in developing countries had, of course, by then generated a vast and critical development studies literature. Killick and Malik (1991) usefully summarised the social impact of IMF-inspired structural adjustment policies in the developing world as:

- having an appreciable effect on the distribution of incomes, although these are apt to be complex and vary from one situation to another;
- meaning that groups of the poor can indeed be among the losers, with the urban working class particularly at risk; and
- permitting governments adopting Fund programmes to adopt specific measures to protect vulnerable groups, although there may be hard negotiations with the Fund over measures which are liable to create large claims on public revenues.

Garunda (2000) subsequently reviewed the impact of IMF lending on 58 countries between 1975 and 1991, and showed that for those countries that had bad pre-loan external balances of payments and other fiscal problems, the effect of fund intervention was a significant deterioration in income distribution and in the incomes of the poor.

As early as 1992 the Fund did acknowledge the shortcomings of some of the structural adjustment programmes it had influenced: 'Mistakes have been made. One of the results, as is well known, is a greater emphasis on social aspects of adjustment and the explicit incorporation of affordable safety nets in an increasing number of instances' (IMF, 1992). However, the underpinning defence made by the IMF of its structural adjustment policies, which are acknowledged to have a negative impact in the short term on some citizens, was that 'social development requires a strategy of high quality economic growth' (IMF, 1995: 1). Such a strategy requires 'macroeconomic stability, a marked based environment for trade and investment, good governance through accountable institutions and a transparent legal framework, and participatory development through active involvement of all groups in society' and 'sound social policies, including social safety nets to protect the poor during the period of economic reform, cost effective social expenditures, and employment generating labour market policies' (IMF, 1995: 1).

The thrust of publicly stated IMF social policy in the mid-1990s was the 'safety net'. This could 'comprise targeted subsidies, cash compensation in lieu of subsidies, improved distribution of essentials such as medicine, temporary price controls for essential commodities, severance pay and retraining for retrenched public sector employees, employment through public works, and adoption of permanent social security arrangements to protect the poorest' (IMF, 1995: 15). In the longer term, the stated aim of the IMF was 'to achieve significant real growth in social expenditures including primary education and health ... [while in some cases] ... shifting resources away from university education or advanced medical care' (1995: 18–22).

The debate between state PAYG and privatized individualized social security systems in middle-income or post-communist countries was not often addressed in IMF thinking on social policy, the IMF preferring to give emphasis to safety nets. Indeed, Etisham Ahmad, who moved from the Bank to work in the Fiscal Affairs Division of the IMF, wrote the chapter on social policy of the OECD/IMF/EBRD/Bank joint study of the Soviet economy. He concluded that 'there are a number of measures available to protect the vulnerable including cash transfers, the provision of specified quantities of certain essential goods at given price, or food stamps' (OECD, 1991: 137). 'The danger to be avoided is to construct an elaborate and expensive social security edifice that provides benefits to a privileged subset of the target population, in the presence of poverty and need' (1991: 192).

Kopits (1993), however, when head of the Fiscal Affairs Division of the IMF, did address explicitly the issue of a longer-term strategy for social security. The perceived crisis of the typical European Bismarckian social security system, he suggests, results from 'generous eligibility for benefits granted for political expediency rather than on the basis of either past contributions or genuine need' (1993: 103), together with 'excessive claims for sick pay, partial disability pensions, early retirement pensions, length of service pensions, and health care benefits' (1993: 105). Reform was required which is cost effective: 'Social security can no longer be viewed simply in terms of magnitude and coverage of benefits, but must be assessed also in terms of fiscal and allocative costs' (1993: 108).

The IMF has, however, provided assistance to some countries in the design of new social security schemes. These include Algeria, Bolivia, Brazil, Greece, Hungary, Indonesia and most former Soviet republics. In proposing reforms, Kopits suggested the following considerations. First, there is the cultural and historical context. In some societies the extended family or village structure 'operates relatively well as an informal social security scheme obviating the need for the urgent introduction of large scale public pensions' (1993: 108). At the other end of the spectrum, where 'households have been atomized ... there is an immediate need for provision of an extended safety net, as in much of the former Soviet Union' (1993: 108). Second, social security schemes should not 'interfere with the efficient allocation of resources and not act as a disincentive to save or to work'. Third, the link between benefits and contributions should be strengthened and at the source time contributions should be kept relatively low. Fourth, they should discourage waste by, for example, introducing user fees in health and education provision. Fifth, a clear distinction should be drawn institutionally between elements of the scheme such as pensions, sick pay and so on. Last, the schemes should be 'financially self sustaining over a long period of time' (1993: 108). The proposals stressed by Kopits point in the direction of greater individual investment funds with individually earned benefits in line with dominant Bank policy.

During the 1990s, the IMF came under more intense scrutiny from members of international civil society with regard to the impact of its policies on poverty reduction. This and the financial crisis in East Asia that led to the further impoverishment of many, led to some self-reflection inside the IMF about its policies. Indeed, the Fiscal Affairs department of the IMF convened a conference on the question of equity and economic policy. The conference background paper written by IMF staff reflected upon the trade-off between growth and equity and concludes that evidence points both ways:

> Large scale tax and transfer programs may, in fact, slow growth, but poverty alleviation and universal access to basic health care and education can simultaneously improve equity and enhance the human capital upon which growth depends. (IMF, 1998: 2)

The conference invited participants to reflect upon whether 'an international consensus [could] be forged on a minimum set of equity conditions that should be met' (IMF, 1998: 2). Among the scholars invited to reflect upon this issue were Amarayta Sen and Anthony Atkinson, who have been associated with views concerning the desirability of universal entitlements to livelihood and to a participation income respectively.

This renewed concern with the impact of adjustment upon the poor led to the World Bank and the IMF collaborating on the Poverty Reduction Strategy Papers (PRSPs) policy. This policy was designed to ensure an integrated approach between the Bank and the Fund to poverty reduction and growth that would also involve countries and their civil societies in shaping country anti-poverty policy when applying for cheap loans and debt relief. The Fund's structural adjustment facility was thus renamed the Poverty Reduction and Growth Facility (PRGF). However, critics continue to point out the contradiction between the IMF's short-term concerns with macroeconomic stability and these longer-term poverty reduction goals. IMF fiscal targets often lead to diminished social spending. Development Assistance from North to South does not arrive to fill the gap, as donors also take their cue from IMF country surveillance reports. In Honduras, disputes with the IMF over teachers' salary increases have cost the country US$194 million in delayed debt relief and donor aid cuts. Zambia was removed from the Fund's credit line for debt relief under the Heavily Indebted Poor Countries Initiative in 2000 and put under the IMF Staff Monitoring Programme instead of the PRGF process because it did not meet the limits imposed for public sector salaries. Under IMF rules, public sector wage to GDP ratio must not exceed 8 per cent, as well as the budget deficit not exceeding 3 per cent. In order for the goal to be met, Zambia is currently not increasing salaries and not increasing teacher and doctor recruitment despite shortages in each field (Bretton Woods Project, 2004). It would seem that despite the change of name from 'structural adjustment' to the 'poverty reduction and growth facility', the requirements the IMF impose in the field of macro-economic stability, in the absence of significant North–South transfers of funds, make it impossible for countries to make real progress either in effective poverty reduction or in the public service provision of health and education.

Nevertheless, in terms of the IMF's own account of its social policy, there has been a significant shift from the structural adjustment days of the 1980s. Its 2002 Fact Sheet on the *Social Dimension of the IMF's Policy Dialogue* now asserts that 'macroeconomic viability must include policies that directly address poverty and social concerns: and that in order to support these objectives, social sector spending should be focused on improving the education and health status of the poor' (IMF, 2001a: 1). Indeed, it insists 'IMF-supported programs have sought to promote universal access to basic social services' (2001a: 1). Furthermore, it cites evidence from its own review (IMF, 2001b) of social spending in a sample of 32 countries that received IMF support between 1985 and 1999, claiming that on average for the entire group of countries real spending on education and health increased at an annual rate of 3.4 and 3.3 per cent respectively. This impacted on improvements in indicators of education enrolment and infant mortality.

The WTO: is 'trade creep' undermining international social standards and privatising public services?

The World Trade Organisation (WTO) is the new kid on the bloc. Its activities and policies also impact upon national social policy. It was created in 1994 after an eight-year period (1986–94) of protracted negotiations under the previous framework for settling international trade issues: the General Agreement on Tariffs and Trade framework (GATT). The WTO is designed to complement the World Bank and IMF and provide an international regulatory framework covering trade in goods and services, trade-related intellectual property rights, and to oversee and settle trade disputes. The prime motivating force for its creation was the belief at the height of the neoliberal ascendancy of the 1990s, that increased global trade was, along with the liberalisation of capital flows, the key to increased world prosperity. It was seen as a force to drive down both tariff barriers and non-tariff barriers to international trade. Prior to its creation, countries established preferential trading arrangements with other selected countries. The future would be one in which the principle of non-discrimination in trade would take precedence. Member countries of the WTO would in general not be able to treat a potential trading partner less favourably than another (the most-favoured nation principle) unless it is a member of its own regional trading bloc, and would be obliged to treat foreign producers as if they were national producers (the national treatment principle).

We are concerned here with the impact of this new organisation upon national social policy-making. What soon became clear was that a process of trade creep was taking place. National social policy was in several respects about to be shaped in part by considerations of trade policy. Suddenly, social policy analysts had to become trade analysts if they were to understand how this issue shaped national social policy. Not that trade and social policy had been entirely separate hitherto; countries and regional blocs such as the EU had already used preferential trading arrangements to try to influence the social policies of their trading partners. The EU had introduced an offer of trade preferences for countries that met ILO conventions on forced labour, freedom of association, collective bargaining and minimum age of employment (Woolcock, 1995). Belgium had way back in 1953 tried to give trade preferences to those countries that had a universal family allowance scheme (Esty, 1994). Even the USA, under its 1984 Trade and Tariff Act, used its trade preferences to enforce its view on labour standards that were somewhat different from the ILO standards to which it does not subscribe. With the completion of the GATT negotiations and the establishment of the WTO, the issue was now to become whether the non-discrimination policy would mean that everybody had to trade with countries that had low labour or social standards, and hence encourage a race to the bottom and the erosion of European or other northern social and labour standards.

Should the WTO uphold labour standards?

The first WTO-social policy issue became the social clause issue. Let's put this issue of the relationship between trade and labour standards in historical context. In the context of the Bolshevik unrest sweeping Europe the Treaty of Versailles, which settled the terms of the peace after the First World War, included an important reference to labour conditions. In a phrase which has resonance today in the context of the drive to free trade and the consequent perceived danger of the race to the welfare bottom, the Treaty noted that 'the failure of any nation to adopt human conditions of labour is an obstacle in the way of other nations which desire to improve the conditions in their own countries' (quoted in Woolcock, 1995). Part XIII of the Treaty was concerned with international effort to establish common provision for: the right of association, wages for a reasonable standard of living, an eight-hour day and a 48-hour week, no child labour, equal remuneration for men and women, and equal rights for migrant workers. Then, as we shall see in the next chapter, when reviewing the contribution of the ILO, the concern was with encouraging countries to sign up to and ratify common labour and social standards. Now the question became: would increased free trade in the context of a neoliberal drive erode those standards that had been achieved? Could, alternatively, a 'social clause' be inserted in trade agreements that insisted that countries could only trade under the WTO regime if they upheld certain standards?

The main proponents of a social clause (the US administration, the French government and the trade unions) faced the main opponents (India, China, Brazil and the employers). The argument from France and the trade unions that a social clause was a good idea had become interpreted by many southern countries within the WTO as an attempt at social protectionism. The developed North was trying to exclude developing countries from entry into the global trading system. The South needed to benefit from the comparative advantage of low labour costs. At the WTO's meeting of ministers in December 1996, the debate was pursued with vigour. A compromise emerged in the final declaration. On the one hand, the conference committed itself to the 'observance of internationally recognised core labour standards' and noted that the ILO is the competent body to set and deal with labour standards. On the other, it was resolved that 'the use of labour standards for protectionist purposes is rejected' and that 'the comparative advantage of countries, particularly low-wage developing countries, must in no way be put into question' (Deacon, 1997: 78–9). The WTO and the ILO will continue to collaborate. The meaning of this declaration was open to different interpretations: the International Confederation of Free Trade Unions (ICFTU) applauded the commitment to core labour standards by the WTO, while the Malaysian Trade Minister concluded that 'there will be no more talk of labour standards in the WTO' (Deacon, 1997: 79). There **was** talk of labour standards in the WTO again at the ministerial meeting in Seattle in 1999. The meeting was surrounded by an army of anti-globalisation protesters, including US trade unions opposed to globalisation on the basis of the fear of job losses. President Bill Clinton suggested in an interview that a social clause should be back on the agenda. This, together with a number of other North–South conflicts of interest, led to the collapse of that particular WTO ministerial meeting. There **has** now been no more talk of labour standards and social clauses within the WTO, although as we shall see in Chapter 6, the idea of global standards continues to be a fraught part of the global social policy discourse.

The impasse on this issue illustrates sharply the complexity of the contending interests converging to shape a global social policy that might be concerned to achieve at one and the same time the increased prosperity of the South (via free trade), the greater redistribution of resources from North to South, and the regulation of the global economy in sustainable ways that preserve and enhance the social achievements of developed welfare states. This issue will be returned to in Chapter 6 when the topic of supranational social policy is examined.

Is the GATS privatising public services?

Soon the issue that was to prove equally controversial was that of the General Agreement on Trade in Services (GATS), an element of the WTO negotiating framework. It would become perceived as a threat to universal public service provision, particularly in the field of health policy. Let's put this in context.

Table 3.1   **WTO agreements impinging upon aspects of health policy**

Policy field	SPS	TBT	TRIPS	GATS
Infectious diseases control	X	X		
Food safety				
Tobacco control		X	X	X
Environment	X	X		
Access to drugs		X		
Health services				X
Food security	X			
Biotechnology	X	X	X	
Information technology			X	
Traditional knowledge			X	

International trade in goods and people impacts on health in numerous ways. The connections between trade and health are many, and four aspects of WTO policy directly impact on areas that were once the sole responsibility of the WHO:

- Sanitary and Phytosanitary Measures (SPS)
- Agreements on Technical Barriers to Trade (TBT)
- Trade Related Intellectual Property Rights (TRIPS)
- Trade in Services (GATS)

A joint working party of the WHO and WTO Secretariats on WTO agreements and public health (WHO/WTO, 2002) listed 11 policy issues which were affected by one or other of these agreements (see Table 3.1).

It is the issue of trade and health services to which the GATS is most relevant that concerns us here. We are interested in the extent to which the WTO is influencing national health service policy.

GATS differs from the agreement governing international trade in goods in several critical ways. At present, some of its rules and requirements do not apply to all services, but only to those sectors that each country has indicated it is prepared to open up to foreign competition. A government thus provides the WTO with a 'schedule of specific commitments' that lists which services and the ways of supplying those services it is prepared to open up to competition under GATS.

The over-arching aim of the WTO GATS agreement is to encourage countries to open up their service sectors to foreign competition, such that once a country has agreed to sign up to GATS for a specific service it must treat equally firms from all nations in terms of market access. Many see this as a back-door route to increasing the private market share of hitherto publicly provided services (Pollock and Price, 2000; Sexton, 2001; Krajewski, 2003).

There are four modes of international trade according to the GATS approach:

- **Cross-border supply:** Services can be supplied from one country to another: international telephone calls; Internet services; telemedicine; purchase of laboratory services from another country; purchase of medicines or advice on the Internet. Only the service itself crosses the border.

- **Consumption abroad:** Individuals or companies can go to another country to use a service there. Tourism is a prime example. This mode encompasses travel to another country to obtain a medical treatment that is better, faster or cheaper than that available domestically.
- **Commercial presence:** A company can set up subsidiaries, branches, joint ventures or representative offices, or can lease premises in another country to provide services there. For instance, banks can set up operations in another country, and US health care companies can set up hospitals or clinics in European countries.
- **The presence of natural persons:** Individuals from one country can be admitted temporarily to another country to provide services there, for instance fashion models, doctors or nurses. GATS does not apply, however, to people seeking permanent employment or to conditions for obtaining citizenship, permanent residence or permanent employment.

One of the issues surrsounding GATS is whether it applies to public services, such as a national health service (NHS). Although GATS encompasses all services, many civil servants and government ministers believe that it makes an exception for public services – those 'supplied in the exercise of governmental authority' (Article 1.3b) – such as health care, education or utilities. But GATS defines government services so narrowly – 'any service which is supplied neither on a commercial basis, nor in competition with one or more service suppliers' (Article 1.3c) – that the exception could be almost meaningless if one country were to challenge another country's **public services** at the WTO dispute panel as contravening GATS. It could be argued that where the NHS exists alongside a small private sector, as in the UK, the government service **is** provided in competition with another provider. Indeed, governments the world over have been deregulating and privatising both the funding and the provision of public services, sometimes on their own initiative, sometimes as a condition of IMF structural adjustment programmes.

However, this challenge to a country to ensure equal treatment of foreign private providers could only apply if the country being challenged **had** signed up to trade liberalisation for its private health services. It is argued by those who regard the concerns over GATS as overstated that few countries in the South have signed up to opening their health services to competition via a GATS commitment. Health and social services are 'trailing behind other sectors' in the rate they are being listed under GATS as open to competition. Of importance, however, are the WTO negotiations in 2005 and 2006. At the Hong Kong WTO meeting in 2005 and subsequently, the EU and the USA were trying to encourage, a more rapid opening of markets in this field in exchange for the North dropping barriers to trade in agriculture (GSP Digest, 2006b: 124).

Clearly, there are conflicting interests between northern companies and their countries wanting to export hospital services to new markets in developing countries, and those in the developing countries who might want to protect public provision. At the same time, there may be niche international health markets that some southern countries can exploit by providing cheaper operations. It can also be argued that foreign presence or cross-border supply is the only way that new health technologies will reach impoverished countries. In addition, the rich in poor countries might go abroad for private services, undermining support for a high-quality universal health service used also by the better-off. Woodward, in an extensive review of the implications of GATS for health care in developing countries, concludes that 'its potential effects on health systems are substantially negative in almost all developing countries' (2005: 511). In particular he argues that 'the stronger domestic regulations needed in an open health market is beyond the capacity of most developing countries' (2005: 511).

While the question of GATS and health services have received most attention, the same questions arise in relation to social protection, education and public utilities. In relation to social security, the exemption principle under Article 1.3 (c) is further reinforced by Artcle 1 (b)(ii) of the Financial Services Annex. Here included in services supplied in the exercise of government authority is specifically 'activities forming part of a statutory system of social security or public retirement plans' (quoted in Yeates, 2005a: 9). The inclusion of this social security exemption was supported by the EU and objected to by India, Pakistan and Egypt. Its inclusion affords legal and political protection of public social security schemes from GATS rules. Its existance 'places the burden of proof on a plaintiff government to demonstrate that any given social-security-related activity or measure of another member is not covered by the exemption' (Yeates, 2005a: 9). However, as Yeates (2005a) explains, the important caveat in Article 1(c) limits the effectivness of this social security exemption. This makes it clear that if any member state allows any of the services listed in Article 1(b) (ii) to be conducted in competition with a financial service supplier, then the exemption does not hold. Given the fact that the market provision of statutory social security benefits either as a complement to, a substitute for or a replacement for public (and employer) provision is happening in a number of countries, there is clearly a wider scope for international competition in the provision of social security schemes than might have appeared. Of course, the scope for such potential competition still depends on governments including such services in the schedule of commitments to international trade in this area they have signed up to. As of September 2003, 81 countries have made some commitments in health and accident insurance, and 64 for pension fund services. However, the overwheleming majority of those have entered caveats about excluding competition with mandatory schemes or insisted on their right to regulate foreign providers according to public policy objectives. So far it would seem that most countries have chosen to limit the penetration of this area of international commercial law into the social protection domain. The issue of the right of foreign providers to compete in this field has yet to be tested in any dispute at the GATS/WTO disputes procedures.

While most discussion about GATS and social security focuses upon the rights it might give multinational service providers to operate across borders and potentially undermine state social security services, an alternative reading of GATS sees it as a mechanism to improve the social security entitlements of temporary migrant service workers (Yeates, 2005a). Some southern governments, notably India, Pakistan and Egypt, have argued that GATS' fourth mode of trade could be expanded and interpeted to ensure that social security provisions for temporary migrant service workers could be made GATS-consistent. This would, for example, end discrimination against foreign nationals proving services by stopping the practice whereby some migrants pay social security in the host country without benefiting from those contributions. This could be done by enabling migrants to repatriate social security contributions, or by setting up a totalising agreement whereby periods of work in the sending and receiving countries both counted towards the qualifying period for benefit (Yeates, 2005a: 19).

In terms of the rights provided under GATS for foreign private education providers to enter the domestic education markets, the same set of principles applies as with health services with regard to Article 1.3 (c) and with regard to the decisions of countries to make trading commitments in this area. There have been some commitments to open markets, 44 countries having by 2005 agreed to do so, while some southern and northern countries have stood firmly against this trend. South Africa has argued strongly against higher education being turned into a global market through GATS, and within the EU certain countries, notably Austria, Cyprus, Finland, Malta and Sweden, have resisted cross-border supply and commercial foreign presence (MacGregor, 2005; Nuthall, 2005). However, there is an increase in provision of private education by all modes of supply. In terms of cross-border supply, web-based courses are growing and the World University Network provides entirely on-line courses not requiring attendance. In terms of consumption abroad, the USA, followed by the UK, Australia and Canada, are market leaders 'exporting' courses to students who travel from a range of countries. In terms of foreign commercial presence, universities from the same group of countries are developing private overseas campuses. In 2000, 35 Australian universities offered 750 offshore programs in Singapore, Hong Kong, Malaysia and China. Finally, in terms of the movement of persons, teachers are lost from poorer countries to richer ones. In sum, already international student mobility accounts for 3 per cent of the global service sector trade, but exporting countries are pushing hard within the GATS negotiations to increase this level of trade in education (Scherrer, 2002). Issues of the regulation of standards in this sector will be returned to in Chapter 6.

Protecting intellectual property: does TRIPS deprive poor countries of cheap medicine?

One aspect of the rules established with the formation of the WTO in 1995 was the global agreement on intellectual property rights: the TRIPS agreement. This agreement established in all member countries of the WTO a patent on **both pharmaceutical processes and pharmaceutical products** for 20 years. Previously only final products were protected, but now the process is protected too, thus eventually making illegal in WTO member countries the production of generic or non-brand-name equivalent drugs by alternative routes (of new drugs invented after 1995 for a period of 20 years). This inclusion of alternative routes to the same medicine was a clause hard fought for by northern pharmaceutical companies, who had long since seen their profit margins eroded by the generic drugs industry developed in places like India. They lobbied extensively to incorororate the idea of a protectionist and cartel approach to intellectual property in an otherwise liberalising trade agreement. In effect they lobbied for a new form of protectionism which went beyond keeping competitors out of your home market to include the idea of keeping your rivals out of the world market altogether by securing monopoly rights (Drahos and Braithwaite, 2004).

Least-developed countries were initially granted until 2005/6 to bring their laws into compliance with the TRIPS agreement. Some might have been affected earlier than this because of the impact on prices of new drugs that they import from countries making generic drugs who are not so poor. These exemptions were later extended to 2016. The impact of these changes will be to raise the price of drugs, as patented drugs are sold at very high prices to cover the cost of research and development into new processes. This issue has been a matter of dispute between poorer countries such as South Africa and Brazil and richer patent-holding countries such as the USA and to some extent countries in the EU. The focus of the disputes has been on HIV/AIDS drugs in the context of the pandemic that is undermining the economies of many African countries, but the issue also applies more generally.

The likely impact on poorer countries was acknowledged when the TRIPS agreement was finalised. Exceptions were provided for in terms of:

- **Compulsory licences**: This provides for a country to grant a licence to a company without the agreement of the patent holder on the grounds of a public health emergency.
- **Parallel importing**: This permits countries to import drugs not directly from the manufacturer but from a third country where those same drugs might be marketed at a cheaper price.

In the light of the controversy surrounding this issue, two other strategies have emerged to attempt to meet the needs of the poorer countries:

- **Voluntary differential pricing**: Some northern drug manufacturers such as GlaxoSmithKline have agreed with the WHO to sell drugs to South Africa and some other countries at a substantial reduction on the normal market price.
- **Global funds for drug purchase**: As we shall see in Chapter 6, the UN has established a global fund for AIDS, TB and malaria which is seeking donations from rich countries to fund anti-AIDS, TB and malaria projects in poorer countries. In principle, this could provide for the purchase of drugs for poor countries by rich countries. Indeed, such a fund to purchase drugs for the South by the North has been established under the Global Finance Facility set up by Gordon Brown (Chapter 6).

The controversy around this issue has arisen because of the global lobby by the main northern pharmaceutical companies, exercised mainly through pressure on the US government, to limit the situations in which countries might use the health emergency let-out clause to produce generic drugs. In 1998, 42 such companies launched a law suit against the government of South Africa, attempting to stop the country from adopting compulsory licensing for life-saving drugs. At the same time, the USA adopted trade sanctions against South Africa for this reason. However, under intense international pressure from NGOs and AIDS campaigners, the US policy was reversed and court action was stopped in May 2000 (Lee, 2003: 76). At the same time, the major drug manufacturers started negotiating 80 per cent cuts in prices in an attempt to stave off the use of compulsory licensing.

The issue came to a head at the next ministerial meeting of the WTO, at Doha in 2001. A Doha declaration resulted that reaffirmed the right of countries to adopt the compulsory licensing regulation and postponed until 2016 the application of the TRIPS agreement for the poorest developing countries. However, the fate of this declaration was put into question in December 2002 when the USA refused to ratify the regulations following from the declaration. It subsequently backed off from its position but this and many other WTO/GATS/TRIPS issues which affect the interests of developing countries were shelved when the Cancun meeting of the WTO collapsed. At Cancun many developing countries, led by Brazil, South Africa and India, objected among other things to the principle embedded in the TRIPS that developing countries must normally (except in a health emergency) pay a tribute to northern pharmaceutical companies. The dispute rumbles on in the context of the 2005 and 2006 Hong Kong WTO meetings (GSP Digest, 2006a: 246, GSP Digest, 2006b: 124).

OECD: Neo-liberal stalking horse in Paris or balancer of social and economic objectives?

The OECD grew in 1961 out of the Organisation for European Economic Cooperation created in 1948 to administer the Marshall Plan aid to Europe after the Second World War. Its membership now embraces all developed countries, and has been described as a 'rich-country club' of some 30 members. It does, however, have a Development Assistance Committee that advises rich countries on the co-ordination and focus of their aid programmes. The OCED describes itself as a forum where governments can pool ideas and expertise to tackle the economic, social and governance challenges of the twenty-first century (Woodward, 2004a). It provides a forum for policy dialogue among Ministers; it enables peer review and exercises surveillance of country policy through its Economic Development Review Committee (EDRC). In the words of one commentator (Marcussen, 2001: 18), 'the OECD ... indirectly compels member states into promoting a certain legitimate discourse even a certain concrete behaviour', and it 'plays the so-called ideas game through which it collects, manipulates and diffuses data, knowledge, visions and ideas to its members and to a still larger extent, to a series of non-member countries' (Marcussen, 2001: 29). So what ideas does it diffuse?

In terms of social policy ideas, the Directorate of Education, Employment, Labour and Social Affairs, established in 1974, achieved at the outset a high profile for the topic of social policy by the conference it convened in 1980 on the welfare state in crisis in OECD countries. While bringing the matter of social welfare higher up the agenda, it concluded that 'Social policy in many countries creates obstacles to growth' (OECD, 1981). The continued association of the OECD with the 'welfare as burden' approach by some commentators stems from that publication. Further work on social expenditures in OECD countries followed from this initiative. The interest in this and the enthusiasm of Ron Gass as the then Director of the Social Affairs Directorate led to the first meeting of social affairs ministers in 1988. OECD work in this field continued and became widely used among scholars. Publications followed and continue on pensions (OECD, 1988, 2002a, 2002b, 2005b), on health expenditure and policy (for example, OECD, 1990, 2004a, 2004b) and on labour markets and 'active social policy' (for example, OECD, 2005a). More recently, work has been undertaken on migration, on balancing care and work (OECD, 2002a, 2003, 2004c, 2005f), and on long-term elderly care. With the more recent creation of the Directorate of Education, work already undertaken in this field (for example, OCED, 1998b) is likely to increase.

The Council of the OECD in 1991, concerned about the burden of taxes on employment to sustain welfare expenditure, gave rise to further work on social policy by the Directorate, under the new Director, Tom Alexander. Concerned not simply to repeat the 'welfare as burden' liturgy and learning perhaps from parallel work of the OECD Development Centre which, in its review of the dynamic South East Asian economies, concluded that 'limited but effective action by the state ... [has led to] ... rapid return to growth' (OECD, 1993: 41), the social affairs official responsible for the draft of the impending ministerial conference fashioned the New Orientations for Social Policy document that asserted, 'Non inflationary growth of output and jobs, and political and social stability, are enhanced by the role of social expenditures as investments in society' (OECD, 1994: 12). This and other sentiments such as 'restrictions on social expenditure could be counter productive if the objectives of social policy are sacrificed. Jeopardising the quality of life ... may be the most costly route of all' (1994: 13), were adopted with minimal change as they progressed from the office in the Social Affairs Directorate, through middle-and high-rank meetings of government ministers, to the 1992 ministerial conference itself. These 'new' orientations reflect the fact that, in contrast to the US-influenced IMF and World Bank, the economic and social policy of the OECD represents a much more balanced set of economic and social considerations more typical of mainstream European social and economic policy. Indeed, the OECD's subsequent review of the role of social policy in the context of globalisation concluded, 'one of the effects of globalization could be to increase the demand for social protection ... a more useful blueprint for reform would be to recognise that globalization reinforces the need for some social protection' (OECD, 1999: 137).

That said, the attempt by the OECD to balance economic efficiency and social protection of necessity has led it to recommend policy changes which have been seen by some defenders of the European Social Model, or more particularly one version of this represented by the work-based welfare states of Germany and France, as evidence that the OECD is a neoliberal stalking horse located in Paris. This is most clearly the case in relation to the OECD's frequent calls to loosen up labour markets, but it is also evidenced by its critics in its insistence on the main purpose of education enhancing employability, its proposals to add a private tier to pension schemes, and its exhorting of countries to consider the options for mixed funding in health care.

Thus with regard to labour markets, Farnsworth reminds us that the 1994 OECD job study 'recommends that governments: tackle inflation, increase wage and employee flexibility, eliminate impediments to the creation and expansion of enterprise, relax regulations on employment, increase employee skills and reform social protection systems to ensure they do not impinge on labour markets' (2005: 223). Indeed, this emphasis in the work of the OECD on social protection continues. However, even within the core issues of labour markets, it is to be noted that in the most recent OECD report on this topic (OECD, 2006c) it is argued that strong trade unions and employment protection laws can go hand-in-hand with low levels of unemployment. Among the OECD activities on social policy during 2003 was ongoing work on employment-related social policies under the title 'Making Work Pay'. The summary report of the most recent work in this field, *Extending Opportunities: How Active Social Policy Can Benefit Us All,* argues: 'Instead of relying on taxes and public transfers alone, OECD countries need to look for other ways to deal with the social challenges of today. In this volume, the policies that aim to do this are called active social policies because they try to change the conditions in which individuals develop, rather than limiting themselves to ameliorate the distress theses conditions cause' (OECD, 2005f: 6). Such polices include giving children a good start in life by enabling people to reconcile work and care, and encouraging welfare-to-work programmes. The 'Babies and Bosses' programme of the OECD (see OECD, 2006c) has undertaken an extensive review of current policies in member countries and has concluded that 'too often policy helps parents of babies take some time off around childbirth and maybe provides some pre-school support when they are around 4 years old, but that is it. In practice, parents of children of other ages also face severe barriers to work. If policy makers want parents to be able to choose to work, they need to provide continuing support as children grow up' (OECD, 2006a: 2). Among the policy options argued for is legislation that entitles parents to change their working hours so that they are more compatible with their care commitments. This aspect of the work of the OECD is far removed from the neo-liberalism with which it has been charged.

The study by Henry et al., of the OECD's education policy in the context of globalisation concludes that globalisation has encouraged a convergence in education policies internationally around:

> An ascendant neo-liberal paradigm of policy in which education has been largely (though not solely) framed as human capital investment and development. Such a paradigm serves to legitimate a set of educational values feeding off and feeding into the broader culture of rampant individualism and consumerism unleashed by the victory of capitalism over communism. Educational purpose has, in large measure, been reduced to a student's calculus of job opportunities or to the state's calculus of maximum return on minimum input. (2001: 175)

They assert 'the OECD has been a key player in sponsoring such a set of values' (Henry et al., 2001: 175). Their analysis of OECD policy and the work of the associated Centre for Educational Research and Innovation (CERI) stops with the publication of its *Pathways and Participation in Vocational and Technical Education* (OECD, 1998). It will be interesting to see how OECD education policy develops now it has an independent Directorate of Education under Donald Johnston. The new strategic objectives of the Directorate agreed at a meeting of Ministries of Education in 2003 are all encompassing: to assist members and partners in achieving high-quality life-long learning for all, contributing to personal development, sustainable economic growth and social cohesion. In terms of the impact of globalisation on higher education, CERI is collaborating with UNESCO to develop guidelines for cross-border tertiary education. We will return to this example of the trans-border regulatory authority of the OECD in Chapter 6.

In terms of pension policy, the OECD does seem to strike a middle ground between that of the Bank with its strong push for defined contribution, fully-funded, privatised pensions and that of the ILO with its continued defence of the PAYG defined benefit systems. Its recent review of pension systems (OECD, 2005b) is a sound analysis of the costs and benefits of country schemes, with a comparative analysis of the pensions citizens might expect from the contributions they make. The earlier report, *Ageing Societies and the Looming Pension Crisis* (OECD, 2002a), pointed to the need to reform state PAYG schemes to '**ensure their sustainability**' by such means as extending working lives and eliminating early retirement provisions. At the same time it pointed to problems in private pension schemes, such as the consequences of stock market slump. Here the OECD has been active in promulgating guidelines for the better management of pension schemes (OECD, 2002b). In terms of the mix of public and private, the OECD argues that 'a higher share of retirement income from private sources makes it less likely that reductions in replacement rates of public pensions leads to an increase in poverty among the elderly' (Casey et al., 2003: 31).

In health service provision and policy too an even-handed approach is evident. A major OECD project on health culminated in a meeting of health ministers in May 2004. The report *Towards High-Performing Health Systems* (OECD, 2004a) was the basis of the meeting. The work programme addressed issues of rising costs and **efficiency**, outcomes of health expenditure and **effectiveness**, and issues of access and **equity**. Sub-projects were carried out on waiting time, emerging technologies, private health insurance, and long-term care. This was a typically thorough and professional OECD piece of work, undertaken in collaboration with professional bodies and the WHO. On how to achieve equity the report summary is clear: 'Ensuring comprehensive coverage of core services and minimising financial and other barriers to access have proven effective in promoting equitable use of health services' (OECD, 2004a: 14). On the temptation to increase consumer choice to ensure greater service responsiveness, the report warns against the cost and equity implications: 'multi-payer systems can raise spending and make it difficult to maintain equity in access' (OECD, 2004a: 15). Co-payments are also seen as having only limited benefit: 'Major savings from user fees are unlikely, particularly as vulnerable populations must be exempted to avoid restrictions on access' (OECD, 2004a: 16). The report is also clear that the benefits of private health insurance are limited: 'Private health insurance premiums are a regressive source of financing compared with income-based taxes or social insurance contributions. Private health insurance has not lead to significant reductions in public spending on health ... and entails trade-offs with equity that is costly to offset' (OECD, 2004a: 17). Given these conclusions, it was surprising to find some prominence given on the OECD website to a policy brief on *Private Health Insurance in OECD Countries*. However, this policy brief (OECD, 2004b) is far from a ringing endorsement of private health insurance, repeating many of the points above about the impact on equity and its failure to reduce public spending.

Even though I have argued that compared to the ideologically driven World Bank, the OECD should be regarded as a source of even-handed technically competent knowledge on aspects of social policy, it still finds itself tarred with that neoliberal brush. To some extent this might be due to the fact that its highest profile activity, the country appraisal mechanism (EDRC), is under the control of the Economics Directorate, and this gives emphasis to the OECD labour market policies which are clearly in favour of flexibility. Certainly the recent review of the social policy advice given by the OECD to 13 European Countries paints a picture that is nearer the neoliberal end of the range than the one painted above. Thus:

> OECD recommendations are to cut budgets, eliminate labour market rigidities, strengthen competition, free international trade, rationalise production, exploit all new technologies, refrain from demand management, strengthen the personal responsibility of individuals and families and reduce generous social security benefits. ... In addition to suggestions concerning labour market policies and social security benefits, the

OECD's general advice regarding health policy has been to allow for more competition. In education policy the principal suggestion is to improve education – particularly vocational training – and to better target higher education towards the labour market. Pension policy recommendations generally consist of a double strategy; increase the average age of retirement and add funded or private pension systems to public pay-as-you-go systems. (Armingeon and Beyeler, 2004: 228)

In sum, in contradiction to my earlier assessment based upon a broader reading of OECD policy analysis as distinct from just the country recommendations, Armingeon and Beyeler conclude:

hence the OECD has a coherent ideational strategy, which resembles the general liberal advice to reduce state intervention in society and the economy and to free markets from public regulations as long as these are not indispensable for the functioning of the economic exchange. (2004: 229)

Finally, the role of the OECD in relation to developing countries needs mentioning. Its Development Assistance Committee brings together Ministries of Development of OECD states with a view to co-ordination of aid policy and practice. We examine in Chapter 4 the UN's adoption of the Millennium Development Goals (MDGs) as goals and targets to be met with the support of OECD's official development assistance (ODA) in this context. These goals and targets were first articulated within OECD-DAC (Development Assistance Committee). OECD discussions about social policy for developing countries have a different location and often arrive at different conclusions and recommendations. Even if it is possible to characterise the OECD in terms of its views on national social policy for **developed** countries as even-handed and concerned as much with universalism and equity as with market efficiency, this isn't the case with regard to its views on social policy in a **development** context. Certainly from the standpoint of social policy ministries of the OECD, many would be very worried if some of the content of the goals and targets in social development policy designed by the OECD for the Global South were to be applied to social policy in the North. The OECD (1997) report *Shaping the 21st Century – The Contribution of Development Co-operation* set a number of specific targets for development policy. This led to a joint venture between DAC, bilateral donors and the World Bank to establish indicators of progress towards their achievement (www.oecd.org/dac/indictors). The OECD-DAC targets, later adopted as the Millennium Development Goals, are ones thought to be realisable by 2015 and focus on the poorest of the poor in poor countries. These targets include the halving of the number of people in extreme poverty, making basic education available to all girls and boys, enabling access for all to reproductive health services, with concomitant reductions in maternal and infant mortality rates and gender inequality. The two positives in this approach are the inclusion in the agreed measures of poverty of one indicator of inequality (the poorest fifth's share of national consumption), which suggest that redistribution policies are not forgotten entirely, and the fact that measurable and attainable targets and the monitoring of them are in place. The other side of the coin, as will be argued when discussing the subsequent Millennium Development Goals, remains the limited goal in terms of public service provision of only universal **primary** education and universal **reproductive** health. This leaves ample scope for the privatisation of the rest of social provision, while international attention is focused on these issues of basic service delivery only.

Further Reading

On the IMF and WTO: Boas, M. and McNeil, D. (2003) *Multilateral Institutions: A Critical Introduction.* London: Pluto.

On the IMF: Lee, S. (2002) 'Global Monitor: The IMF', *New Political Economy*, 7(2): 283–98.

On the WTO: Wilkinson, R. (2002) 'Global Monitor: The WTO', *New Political Economy*, 7(1):129–41.

On the OECD; Armingeon, K. and Beyeler, M. (2004) *The OECD and European Welfare States.* Cheltenham: Edward Elgar.

And Woodward, R. (2004) 'Global Monitor: The OECD', *New Political Economy*, 9(1): 113–27.

Global Social Policy: GSP Digest Section on International Organisations and Social Policy. (www.garpp.org)

Related Websites

www.imf.org
www.wto.org
www.oecd.org
www.unctad.org
www.brettonwoodsproject.org

4

The Social Policy of the UN and Its Social Agencies

This chapter

- Describes the social protection policies of the ILO
- Describes the policies of the WHO in the fields of health services and the global trade in health
- Reviews the approach of UNESCO towards education policy
- Reviews the significance of the MDGs and the role of the UNDP in helping countries meet them
- Evaluates the contribution of the UNDP Human Development Reports regarding national social policies
- Assesses the role of UNDESA and commends its new social policy guidelines
- Notes the role UNICEF has played in global social policy issues
- Draws interim conclusions from Chapters 2, 3 and 4 regarding the Bretton Woods Institutions and the UN

The ILO: promoting and defending international social security and labour standards?

In refreshing contrast to the neoliberal preoccupations and orientation of the IMF and the World Bank, the International Labour Organisation (ILO) derives its brief to set and keep common international labour and social standards from the social democratic climate of the period after the First World War when it was established. The ILO strategy has been to persuade governments by peer and moral pressure to sign up and ratify conventions of good practice in labour standards and social security. Only when governments ratify conventions has the ILO any power to seek an enforcement of them.

Initially the ILO conventions were concerned strictly with labour standards, although by 1934 convention 44 required that those states ratifying the convention maintain a system of unemployment benefits or allowances. Just as the political climate of 1918–20 established the ILO, so did the next phase of social optimism in the wake of the Second World War provide greater scope for the work of the ILO. The Keynesian climate encouraged the ILO at its Philadelphia meeting in 1944 to declare the convention on freedom of association and the protection of the right to organize. The declaration also asserted that lasting peace was only possible on the basis of social justice, and this required the right of human beings to economic security and equal opportunity. As a consequence, the ILO was to be responsible for 'examining and considering all international economic and financial polices and measure in the light of this fundamental objective' (Plant, 1994: 158). At the same time, the ILO was instrumental in enabling the UN to convert its 1948 Declaration of Human Rights into the 1966 Covenant on Economic, Social and Cultural Rights (see Chapter 6).

Throughout the 1950s, 1960s and 1970s, therefore, the ILO established a large number of conventions which, if ratified, provided for a well-functioning system of social insurance, social support and social assistance. The conventions, nearly 200, cover employment policy, human resource development, social security, social policy, wage-fixing machinery, conditions of work, industrial relations, labour administration, and the protection of women, children and indigenous peoples. An important emphasis in the internal workings of the ILO and in its policy prescriptions is tripartism, that good governance to secure social security requires the consensus of industry, workers and government. At that point the ILO could claim some success over the years of its existence. By 1994 the average number of ratifications per country had reached 41 (ILO, 1995: 115), although they have come under threat in the context of globalisation. Bohning (2005) has shown – assessing progress in four core labour standards: freedom of association, forced labour, child labour and discrimination – that continued implementation of these is a growing problem, especially in terms of freedom of association and discrimination (see also Chapter 6).

It comes as no surprise that this European welfare policy orientation of the ILO should have come under challenge in the 1980s with the ascendancy of neoliberal thinking and the increased influence of the IMF and the World Bank in shaping structural adjustment policies in many developing countries. How has the ILO held up to this challenge? What are the prospects for the continued influence of the ILO? What rethinking, if any, has it engendered inside the ILO? Here we examine the ILO policy and influence on pensions, social security and social protection, and how it has been modified in the light of the challenge from the World Bank's view that we described in Chapter 2.

From PAYG to four-tiered pensions, the 'extension of social security' and new policies for socio-economic security

We examined in the last chapter the challenge that the World Bank mounted to the Bismarkian PAYG work-based wage-related pension system defended by the ILO. This challenge was not just to the idea of a scheme embodying inter-generational solidarity, it was also to the widely established practice of this type of scheme. Orenstein (2003) reviewed the diffusion of pension policy across the world between

1989 and around 1990. He notes that countries gradually adopted either the Bismarkian framework or a Beveridge-type tax-based universal pension system, or more usually a combination of both. First to adopt the systems were European countries including the pre-communist Austro-Hungarian Empire, second were the leading Latin American countries in the 1930s, then the Caribbean. South Africa and other African countries, and the Middle East followed, as did Japan, in 1940 and later other East Asian countries. Adoption followed an S-shaped curve with, by 1920, 40 countries 'signing up', by 1940, 60 and by 1970, 140. Orenstein explains:

> The ILO ... vigorously promoted these aims (of a unified national insurance pension system) in regional conferences, through the dispatch of consultants, the publication of reform templates and the articulation of principles ... Activities of the ILO were a major factor in the export of pension ideas to the rest of the world ... all in all the organisation played a major role in the establishment of social welfare states. (2003: 175–81)

As we saw in the last chapter, it was the World Bank that was to take over this global leadership role in the 1980s and 1990s and gradually rolled back this state system of pensions in favour of privatised and individualised forms of pensions on the basis of its criticisms of the PAYG model.

The ILO fought long and hard to expose what it regarded as the flaws in the dominant World Bank thinking on pensions by arguing that there is no demographic imperative leading to privatisation, that the European-type schemes are reformable and sustainable, and that the privatisation strategy is merely a cover to increase the share of private capital savings. Moreover, it is argued that the strategy is risky in the context of unregulated capital markets and imposes a heavy burden on current workers who have to finance the existing PAYG system as well as funding their own schemes (Beattie and McGillivray, 1995).

However, within the context of the global debate about pension policy, the ILO came under pressure from the Bank to make concessions to its view that there was a role for private savings in the context of pensions. A major review and restatement of ILO pension policy by Colin Gillion, who was then head of the ILO Social Security section (Gillion et al., 2000), accepted some of the criticisms by the Bank of the ILO approach. In particular he acknowledged that pension schemes, especially in Latin America, had come under pressure to promise more benefits than could be sustained, and that in some countries the administration of the schemes left much to be desired. He uses the language of the Bank in the new ILO formulation, and even suggested the need for a four-tier pension policy. The first tier would be a state welfare pension that could be means-tested – a remarkable retreat from the ILO support for universalism. The second should be a compulsory PAYG-defined benefit pension with a moderate replacement rate of around 40–50 per cent of lifetime average earnings. The third should be a mandatory capitalised defined contribution pension. The fourth would be a voluntary private addition. The concession that the first tier could be means-tested, and the acknowledgement that there is a large role for individualised and capitalised private pensions, suggested that at that point the social security department of the ILO could no longer be regarded as a bulwark against Bretton Woods's policies.

Collin Gillion died suddenly soon after this major restatement of ILO pension policy was published, which perhaps goes some way to explaining a certain loss of direction regarding ILO pension policy subsequently. The ILO's annual conference in 2001 discussed a report on *Social Security: Issues, Challenges, Prospects* (ILO, 2001) that interestingly makes not one explicit reference to Gillion's work. The report reviewed some of the global debate about pension and other social protection policies, noting that 'Recent years have seen an intense international debate on the merits of increased advanced funding of national pension schemes' but concludes rather lamely that if countries shift from defined benefit schemes to defined contribution schemes 'certainty concerning contributions is achieved at the cost of uncertain benefit levels. This represents a complete reversal of previous objectives' (ILO, 2001: 87). The agreed resolution after the debate merely notes that in paragraph 4 'There is no single right model of social security … each society must determine how best to secure income security' (ILO, 2001: 2).

The concern and thrust of the report and concluding resolution was not so much with the debate about funded or PAYG, but rather with the extension of social security to those not covered. One of the reasons, as we saw in the last chapter, as to why the Bank could so easily win its argument in Latin America about reforming the state system was its low coverage. PAYG pensions had become a privileged source of income in old age for a small fraction of the population previously working in the state sector or the small formal economy. The schemes had become a source of inequity. In sub-Saharan Africa and South Asia more than 90 per cent are not covered, while in middle-income countries the percentage not covered ranges from 20 to 60 per cent. The 2001 ILO report foresaw four ways in which social security entitlement might be expanded in lower and middle-income countries: extending (existing) social insurance schemes; encouraging micro-insurance; introducing universal benefits or services financed from state revenues; or establishing means-tested benefits or services. Indeed, the ILO subsequently then launched a campaign to extend social security (www.ilo.org/coverage4all) and has published series of policy papers (for example, Reynaud, 2002) mainly focused on case studies of the extension of formal schemes or case studies building on micro-credit schemes and local collective self-insurance schemes.

This concern with not only the formally employed and insured but also with the wider poor was partly a response to the Banks' focus on the poor and partly a reflection of the fact that the new ILO Director General was Juan Somavia, who had been responsible for the 1995 Copenhagen UN World Summit on Social Development. He brought the concerns of the wider INGO community to the ILO to sit not always easily alongside its 'workerist' tradition. However, while the campaign to extend social security has had some impact in this direction, it was left to a separate and often overlooked section of the ILO to really advance thinking and practice in this area. Under the leadership of the new Director-General, a number of In-Focus work projects were specified. One of these on 'Economic and Social Security in the 21st century' (www.ilo.org/ses) took a broad brief to examine the policies in the twenty-first century that might contribute to universal citizen (and resident) security in the context of global labour flexibility. This programme tracked and argued for the emergence of a new universalism from below embodied, for example, in the provision in Brazil of universal cash income benefits conditional on their children's attendance at school to all families, or on universal categorical pensions in some southern African countries. The work programme was under the intellectual leadership of Guy Standing (for example, Standing, 2002), who argues that the century of the labouring man has come to an end, yet governments still try to link benefits to labour performance. To compensate for the workplace and livelihood insecurities of a globalised economy, a new system of income security for all citizens and residents is required which would provide for flexi-security.

The first and only major ILO-endorsed publication of this work programme was a report on *Economic Security for a Better World* (ILO, 2004a). Much of its focus was on several aspects of insecurity and how they are manifested: income insecurity, labour market insecurity, employment insecurity, work insecurity, skills insecurity, job insecurity, and voice or representation insecurity. Of most relevance to our concerns here is the report's analysis of the several ways in which income security might be enhanced. It is sharply critical of several of the conventional schemes for attacking income insecurity, such as social funds, means-tested benefits, public works and micro-credit. It suggests on the basis of their already existing reality that there are a number of promising avenues to universal income security. Among these are:

- **Social pension**: 'If a pension were set at about 20 per cent of the average earned income, it is fiscally feasible and would cost about 1–2 per cent of GDP'.
- **Minimum-income-with-schooling schemes**: 'The success of cash-for-schooling schemes in Brazil and Mexico suggests they could be copied elsewhere'.
- **Capital grants**: 'Some governments and some social scientists have been enthusiastic about new efforts to universalise access to capital such as the baby bond in the UK ... and the Alaskan Permanent Fund which allocates all citizens US$2,000 annually'.
- **Care work grant**: 'One of the greatest changes in the world of work has been the recognition that care work is work. One context that might help to legitimise giving basic security to care workers is the scourge of HIV/AIDS ... the catastrophic social and economic effects of the disease on communities in Africa will be addressed only if a systematic approach to social support policy is adopted'.
- **Basic income as of right**: 'Finally there is a growing advocacy for policies that would provide a basic income for everybody – or at least for specific vulnerable groups gradually to be extended to all – as aright without conditions'. (Schemes that bear this name are under serious consideration or partial implementation in Brazil, South Africa and Peru. (ILO, 2004a: 380–9))

It remains to be seen if this kind of policy advocacy becomes mainstreamed within the ILO or whether political resistance to such ideas inside the ILO will win out in favour of the far more conventional, and some would say far less convincing, campaigns to merely extend social security. At the time of writing the ILO's Social and Economic Security Programme (ILOSES) was being wound up. A new head of social security has been appointed, Michael Cichon. While Cichon has in the past been very critical of some of the more radical ideas, such as citizen's income argued for by Guy Standing of ILOSES, he is more than a defender of simply extending contributory social security. Not only has he been instrumental, as we shall see in Chapter 6, in working for a global social solidarity fund to finance social protection, he has also published papers (Pal et al., 2005) which demonstrate that universal categorical benefits are affordable in poorer countries. The ILO's Social Security Department is now developing a new department policy paper on social protection. A first indication of its contents was provided at an ILO-convened inter-agency 'Show and Tell' seminar on 20 February 2006. The ILO presentation by Cichon stated it was now developing 'a vision of national social security systems that countries on different levels of development can afford' (Cichon, 2006: 3). These would, for the poorest countries, ensure access to basic health care, provide a system of family benefits that permit children to attend school, involve a system of self-targeted basic social assistance (cash for work) for the able bodied, and a system of basic universal pensions in old age, invalidity and survivorship that in effect support families. It appears that the new terrain of struggle between Holzmann in the Bank and Cichon in the ILO might be the affordability and utility of 'universal' cash transfers or income support systems conditional on school or clinic attendance. As the ILO publishes its case for universal cash benefits, the World Bank Institute was organising in June 2006 a major global workshop on lessons to be learned from 'universal' conditional cash transfers. In Bank-speak, the blurb to the event (www.worldbankinstitute.org) agreed that 'evaluation from the first generation of programs show that CCTs programs are an effective means of promoting human capital accumulation among poor households. [But] there are concerns regarding [their] effectiveness and appropriateness ... for low income countries' (World Bank Institute, 2006).

The WHO: from health for all to health markets for all?

Several international organisations have a stake or role in shaping national health policies. Over the past 20 years from the 1980s to the first years of the twenty-first century, the situation has changed from one in which the World Health Organization (WHO), overseen by the World Health Assembly, was *the* paramount international agency, with the mandate to make both global health policy and to advise governments on national policies, to one in which the World Bank and the World Trade Organisation (WTO) have come to play an equal and some would say a more dominant role. This in turn has influenced the policy orientation of the WHO as it has tried to catch up with the terms of the policy debate set by the other actors, as is demonstrated below.

A WHO view on desirable national health system policies?

Although only established in 1948, the WHO idea has a longer history stretching back to the first International Sanitary Conference in 1851. Its initial focus was on preventing the spread of communicable diseases rather than a concern with the health systems of governments. Indeed, Siddiqui (1995) argues that when the WHO was being established, the USA was opposed to the WHO having anything to say about socialised medicine or health insurance, although the Soviet Union and some European countries argued otherwise. In practice the early years of the WHO were dominated by the medical profession's concern to use it as an instrument to eradicate and control major diseases about which there was little professional controversy.

However, the failure of the malaria eradication programme led to a refocusing on the broader social and policy determinants of health and disease (Walt,

1993; Koivusalo and Ollila, 1997). The WHO's *Alma Ata Declaration of 1978* (WHO, 1978) focused on the right to primary health care, and the subsequent adoption in May 1981 by the WHO General Assembly of the policy document *Global Strategy for Health for All by the Year 2000* (WHO, 1981) brought issues of access to and equity of health services centre stage. Among the clauses of the Alma Ata declaration was the assertion that 'the existing gross inequality in the health status of the people, particularly between developed and developing countries as well as within countries, is politically, socially and economically unacceptle' and 'Governments have a responsibility for the health of their people which can be fulfilled only by the provison of adequate health and social measures' (WHO, 1978). According to the 1981 policy, among the minimum requirements to secure 'the attainment by all citizens of the world of a level of health that will permit them to lead a socially and economically productive life' was in each country access to 'local health care, including availability of at least 20 essential drugs within one hours travel' and 'trained personnel to attend child birth and to care for pregnant mothers and children up to one year old' (WHO, 1981). The limited effectiveness of the WHO at this time, however, reduced the impact that this new concern with health services and their equity might have had on country policy. During the late 1970s and 1980s at the height of the cold war, the World Health Assembly (WHA) was seen by its critics, including the US government, as having become politicised. The WHO was at this time campaigning against infant feed manufacturers and linking the health status of the Arab population to the Isreal–Palestine conflict (Koivusalo and Ollila, 1997: 12). At the same time the funding for the WHO was reduced.

This 'universalist–normative' phase of the WHO focus on health policy came to an end in 1988 with the appointment of Hiroshi Nakajima as Director General. There followed a more 'technological and managerial approach to health issues' (Walt, 1993; Koivusalo and Ollila, 1997). 'In the 1980s the World Health Assembly (WHA) policies came closer to the more selective approach on some issues ... it produced its own modification of selective health care policies in the form of a risk approach ... to target health interventions at those with the higest risk' (Koivusalo and Ollila, 1997: 117). However, the pendulum swung again and with the ending of the cold war and with the subsequent sober reflection upon the impact of the 1990's neoliberalism there was a restatement of the universalist approach to health service policy at the 1998 WHA. A new global strategy should be effected, through regional and national health policies. This 'Health for all in the 21st Century' initiative was to build on the primary health care approach of the 'Health for All' strategy, but was to strengthen the emphasis on quality of life, equity in health and access to health services. However, in July 1998, Dr Gro Harlem Bruntland from Norway took over as Director General. She had a significant impact upon the organisation and priorities of the WHO, and it is a matter of controversy as to whether her influence can be seen as continuation and more effective implementation of the renewed health-for-all policy or a retreat from it. Three policy reports produced during her period of office exemplify the controversy: two are dealt with here, the third concerned with trade in health is examined in the susequent section.

Bruntland was concerned to rescue the WHO from the margins of internatioanl influence and establish it as an agency able to compete with, or at least stand alongside, the Bank as an authorative voice on global health issues and national health policies. To do this she believed it necessary to shift the WHO discourse from a purely normative one to one which engaged with economists. Health expenditures were to be encouraged not because they were morally desirable but because they were a sound investment in human capital. Indeed, for a period of time after she took over it was hard to find on the WHO website the earlier documents on Alma Ata or Health for All. In fact, according to one observer (Richter, 2004a: 79), Health for All was 'censored' from the WHO's headquarter's language. From Bruntland's point of view, what better way to focus the debate upon the investment function of health expenditure than to appoint a Commission on Macro-Economics and Health under the chair of Jeffrey Sachs?

Sachs, a Harvard economist, had shot to international fame or notoriety in the late 1980s and early 1990s when, together with his Harvard mate Larry Summers (who was in 1991 to become Chief Economist at the World Bank and later Chief Secretary of the US Treasury, where he was influential in sacking Stigletz (see Chapter 2)), he advised Poland and then the USSR on the shock therapy route to privatisation. Janine Wedel (1998) argued that Harvard's best and brightest entrusted with millions of aid dollars colluded with a Russian clan to create a system of tycoon capitalism.

With the appointment of such a person to steer the WHO Commission, no wonder Bruntland began to be seen by some critics as selling out to the Bank (Ollila, 2003; Richter 2004b). Indeed, some of the authors of the earlier Bank's World Development Report of 1993, *Investing in Health* (see Chapter 2), were transferred by Bruntland to the WHO. One commentator noted that the WHO had become 'a branch of Harvard and the World Bank' (Richter, 2004a: 78). Despite this controversy it needs to be said that Sachs has clearly been concerned to transform the negative image he developed during the shock therapy days. He subsequently became, after the work for the WHO Commission, advisor to the UN Secretary-General on how to realise the achievement of the Millennium Development Goals and lead author of the UNDP's 2003 Human Development Report: *MDGs, A Compact Among Nations to End Human Poverty*. His own most recent book (Sachs, 2005) sets out to show how to end world poverty and is very critical of both the US government and aspects of World Bank policy, as we will see later in this chapter. Given this change of political stance, it is not so surprising that the section of the WHO Report on Macroeconomics and Health is supportive of a universalistic approach to health investments in countries. The report (WHO, 2001b) called for massive additional financial resources to be committed to health both by developing and middle-income countries and by donors to support the poorer countries. A shift in health-related official development assistance (ODA) from US$6 billion in 2002 to $27 billion in 2007 and $38 billion in 2015 was called for. Significant was what the report had to say about within-country policy, especially in middle-income countries:

> Since many middle income countries provide inadequate financial protection for large portions of their population, catastrophic medical expenses impoverish many households. In view of the adverse consequences of ill health on overall economic development and poverty reduction, we strongly urge the middle-income countries to undertake fiscal and organisational reforms to ensure universal coverage for priority health interventions. We also believe that the World Bank and the regional development banks, through nonconcessional finance, can help these countries to make a multi-year transition to universal coverage for essential health services. (WHO, 2001b: 6)

Of course, a lot hangs on the interpretation of 'essential', and some fear that when linked to the MDGs (of which more later in this chapter) it might mean only a focus on basic health services. In any event it is not a call for privatisation and targeting.

The other significant WHO report with a focus on national health systems produced under Bruntland's leadership was the World Health Report of 2000: *Health Systems: Improving Performance*. In an ambitious, and some (Hakkinen and Ollila, 2000) say methodologically flawed, report the WHO sets out to compare and evaluate health systems within countries on the basis of five criteria:

- Level of health of population (disability-adjusted life expectancy).
- Distribution in health (equity in child survival).
- Responsiveness (seven elements).
- Distribution of responsiveness (responsiveness to minorities).
- Fairness of financing (household contributions compared to ability to pay).

These five criteria were weighted and averaged into one index, which was then compared to health input data (for example, health expenditures) to calculate an efficiency for the particular health care system. In the event, France was 'shown' to have one of the best health care systems, and the USA (and Finland!) one of the worst among the developed countries. The report has been important not so much for its findings but for the claims that its methods are suspect and do not stand technical comparison with those of the OECD or the World Bank or of independent scholars. Hakkinen concludes:

> The publication of this poor-quality report ... undermines WHO's authority as a producer of reliable information. In addition there is the risk that international comparative studies of considerably higher quality ... are overlooked ... Such studies include a range of comparative studies on equality in health, health care financing and the use of health care services (e.g. Wagstaff et al., 1999) to which no reference is made in the report. (2000: 13)

This raises the issue of the resources, both financial and technical, available to competing international organisations and touches upon the question of how global knowledge about social and health policies is produced. The OECD's work on health systems was initiated following this debate (Chapter 3).

WHO and WTO do a deal on trading in health

This issue of the technical competence of competing agencies figures again in the issue of the WHO's attempt to establish its policy on the vexed question of whether international trading in aspects of health care is a good thing. In Chapter 3 we reviewed the several ways in which international trade might impact upon issues of health. In 1995 the WHO produced its first report on the possible implications for health of the formation of the WTO. The issue only rose to a higher profile, however, after the appointment of Bruntland in 1998 and the emergence of a growing body of INGO and scholarly concern about the impact of trade creep on health and health policy. Bruntland herself argued that trade in health was here to stay. The issue was how to maximise its benefits. In 2000 a working group within the WHO under Nick Drager of the Globalization, Cross-Sectoral Policies and Human Rights team began work. By January 2001, the WHO's substantial draft report *Public Health and Trade: A Guide to the Multilateral Trade Agreement* (WHO, 2001a) emerged and was circulated for comment. It contained some quite serious warnings about the possible negative impacts upon health service policy. Thus, on the growth of private foreign investment in health service provision in poorer countries, it noted that:

> Greater, not less, regulation in general has accompanied more open markets … this can be expected for health services as well. For example, unless prevented by law, regulation or contract, private health insurance companies in order to be more profiable will drop high-cost patients, refuse coverage for those with pre-existing conditions and diseases, and limit benefits. Similarly, for profit hospitals will not provide free care to the poor unless required by law to provide a minimum amount. (WHO, 2001a: 72)

Similarly, with regard to the strategy of poorer countries attracting richer people to buy lower cost health care abroad, it worried that:

> Such services … have the potential to crowd out domestic need and skew health services towards procedurally complex services for foreign consumers and away from public health services needed by national citizens, especially the poor. (WHO, 2001a: 73)

The work was, however, continued and finished as a joint effort between the WHO and the WTO. Indeed, the WTO team was led by the Deputy Director-General Miguel Rodriguez Mendoza. The final document bears a number of WTO hallmarks, with most of the concerns which were being articulated by the WHO being balanced by and set aside by WTO-related considerations. Thus with regard to both foreign investment and consumption abroad, 'trade liberalization can contribute to enhancing quality and efficiency of supplies and/or increased foreign exchange earnings' and anyway 'there is no obligation on any WTO member to allow foreign supply of any particular service nor even to guarantee domestic competition' (WHO/WTO, 2002: 18). Indeed, the joint editorial by Gro Harlem Bruntland of the WHO and Mike Moore of the WTO asserts that: 'The multilateral trading system has a lot to contribute to increase global welfare' (WHO/WTO, 2002: 1).

UNESCO: The case for humanistic education – swimming against the tide?

The United Nations Education Scientific and Cultural Organisation (UNESCO) is the third of the UN social agencies we are considering in this chapter. It was established in 1945 and is housed in Paris. Although, as we shall describe later, it is centrally involved in the global campaign to achieve education for all, the emphasis of its work is not on **funding** education but on its **content**. This is also in part because it is one of the poorer UN agencies and suffered between 1984 and 2002 in not having the USA as a member and between 1984 and 1997 in not having the UK as a member. UNESCO in its education work assists countries formulate education policies, develops and disseminates manuals and teacher training packs on environmental and peace issues, and establishes norms and standards for vocational and technical education.

Its approach to education as a contributor to peace and tolerance rather than economic growth is reflected in the words of the Director-General of UNESCO, Koichiro Matsuura, in his foreward to the 2002–2007 work programme: 'The Medium-Term Strategy is formulated around a single unifying theme – UNESCO contributing to peace and human development in an era of globalization through education, the sciences, culture and communication' (UNESCO, 2002b). Thus, it seeks to create a link between UNESCO's mandate and role on the one hand and globalisation with a human face on the other hand. He goes on to argue that there should be three axes to the work of UNESCO: developing universal principles and norms while promoting pluralism and promoting empowerment. UNESCO's functions are listed in this work programme as being a laboratory of ideas, a standard-setter, a clearing house, a capacity builder in member states and a catalyst for international co-operation. A funding agency it is not.

Education for all: resources or quality?

UNESCO was centrally involved in the conference in Jomtien, Thailand, in 1990 which formulated the World Declaration on Education for All (EFA). The vision set out then declared that all children, young people and adults have the right to benefit from an education that will meet their basic learning needs in the best and fullest sense of the term, an education that includes learning to know, to do, to live together and to be. It is an education geared to tapping each individual's talents and potential, and developing learners' personalities so that they can improve their lives and transform societies. Article 1 of the declaration asserted:

> The satisfaction of these needs empowers individuals in any society and confers upon them a responsibility to respect and build upon their collective cultural, linguistic and spiritual heritage, to promote the education of others, to further the cause of social justice, to achieve environmental protection, to be tolerant towards social, political and religious systems which differ from their own, ensuring that commonly accepted human-istic values and human rights are upheld, and to work for international peace and soli-darity in an interdependent world. (UNESCO 1990: 1)

This was a classic restatement of the role and purpose of a rounded humanist edu-cation, far removed from the instrumental and economic growth-driven purposes of education we found articulated by the OECD. A decade later a subequent World Education Forum took place in Dakar, Senegal, which began to make rather more concrete the educational goals that should be achieved in the coming years. An Education For All (EFA) assessment provides the starting point of deliberations. Although there had been significant progress in some countries, it remained the fact that 113 million children had no access to primary education and that 880 million adults were illiterate (UNESCO, 2000). At the turn of the millennium, the UN was about to adopt the Millennium Development Goals (see below) that had already been articulated by OECD–DAC (see last chapter). In this context the Forum collectively commited itself to six EFA goals:

* expanding comprehensive early childhood education;
* ensuring access to free compulsory primary education by 2015;

- ensuring the meeting of the learning needs of young people and adults;
- achieving a 50 per cent improvement in levels of adult literacy by 2015;
- eliminating gender disparities in primary and secondary education by 2005; and
- improving all aspects of the quality of education.

It aimed to meet these goals by, among other things, increasing external financial assistance, improving donor co-ordination and ensuring earlier debt relief. UNESCO would co-ordinate EFA partners to achieve these ends.

To this end an international task force on EFA was set up in December 2001 to develop a comprehensive strategy to operationalise the Dakar Framework for Action. It resolved upon an international strategy in March 2002 that included five major actions which it regarded as essential to the achievement of the Dakar goals:

1. Countries would be urged to develop EFA plans as part of the PRSPs if they were party to these.
2. Increased global advocacy for EFA.
3. Increased international financing focused first upon primary eduation with the World Bank to launch and manage a fast-track initiative (see the education section of World Bank in Chapter 2).
4. Improved monitoring.
5. Speed up progress by paying attention to the international and regional mechanisms.

UNESCO adopted at its 32nd Session in October 2003 a programme and budget for further planning and implementation of the EFA goals that focused on its comparative advantage in country capacity building. Its regional offices would play a larger role. It would also focus on flagship programmes such as the support to countries in post-conflict situations, particularly in Africa, and its support to civil society groups to enhance the quality of EFA planning. The big question of money was in effect left to the Bank. In a rather similar way, UNESCO reveals its take on the EFA issue with its EFA Global Monitoring Report of 2005 (UNESCO, 2004). It addresses the quality imperative and asserts that 'In the many countries that are striving to guarantee all children the right to education, the focus on access often overshadows attention to quality' (UNESCO, 2004: 34). It concludes that in many parts of the world there is 'a huge gap between the numbers who are graduating from school and those among them who have managed to master a minimum set of cognitive skills' (UNESCO, 2004: 35).

UNDP: facilitating the realisation of the Millennium Development Goals?

The UNDP used to act as a grant-giving agency, mainly for the poorest countries, with the aim of capacity building to enable countries to reassess their development priorities. Among the five priorities agreed by the UNDP in 1994 was poverty elimination. To this end it established in 1996 its Poverty Strategies Initiative (PSI) to strengthen government capacity in analysing the extent and causes of poverty as well as improving policy articulation. Reviewing the outcome of PSI work in a number of countries for the UNDP, Grinspun concluded that:

- poverty 'stems from disparities in the distribution of power, wealth and opportunities. Changing these disparities always risks pitting certain groups against others';
- 'institutions (to address this issue) take time to develop';
- 'development agencies need to emphasise a capacity development agenda'; and
- 'to the extent that poverty reduction is politically charged, multilateral organisations, especially those of the UN, may be better placed than bilateral donors or development banks to act as trusted impartial advisors of governments and civil servants in convening national debates on the topic' (2001: 16–20).

These conclusions prefigure the subsequent decision to give the UNDP working with UNDESA (see below) the lead role in enabling countries to meet the Millennium Development Goals (MDGs) targets and to develop social polices to facilitate this. Another outcome of this UNDP poverty focus was the establishment of the UNDP International Poverty Centre in Brazil in 2004, which aims to facilitate South–South co-operation and analysis of policies to combat poverty. The latest issue of its *Poverty in Focus* newsletter addresses the issue of universal and conditional cash transfers (reflecting the renewed focus on this in the ILO and World Bank). Articles by Mkandawire (2006), Barrientos (2006), Bhorat (2006), Mehrotra (2006) and others all stress an equity approach to the question.

MDGs: global social progress or a narrowing–down of development goals?

The UNDP has been designated the UN agency with prime responsibility for enabling countries to meet the MDGs. What are the MDGs? Where did they come from? Are they a step forward or a step back? How does the UN think they can be met? What is the UNDP doing about them? How does this inititiative square with the work of the Poverty Reduction Strategy Papers (PRSPs) of the World Bank?

To understand the debate about whether the MDGs, which became a major plank of UN policy in 2000, are progressive or not it is necessary to put them in the context of earlier UN conferences, and in particular the Social Summit of 1995. The Social Summit of the UN held in Copenhagen in 1995 was the most significant in a line of recent summits. In 1990 there had been the World Conference on Education for All, and the World Summit for Children. In 1992 there was the Rio Summit on Development. In 1993 in Vienna there was the World Conference on Human Rights, and in 1994 the International Conference on Population and Development (see Schechter, 2005, for an account of these and other UN conferences). The all-encompassing theme, however, of the 1995 Social Summit represented the most significant global accord on the need to tackle issues of poverty, social exclusion and social development, North and South.

The summit concluded with ten commitments embracing poverty eradication, full employment and social integration. It also resolved a commitment to strengthen the framework of international co-operation and a commitment to create a (global) economic and political environment that would enable social development to be achieved. Most important from the point of view of the comparison of the Social Summit with the MDGs was the commitment to 'promote and attain the *goals of universal and equitable access to quality education, the highest attainable standard of physical and mental health and the access of all to primary health care,* making particular efforts to rectify inequalities relating to social conditions and without distinction as to race, national origin, gender, age or disability' (United Nations, 1995). It is against this commitment to a universalistic approach to social provision that the MDGs have to be measured.

It was actually in 2000 in the context of a five-year review of progress in meeting the Copenhagen Commitments that the MDGs were declared by the UN Secretary-General to be the shared goals of the UN system, the World Bank, the IMF and the OECD. Their origin lay, however, as we saw in Chapter 3, in the work of the Development Assistance Committee of the OECD. The MDGs and associated targets are:

- **Goal 1 Eradication of extreme poverty and hunger** with a target of halving, between 1990 and 2015, the proportion of people whose income is less than US $1 a day, and halving between 1990 and 2015 the proportion of people who suffer from hunger.
- **Goal 2 Achieving universal primary education** with a target of ensuring that by 2015 children everywhere, boys and girls alike, will be able to complete a full course of primary schooling.
- **Goal 3 Promoting gender equality and empowering women** with a target of eliminating gender disparity in primary and secondary education preferably by 2005 and in all levels of education no later than 2015.
- **Goal 4 Reducing child mortality** with a target of reducing the under-five mortality rate by two-thirds between 1990 and 2015.
- **Goal 5 Improving maternal health** with a target of reducing the maternal mortality ratio by three-quarters between 1990 and 2015.
- **Goal 6 Combating HIV/AIDS, malaria and other diseases** with a target of halting and beginning to reverse the spread of HIV/AIDS by 2015.
- **Goal 7 Ensuring environmental sustainability** by integrating the principles of sustainable development into country policies and programmes and reversing the loss of environmental resources.
- **Goal 8 Developing a global partnership** for development by:
  - developing further an open, rule-based, predictable, non-discriminatory trading and financial system. This includes a commitment to good governance, development and poverty reduction, both nationally and internationally;
  - addressing the special needs of the least developed countries, including tariff- and quota-free access for least-developed countries' exports, enhanced programme of debt relief for heavily indebted poor countries (HIPC) and cancellation of official bilateral debt, and more generous official development assistance (ODA) for countries committed to poverty reduction;
  - addressing the special needs of landlocked developing countries and small island developing states; and
  - dealing comprehensively with the debt problems of developing countries through national and international measures in order to make debt sustainable in the long term.

In sum these MDGs represented both progress and retrenchment. The progress was in the timelines for meeting them and for the commitment embodied in Goal 8 of the development of global partnership for development. The retrenchment was in the focus on targeting the poorest of the poor and in its focus only on primary education and reproductive health.

However, the world is now focused on the MDGs, and the UNDP is charged with their meeting. Once they were formally adopted by the UN general assembly in September 2000, Kofi Annan appointed Jeffrey Sachs (of Russian privatisation and the WHO Macroeconomics and Health Commission fame!) to lead a team of ten working parties charged under the auspices of the Millennium Project (www.unmillenniumproject.org) to examine the surest way of realising the MDG targets. The ten task forces were drawn from a range of scientific and policy communities, North and South as well as from the UN agencies themselves, and included ones on poverty and economic development (task force 1), primary education and gender equity (task force 3), child health and maternal welfare (task force 4) and water and sanitation (task force 7). Each of these task forces produced background state-of-the-art and progress papers during 2003 and final recommendations in 2004 that were in turn compiled into an overall report to the UN.

There are two features of the final report that are of interest to us. One is concerned with the action needed by donor countries and international organisations to help poorer countries achieve the MDGs. This will be addressed in Chapter 6 on global social policy. The other is concerned with the action needed by countries to make their contribution to the same end. First among the recommendations for countries is that they should take seriously the MDGs and should 'adopt development strategies bold enough to meet the MDG targets by 2015. We term them MDG-based poverty reduction strategies. To meet the 2015 deadline, we recommend that all countries have these strategies in place by 2006. Where Poverty Reduction Strategy Papers (PRSPs) already exist, those should be aligned with the MDGs' (UN Millennium Project, 2005b: xiv). These strategies should seek to strengthen governance, promote human rights, engage civil society and promote the private sector. There should be a focus among other things on health, education and gender equity. They should plan for a 4 per cent increase in GNP committed to such investments and 'calculate the need for official development assistance'. Among the recommendations was one for a series of quick-fix actions to be launched with the support of UNDP in 2005. These include:

- Ending user fees for primary schools and essential health services, compensated by increased donor aid as necessary, no later than 2006.
- Free mass distribution of malaria bed-nets and effective anti-malaria medicines for all children in regions of malaria transmission by the end of 2007.
- Expansion of school meals programmes to cover all the children in hunger hotspots using locally produced foods by no later than the end of 2006.

The reports recommendations on health and education policy are firmly within the paradigm of public responsibility for universal access to, and in some cases provision of, such services. The condensed recommendations on education in the final report derives from the excellent task force report, *Towards Universal Primary Education: Investments, Incentives and Institutions* (UN Millennium Project, 2005a).

This comprehensive report, whose lead authors included Nancy Birdsall of the US-based Centre for Global Development, notes after extensive analysis that 'For donors the task force has a simple message; fulfil commitments already made and deepen commitments to countries moving strongly towards more and better education for all ... There is little need for even better-documented recommendations if simple promises are not kept' (2005a: 10). Here Birdsall is in effect linking the work of the task force to the already existing work of UNESCO and the World Bank in its EFA campaign, and in particular the EFA-FTI and its associated catalytic fund discussed earlier (see section on UNESCO and World Bank). Indeed, the report's first recommendation for donors is 'to display bold political leadership and make firm financial commitments to make Education for All and the Fast Track Initiative work ... The expected resource needs estimated by the FTI Secretariat expected funding contributions and actual disbursements should be made public' (UN Millennium Project, 2005b: 12) There is much in the final report too about the international agencies identifying and supporting fast-track countries not only for EFA but for all the MDGs to serve as role models for the others.

The UNDP is now charged with enabling countries to work towards the meeting of the MDGs. How can this be done? Reflecting the recommendations of the report he steered, Sachs argues, 'each low-income country should adopt a poverty reduction strategy (PRS) specifically designed to meet the Millennium Development Goals' (2005: 270). Charles Gore, however, who is responsible within UNCTAD for producing their report on least-developed countries, believes that poor countries are caught in a double bind between the demands of the PRSP process and the aspirations of the MDGs. To realise the MDGs, countries would have to plan increased public expenditures. To have their PRSPs approved by the Joint Staff Assessment of the World Bank and IMF, countries will bear in mind that these two institutions are still basically wedded to the Washington Consensus involving macroeconomic stability and privatisation. However much countries are now supposed to own their own policies, 'the mere awareness of dependence on the Joint Staff Assessment ... [means] there is an inevitable tendency for Government officials to anticipate the endorsable' (Gore, 2004: 282). Indeed, Sachs acknowledges this:

> Alas, the international community's approach remains incoherent in practice. On the one side, it announces bold goals, like the MDGs, and even ways that the goals might be achieved, such as the pledge of increased donor assistance. Yet when it comes to real practice. Where the rubber hits the road, in the poverty reduction plans, the MDGS are expressed only as vague aspirations rather than operational targets. Countries are told to go about their business without any hope of meeting the MDGs. The IMF and World Bank have split personalities, championing the MDGs in public speeches. Approving programs that will not achieve them, and privately acknowledging, with business as usual that they cannot be met. (2005: 270)

The Bank on the other hand, in its publications for public consumption, insists that its social policy prescriptions for countries are designed to contribute the meeting of the MDGs. The social protection section (World Bank, 2003c) has set out how each of the goals can be advanced by adopting aspects of the Bank's social protection strategy. An acknowledgement of the tensions described by Gore and Sachs between the PRSPs and the MDGs is made in a paper by the more radical Social Development Department of the Bank (see Chapter 2 regarding the SDD).

Reviewing the extent to which the Bank is enabling countries to meet not only the narrower MDGs but also the broader goals of the 1995 Copenhagen Declaration, it notes that:

> Important challenges remain, however, including ... balancing the tension between the need for realism in the PRSP and the need to aspire to more ambitious results related to the MDGs. [It concludes that] The Bank will continue to be a strong supporter of the MDGs, assisting countries to reach the targets imbedded in the MDGs, supporting country-owned development and poverty reduction strategies, but also continuing to call global attention to the funding gaps, which if not closed will continue to constrain developing countries and the poor that live within them from attaining the MDs. (World Bank 2004b: 5,16)

It remains to be seen if the Sach's strategy that countries should build increased aid into their PRSP plans combined with the pressure being mounted on the international community to forgive debt and increase aid will turn the tables and ensure that PRSPs are MDG-realistic. Certainly after the G8 gathering in Scotland in July 2005,which cancelled the debt of HIPC countries, and after the UN Millennium plus 5 summit in September 2005, there does appear to be a turning of the tide in terms of international commitments. Indeed, within the context of the planned reforms of the UN subsequent to the September 2005 summit that we examine in Chapter 7, it appears that the UNDP will gain a more central role within the projected 'one UN', and moreover there are currently discussions ongoing to inject MGD planning into the PRSP process. UNDP and UNDESA are preparing guidelines for the PRSP process including in the area of social policy. Sundaram of UNDESA (see below) asserted at a recent UNICEF conference that 'it is important that the UN offers meaningful and superior social policy alternatives to those so far used within the PRSPs' (Sundaram, 2006). We examine these guidelines in the section on UNDESA later.

The UNDP Human Development Reports: championing human, not economic, development

In addition to the operational section of the UNDP, the organisation is also noted for its annual *Human Development Report (HDR)* produced since 1990 by its separate HDR Office. Strictly speaking, the report is a report to the UNDP. This annual publication is read as keenly by development studies experts as the *World Bank Development Report* with which it is often in competition. It fashioned, out of an earlier debate among development analysts, a new measure of social progress, the Human Development Index (HDI). This combines longevity with educational attainment and a modified measure of income to rank countries on a scale somewhat differently from the rank order that would pertain if gross national product (GNP) alone were used. For this reason alone it helped reinforce the paradigm shift in the late 1990s from fundamentalist liberalism towards some kind of socially orientated adjustment and development policies. Over the 15 years of its publication it has recommended a number of international policy recommendations, some of which will be reviewed in Chapter 7 dealing with global governance and its reform. At the same time it has occasionally advised national governments in areas related to social policy. In 1991 the report called for a restructuring of social expenditures away from military expenditure towards social spending. The 1995 report called for countries to ensure that women had at least achieved a 30 per cent threshold in decision-making processes. The 1996 and 1997 reports concentrated on pro-poor growth and poverty reduction. The 2000 report lent its weight to the importance of a rights-based development strategy for countries. The 2004 report addressed the issue of how countries might secure both equitable development and a respect for cultural diversity.

An offshoot of the UNDP HDR Office activities was a publication in 1997 resulting from the collaboration of one of the UNDP HDR advisors, Richard Jolly, and Santosh Mehrotra, then of UNICEF (Mehrotra and Jolly, 1997). The book drew upon the lessons of those countries that the UNDP HDR had reported over the years as having higher than expected measures of human development given their measures of economic development. Reviewing the positive experience that combined economic growth with conscious social development in Botswana, Mauritius, Zimbabwe, the Indian state of Kerala, Sri Lanka, the Republic of Korea, Malaysia, Barbados, Costa Rica and Cuba, Chen and Desai concluded:

> The key ingredients to successful social development appear to be responsive governance, socially friendly economic policies, and the universal provisioning of social services. In all these endeavours the role of government is central. (1997: 432)

It was therefore of interest that in 2003 the UNDP HDR was to be focused upon the MDGs, and that among the team tasked to prepare the report were not only Jolly and Mehrotra but also, as guest contributing editor, Jeffrey Sachs. How would the drive and focus of Sachs's concern to target limited public expenditures on those areas such as primary education identified in the MDGs square with the confessed commitment of Mehrotra and others to universal public spending? Chapters 4 and 5 of the report address respectively public policies to improve health and education and private finance and provision of health, education and water. The tension between the authors and the real policy dilemmas posed in the context of limited resources within countries is captured well in this quotation about education:

> Despite improvements in the 1990s, the countries with lower primary enrolments spend more per pupil for higher education than primary education ... These countries need to focus on primary education, not spend more on higher education. Still, additional resources are needed for higher education as well if countries are to build capacity to compete in the global economy – but not at the cost of primary education. Entire education budgets need to increase. (UNDP, 2003: 95)

The report is also clear that user fees for primary education are counterproductive from the point of view of meeting the MDGs. But in the comparable paragraph dealing with health expenditures and equity, no such compromise between public expenditures on primary health and hospitals appears to be struck:

> Spending on basic health care is shared more equitably than total health spending ... Thus if poor people are to benefit, more resources must go to primary health care. (UNDP, 2003: 101)

However, the issue is addressed in the subsequent chapter dealing with the contribution of the private sector. It states again that all citizens should have access to basic health services and goes on to suggest that 'Private provision can help meet different needs. But is equity ignored in this process?' (UNDP, 2003: 113). After reviewing the impact of privately managed care organisations in parts of Latin America, the section concludes that equity is ignored 'Because managed care organizations attract healthier patients, sicker patients are being shifted to the public sector. This two-tier system undercuts the pooling of health risks and undermines cross-subsidies between healthier and more vulnerable groups' (UNDP, 2003: 113).

Freed of the constraints of the collaboration with Sachs, Mehrotra and a UNICEF colleague were able to articulate more clearly their concerns about the negative impacts of leaving the private sector free to enter those sectors of education and health provision not covered by targeted public spending. In *Eliminating World Poverty: Social and Macroeconomic Policy for the Millennium Goals* (Delamonica and Mehrotra, 2006), drawing lessons from the early industrialising countries in Europe, they argue that the experience of the now-industrialised countries suggests that the sequence for social services should be comprehensive provision by the state early on, followed by more targeted interventions to reach the unreached, and then public–private partnerships to serve different markets, depending upon the nature of the services in different sectors. They reject state abdication in the presence of pre-existing markets in developing countries that is typical of neo-liberal reforms. The book goes on to discuss how to ensure the appropriate level, equity and efficiency of public spending and how to raise **additional** resources domestically, privately and internationally.

UNDESA: from side show to the Bank and UN social agencies to lead formulator of UN social policies?

As we shall learn in the chapter on global social governance, formally speaking it is the Economic and Social Committee (ECOSOC) of the UN that holds responsibility for developing the economic and social policies of the UN. This authority does not in practice stretch to embrace the policies of the UN social agencies that have been described earlier who have their own policy-making assemblies. So what does the UN have to say about social policy apart from that which is articulated by the constituent social agencies? It is to the Secretariat of the Department of Economic and Social Affairs based in New York, and in particular to the divisions within it of Social Policy and Development and also of Public Economics and Public Administration that we need to turn to find an answer. The Department as a whole was, until 2004, under the responsibility of Nitin Desai, under-secretary-general for economic and social affairs. It is now led by Jose Antonio Ocampo, who had previously been executive secretary of the UN Commission for Latin America and the Carribean. In that job he had been a well respected critic of neoliberal globalisation. In *Globalization and Development: A Latin American and Caribbean Perspective* (Ocampo and Martin, 2003), he had argued for an agenda for the global era that 'needed to achieve three foremost objectives of a new international order; a supply of global public goods, the gradual correction of international asymmetries, and the progressive construction of a rights-based international social agenda' (2003: xv). Following a reform proposed by Kofi Annan to strengthen the policy articulation capacity of the UN in the economic and social field, Ocampo now has been allocated an assistant under-secretary, a post taken up in 2005 by Jomo K.S. (Jomo Kwame Sundaram), who equally has earned respect as a critic of neoliberal economic and social policies in Malaysia (Jomo K.S., 1998). He was founder of the respected website www.ideaswebsite.org which explored alternative development models. At the time of writing it is perhaps too early to see what impact these two intellectuals will have on the global standing of UN economic and social policy when compared to that of the Bank. A straw in the wind, however, is indicated by a contribution made by Jomo K.S. to a UNICEF workshop on social policies (see below). Here he noted, 'we now have agreement that the Washington Consensus failed. The World has done more poorly in the last quarter of the the last centry than it did in the 1950s and 1960s: this is no small indictment of the Washington Consensus' (Sundaram, 2006). At the same time, he noted with approval the debate underway on universalism and targeting, the recent work of the ILO suggesting that universal provision was not actually unaffordable and the shift in thinking about this in the World Bank. We return at the end of this section to the significant new initiative under the direction of Jomo K.S. to develop within UNDESA a set of social polcy guidelines for use by countries in their attempts to meet the MDGs. These have been developed in part on the basis of the earlier work of UNDESA's Division of Social Policy and Development.

The Division of Social and Development Policy was until recently headed up by John Langmore, who has now been replaced by Johan Scholvinck. This division is important to us for its role as secretariat to the Commission for Social Development. The Commission, consisting of government representatives, meets annually in February to articulate policy in one or other aspect of social development policy as agreed by its multi-annual work programme. Background policy analysis is undertaken by expert working groups and seminars, and the Commission usually has on its agenda a non-paper in draft prepared by the secretariat based upon these earlier considerations. The choice of experts and the drafting by members of the team, including in recent years Serge Zelenev in particular, is important in framing the political debate.

Two recent reports to the Commission prepared in this way are of interest. The report of the UN Secretary-General (2001) on *Enhancing Social Protection and Reducing Vulnerability in a Globalizing World* prepared for the February 2001 Commission for Social Development almost became an important milestone in articulating a progressive UN social policy. Among the positive features of the report were: a) the fact that it was the first comprehensive UN statement on social protection; b) the thrust of its argument was that social protection measures serve both an equity-enhancing and an investment function and such measures need to be a high priority of governments and regions; and c) it argued that social protection 'should not [serve only] as a residual function of assuring the welfare of the poorest but as a foundation for promoting social justice and social cohesion' (UN Secretary-General, 2001) . It has to be said, however, that discussion on this paper became bogged down at the Commission and was never approved. It remains a non-paper. While the EU were supportive, the G77 wished to link it to issues of global financing and global governance arrangements (Langmore, 2002). The

North–South impasse on global social standards (examined in more detail in the chapter on global social policy) stemming from the labours standards and global social policy principles stand-offs bedevilled this Commission's work.

A more recent meeting of the Commission for Social Development (CSD) (47th Session on 4–13 February 2004) seems to have partly managed to avoid this pitfall in terms of its discussion of the issue of improving public sector effectiveness. The Report of the UN Secretary-General (2004) on this topic did contain among its recommendations the sentiment that international co-operation should 'include the elaboration of norms and guidelines ... on the respective roles and responsibilities of the public and private sector' (2004: para. 59a), but such an idea did not find expression in the agreed conclusions. These agreed conclusions rather stress 'that each government has primary responsibility for its own economic and social development, and the role of national policies and development strategies cannot be overemphasised' (2004: para. 7). On the more central question of the issue of universalism versus targeting in social provision and the balance of public and private provision, the agreed conclusions are very much in favour of universalism and equity: 'The Commission emphasise the crucial role of the public sector in, inter alia, the provision of equitable, adequate and accessible social services for all so as to meet the needs of the entire population' (2004: para. 1), and again in the context of assessing the choice between public and private provision the Commission notes that while services can be provided by private entities it also 'reaffirms that any reform of public service delivery should aim at promoting and attaining the goals of universal and equitable access to those services by all' (2004: para. 12). A review of this report is to be found in Scholvinck (2004).

The other vehicle the Division and Department commands for contributing to the global discourse on desirable national social policies is the *Report on the World Social Situation* that it presents to the General Assembly. Unfortunately this report does not receive the attention given by the press, scholars and the development community to the two annual report giants, the *World Development Report* of the World Bank and the *Human Development Report* of the UNDP, nor for that matter the attention afforded in the more specialist circles to the annual reports of the WHO and ILO. This is partly because the reports have been produced since 1952 only every four years (from 2003 on a biennial basis), have not been marketed with a catching theme, and because the technical resources allocated for their production are minimal. Each issue has been very wide-ranging, although themes have been selected over the years for special attention. From 2003 the move was made to improve the profile of the report and to enhance its policy relevance and impact by focusing on one theme. The 2003 report (UNDESA, 2003b) addressed the issue of vulnerable population groups. Policy recommendations for countries, often drawn from the conclusions of various UN social conferences under the three headings of 'addressing barriers to employment', 'promoting social integration and social protection' and 'rights-based approaches and rights deficit', were specific and often challenging, especially for example with regard to the rights of indigenous peoples to benefit from their own intellectual property (2003b: para. 32). With an eye to more global attention, the report in 2005 (UNDESA, 2005c) was focused upon inequality, as was that of the 2006 *WDR* of the World Bank, also published in 2005. It sounded an alarm over persistent inequalities world-wide and argued that it is difficult to advance development within countries without first addressing and overcoming social segmentation in society.

Even less attention is normally given by UN commentators to the parallel Division of Public Administration and Development Management under the Direction of Guido Bertucci. This division exists to 'assist member states in ensuring their governance systems function in an open and participatory manner'. In 2001 under its former name of the Division for Public Economics and Public Administration it embarked with the authority of ECOSOC on another biennial report: the *World Public Sector Report* that is intended to analyse the challenges faced by governments in reforming particular areas of their public sector. The theme of the first report in 2001 (UNDESA 2001) was, unsurprisingly, 'globalization and the state'. It is actually both a rather good primer on the case for strengthened state capacity in an era of economic globalisation and a valuable critique of the shortcomings of the new public management theory that appeared as the little brother of neoliberal economics in the 1980s. It argues that 'the assumption that globalization reduces the size of government is not supported by the evidence' (UNDESA, 2001: 5) but agrees that the 'state is called upon to act as linking pin of processes of planning, consultation and negotiation and decision making involving diverse players' (UNDESA 2001: 31) and that in the case of developing countries there is a need to strengthen state capacity to maximise the benefits that are to be gained from globalisation. An important thrust of the report is the need in some developed countries to re-establish, and in some developing countries to establish for the first time, an ethic of public service among officials. This report of the Division of Economics and Public Administration is being followed up in practical work via its Online Network in Public Administration and Finance (UNPAN) (www.unpan.org).

This brings us to the significant initiative of UNDESA working with UNDP to develop in 2006 guidelines for countries in six policy fields including social policy. These guidance notes are being critically reviewed by Joseph Srtiglitz. At the time of writing the first draft of the social policy guidance notes was available for public consultation at http://esaconf.un.org/WB/?boardid=ndsnet. These are being drafted by Isabel Ortiz. She had previously worked on a social protection strategy for the Asian Development Bank (ADB, 2001) which was subsequently adopted by ESCAP (Economic & Social Commission for Asia & the Pacific). The UNDESA/UNDP guidelines stress the importance of social policies being inclusive and equitable and a necessary development initiative. The guidelines are framed within an account of the damage done by the World Bank and other actors to earlier attempts in developing countries to fashion sound employment, social protection, education, health and social cohesion policies:

> Many of these initiatives were weakened after the 1970s, when redistributive policies lost popularity with the rise of market-orientated reforms and critical attitudes towards state intervention. Social polices were left to a bare minimum, only to be reconsidered during the 1990s with renewed attention, or rhetoric at least, of development polices to poverty reduction. Even then, social policies have been treated as marginal; the idea of 'adjustment with a human face', social safety nets in times of economic crisis, or many donor-funded social investment programmes, were good initiatives developed by committed and concerned professionals in attempts to assist populations, but not adequate lasting solutions. These interventions did not address the structural causes of social tensions or build institutions to ensure adequate and sustainable development and social cohesion. (Ortiz, 2006: 3)

The guidelines are extensive and draw upon ILO, WHO, UNESCO, UNICEF and other UN policies and, where useful, some recent World Bank work. The first draft did, however, show signs of being written in the context of the MDG preoccupation with only basic services; the education and health sections making as yet no reference to necessary investments in secondary and tertiary education or hospital-based health services. The next draft took account of this criticism, remedied this oversight and calls for 'comprehensive universal health and education systems for nation building' and stresses, the importance too of regional and global social governance. It will be fascinating to watch the progress of these guidelines through the UN policy-making system. At the time of writing, UNDP are questionning some of the contents. I trust that because they are a central part of the UN MDG push and because they are being driven by actors within UNDESA who have the respect of the Global South they will not suffer the fate of an earlier attempt within the UN in 2000 to establish a set of global social policy principles. These, as we shall see in Chapter 6, were objected to by many in the Global South for fear that they might become new conditions for receipt of loans and grants.

It will be argued in Chapter 7 that the role of the UN must be strengthened in the social policy field vis-à-vis that of the World Bank and IMF. If that is to be achieved it is the work of the Department of Economic and Social Affairs in New York together with the UNDP that will carry the increased analytical and administrative burden. Additional technical and analytical resources will be needed by them to meet this challenge.

UNICEF: children's rights as a vehicle for global social reformist policies?

Long before the World Bank invented its poverty programme, in the decades of unreformed fundamentalist structural adjustment that did so much to further indebt the South to the North, it was dedicated professionals such as James Grant, head of UNICEF until his death, Richard Jolly, Frances Stewart and Andrea Giovanni, UNICEF economists, and others inside UNICEF who did so much to monitor the impact on children of the global economic conditions of the 1980s, articulate an alternative strategy of adjustment with a human face (Cornia et al., 1987) and engage not only in public polemic but directly with the World Bank and IMF professionals to attempt to shift thinking. Jolly (1991) reports that as early as 1982 James Grant was in discussion with leading Bank and Fund personnel on the impact of adjustment policy. As a consequence, a joint Bank/UNICEF meeting took place in 1994 at which the UNICEF paper entitled 'IMF Adjustment Policies and Approaches and the Needs of Children' was presented. To cut a long story short (detailed in Jolly, 1991), the influence that began then and continued through, for example, the annual UNICEF publication on *The State of the World's Children* (1995) led to the reform of World Bank policy and the adoption by it of lending strategies that aimed to protect the poorest as we described earlier. By 1995 UNICEF was able to make the following claim: 'In 1990 the World Summit for Children set goals for reducing deaths, malnutrition, disease and disability among the children of the developing world. Four years later, a majority of nations are on track to achieve a majority of these goals' (UNICEF, 1995). Within the East European region after the collapse of the communist project, the regional child development centre attached to UNICEF in Florence played an important part in shifting thinking in that region from the neoliberal agenda of the Bank and IMF towards a set of policies that addressed the social costs of the transition (UNICEF, 1993 et seq.).

UNICEF, in particular its Division of Policy and Planning in New York, has continued to provide an institutional home to a number of significant international social policy analysts who have from time to time had a marked impact upon the global social policy discourse. Perhaps foremost among these has been Santosh Mehrotra. With Richard Jolly he wrote, as we reported in the section earlier on the UNDP, the influential *Development with a Human Face* (Mehrotra and Jolly, 1997) that drew lessons from developing countries that had achieved a higher HDI than would have been expected from their level of economic growth. Subsequently, he collaborated with Enrique Delamonica at the UNICEF office on *Eliminating World Poverty: Social and Macroeconomic Policy for the Millennnium Goals* (Delamonica and Mehrotra, 2006). UNICEF Division of Policy and Planning is likely to continue to provide significant inputs to the global debate on how best to achieve the MDGs. In May 2005 it contributed together with the UNICEF-ICDC in Florence to a South Asian Regional UNICEF conference on social policy among the speakers at which were Richard Jolly, Jomo K.S. of UNDESA, Santosh Mehrotra, Enrique Delamonica and others. The conclusions of this workshop were that there were key social policy issues that needed to be taking account of in seeking to attain the MDGs. Among these were the multiple roles that social policy played as 'a key instrument for social protection (through social service provisions and social security), economic development (through human capital formation and generating consumer demand), equity through redistribution, social reproduction (assisting with care), and social and national cohesion' (Lotse, 2006: 54). This work will be reviewed in a conference on social policy to be organised by UNICEF in New York in late 2006.

That is not to say that UNICEF has been immune from criticism. Other aspects of its work, in particular its collaboration with corporate partners (www.unicef.org/corporate_partners/index.html), have led it to be accused of unprincipled collaboration with companies who themselves have contributed to the ill-fair of children (Ollila, 2003; Richter, 2004a). Set against this is the role of UNICEF in developing and working for the Convention on the Rights of the Child. This Convention, agreed upon in 1989 and subsequently becoming the most ratified UN Convention of all time, was the first legally binding instrument to incorporate the full range of human rights – civil, cultural, economic, political and social. Its four core principles are non-discrimination, devotion to the best interests of the child, the right to life, survival and development and respect for the views of the child.

Conclusion: contending views, differential clout

The World Bank, the IMF, the OECD and the UN agencies therefore present us with a picture not of the slow diffusion of agreed social policy ideas and practices across the globe as the world society theorist might have us expect. Rather, the picture is one of a contest of ideas and principles in each sector of social service. The disputes take place between agencies and within them. The disputes about pension policy have been the most heated, but that concerning the proper role for the private sector in health and education provision comes a close second. While there has been more consensus between some parts of the Bank and the UN system around the intellectual case for universal public provision the IFC activities of the World Bank Group, the impact of the WTO GATS and the MDGs target may conspire to continue to push countries towards limiting public expenditure on services only for the poor. Certainly, as we shall explore in Chapter 7, we are faced with a complex set of global agencies all contending for the right to influence national policy and for the content of that policy. Moreover, the agencies have differential capacity to influence national social policy in terms of the instruments at their disposal; the World Bank and IMF's conditional lending versus the UN's moral persuasion, their command of resources; the richer Bank versus the poorer UN and, as we will explore further in Chapter 5, their organisational links to international epistemic communities and think tanks, for example, the World Bank's Institute and global development networks (GDN) versus the UN's Research Institute for Social Development (UNRSID).

Further Reading

On UN conferences: Schechter, M.G. (2005) *United Nations Global Conferences.* London: Routledge.

On ILO and social security issues: Sigg, R. and Behrendt, C. (2002) *Social Security in the Global Village.* London: Transaction.

On WHO and health issues: Lee, K., Buse, K. and Fustukian, S. (2002) *Health Policy in a Globalising World.* Cambridge: Cambridge University Press.

On the MDGS: Sachs, J. (2005) *The End of Poverty.* London: Penguin; and Mehrotra, S. and Delamonica, E. (2005) 'The Private Sector and Privatisation in Social Services: Is the Washington Consensus Dead?' *Global Social Policy,* 5: 141–74.

Global Social Policy Digest section on International Organisations and National Social Policy (www.gaspp.org)

Related Websites

www.ilo.org
www.who.org
www.unesco.org
www.undp.org
www.un.org/esa

5

The Social Policy of International Non-state Actors

This chapter

- Assesses the contribution to global social policy of think tanks, policy advocacy coalitions, knowledge networks and epistemic communities
- Describes the role of INGOs and consulting companies in the global social policy-making process
- Assesses the views of global business on social policy
- Analyses the contribution of old and new social movements and global civil society to social policy thinking

The part that non-state international actors are increasingly playing in world politics and global governance has been recognised by a number of international relations scholars including Rosenau (1997), Camilleri and Falk (1992) and Cerney (1995). Josselin and Wallace (2001) usefully reviewed this literature in a volume that examined the part played by global policy networks, the global knowledge elite, transnational corporations, the Catholic Church, international trade unions, the global underworld, global diasporas and other trans-border actors in specific policy fields. Hall and Biersteker (2002) covered a similar terrain but with more of a focus on how such actors were increasingly involved in the actual practice of international regulation. Stern and Seligmann (2004) argued forcefully for the 'partnership principle' whereby a part had to be played in governance in the twenty-first Century by business and civil society in fields such as poverty and disease eradication, human rights attainment, peace and security, and the economy.

Global think tanks, policy advocacy coalitions, knowledge networks and epistemic communities

Knowledge is politics and politics is knowledge

The review in Chapters 2, 3 and 4 of the ideas about social policy carried and argued for by the international organisations demonstrated something approaching a 'war of position' between those agencies and the actors within them, who argued for a more selective, residual role for the state together with a larger role for private actors in health, social protection and education provision, and those who took the opposite view. This division of opinion often reflected a disagreement as to whether the reduction of poverty was a matter of targeting specific resources on the most poor or whether it was a matter of major social and political-institutional change involving a shift in power relations and a significant increase in redistribution from rich to poor.

These and related social policy controversies are reflected in the wider global contest of ideas taking place between different global think tanks, global policy advocacy coalitions, global knowledge networks and global epistemic communities (Stone, 2001). Clear distinctions between these four categories of ideas-based non-state actors are not easily made. Think tanks are 'independent, or private, policy research organisations, containing people involved in studying a particular area or broad range of policy issues, actively seeking to educate or advice policy-makers and the public through a number of channels'. Among those that have achieved a global reach may be listed the Brookings Institute in Washington, DC and The World Economic Forum in Davos. 'Global policy advocacy coalitions' are a temporary or more permanent alliance between think tanks, some governments and international agencies to achieve particular policy transformation. The coalition between the US government, the World Bank and the Inter-American Development Bank (IADB) to introduce privatised pensions across Latin America was one such that we described in Chapter 2. 'Knowledge networks' or KNETs was defined by Parmar as 'a system of coordinated research, study and often graduate level teaching, results dissemination and publication, intellectual exchange and financing across national boundaries'. These are usually less explicitly concerned to advocate particular policies and tend to include professional bodies, academic research groups and scientific communities organised around a particular subject matter. Stone (2005) has reviewed a range of global policy KNETs such as the Open Society Institute, the South Asian Research Network (SARN) on Gender Law and Governance and the Global Development Network (GDN) to which we will return.

Lurking behind all of these types of intellectual knowledge and policy advocacy networks are the more fundamental units for our analytical purpose, epistemic communities. Epistemic communities as a concept (re-)entered the international relations literature with the publication in 1992 of a special issue of *International Organisations* edited by Peter Haas, addressing the topic 'Knowledge, Power and International Policy Coordination'. Haas defined such communities as 'a network of professionals with recognised expertise and competence in a particular domain and an authoritative claim to policy relevant knowledge within that domain' (1992: 3). For Haas, what was important about such communities was that they shared normative and principled beliefs, causal beliefs, common notions of validity and a common policy enterprise (Stone, 2005: 94). Epistemic communities intervene in and influence the policy process by defining the way in which that reality is defined and understood, by enabling states and other actors to define their interests and by agenda setting. Such 'knowledge elites' contain within them people with different and often antithetical normative beliefs, and visions about society and world politics. Thus, these communities struggle with each other in their effort to establish their discourse and vision of societies.

Asuncion Lera St Clair explores this contest of knowledge claims in the field of global poverty analysis. She argues:

> Expert claims are usually determined by the interrelations between audiences, experts and the legitimacy of knowledge. But in most cases these, these inter-relations are a mere circular process where experts seek legitimacy of their knowledge claims among audiences that have been created by or are dependent on the same experts that seek legitimacy in the first place. (2006: 59–60).

As a result, she suggests, 'the most we can say about the current state of knowledge about global poverty is that it reflects a "consensus among certain scientists" rather than a scientific consensus' (2006: 60). A resolution of this problem, she agues, is to establish a more open and accountable mechanism where contesting scientific (and value) claims made by the Bank, the UN and other stakeholders are assessed within a transnational body 'where research on global poverty could be reviewed and coordinated in analogous ways as knowledge about climate change is managed by the Intergovernmental Panel on Climate Change and its Subsidiary Body for Scientific and Technological Advice' (2006: 72). The alternative, she says, is to leave it as now to a situation where the most powerful actors 'win' the argument.

The rational solutions of the 'World Bank's' Global Development Network (GDN)

Are there particular global think tanks or global knowledge networks that have played a part in the contest of ideas about desirable social policy? What is their relationship to the titanic struggle between the dominant neoliberal tendency in the World Bank and the more social-solidarity tendency around the ILO and other UN agencies? To understand just how closely the Bank has been directly involved in sponsoring one such 'independent' knowledge network, we have to look no further than the Global Development Network (www.gdnet.org) established in 1999. The World Bank, at that time selling itself as the 'knowledge bank', set up the GDN in part to co-ordinate the work of seven older regional research networks (such as the African Economics Research Forum) it had itself already sponsored. At the launch, a number of criticisms were levelled at the organisers (Page, 2000b; Stone, 2000, 2004). It was seen as a creature of the Bank, development economists as distinct from other social scientists dominated the governing body and conference, and it had a technocratic approach to the link between research and policy. Good technical research would lead to better development policy. The notion that there might be an implicit political content to research questions and methodologies was not understood. To quell disquiet, the GDN became independent of the Bank in 2002 and moved to New Delhi to reflect its concern to bring the Global South into the centre of the frame. The governing body now involves the International Sociological Association and the International Political Studies Association. Now, however, it is being transformed again into an international organisation like the Bank and IMF under the patronage of governments. Lyn Squire from the Bank, GDN's driving force, will then become President. Subsequent conferences have been more inclusive of non-economists, and its approach to globalisation is to search for a more equitable globalisation (Dinello, 2004; Dinello and Squire, 2005).

Nonetheless, Diane Stone, one of the GDN's governing body members, still feels that:

> The knowledge that is generated and transferred, research results, data, information about 'best practice', etc is considered by some to be flavoured by the values of the post Washington Consensus. The policy paradigm involves political choices in favour of certain policies such as privatisation, liberalization, deregulation, and public sector reform overlain with new concerns about transparency, engagement with civil society and local ownership of development policy. (2004: 7)

The GDN is well resourced and offers funding for local research, global awards and sponsors research projects. Its focus on the Global South is a two-edge sword. On the one hand it tries to steer funds to the southern research community. But by doing this it pulls perhaps the best researchers into a knowledge network driven by the priorities and paradigm of northern development economists. In supporting the South it might be undermining the autonomous generation of alternative perspectives on economic and social development more in keeping with the interests of the Global South. In this sense, the GDN acts little differently from the World Bank itself or indeed its sister research and teaching organisation, the World Bank Institute. It is creating a global cadre of development economists schooled in a particular view of development policy.

The counter-challenge from other knowledge networks

If the World Bank works with its own World Bank Institute and gave birth to and supports a formally independent economist-dominated GDN, then the UN system works with its UN Research Institute for Social Development (UNRISD), which among many other projects is currently undertaking a multi-year research programme on social policy in a development context. The UNRISD networks with regional networks of social science scholars such as the Latin American Council of Social Sciences (CLASCO) and the West African network CODESRIA. Their 'Social Policy in a Development Context' programme set out to:

> rethink social policy and move it away from its conception as a residual category of 'safety net' that merely counteracts policy failures or development disasters. Social policy should be conceived as involving overall and prior concerns with social development, and as a key instrument that works in tandem with economic policy to ensure equitable and social sustainable development. (Mkandawire, 2004: 4)

Several volumes are being published as a result of this work, all of which directly or indirectly contribute to this end (Kwon, 2004; Kangas and Palme, 2005; Mackintosh and Koivusalo, 2005; Razavi and Hassim, 2006).

Within this context of the struggle of ideas to influence social development discourse and practice, the conference held by UNRISD in 2004 to address the issue of knowledge for development is of interest (Utting, 2006b). Papers and contributions (King, 2006; Toye and Toye, 2006) lamented the domination in development discourse of a certain brand of economics, whose paradigm left no space for structural or institutional blocks to poverty alleviation. These papers echoed in effect the similar lament of Kanbur who, as we saw in Chapter 2, resigned from the World Bank when his views about its report on poverty were being sidelined. Others lamented the erosion of an independent source of scholarly endeavour in these fields in parts of Africa and South Asia as a result of the erosion of public universities in these regions in the aftermath of structural adjustment policies that focused education spending only on primary schools. Nonetheless others expressed more optimistic views about the impact that often UN-sponsored good social and political science research and networking had on international social policy. Gita Sen (2004, 2006) demonstrated how global networks of feminist scholars and activists had led to the mainstreaming of gender issues in much of the World Bank's work on development. Emmerij and Jolly (2006), reviewing the first phases of the 'intellectual history of the UN' project, argued that UN-sponsored scholarships had often been ahead of the curve and later came to be mainstreamed (see more in Emmerij et al., 2001). Certainly this applied to some of the work of James Grant and Richard Jolly influencing the work of UNICEF and then creating the UNDP Human Development Index (HDI). Indeed, the social policy guidance notes (see Chapter 4) being drawn up by UNDESA and UNDP (Ortiz, 2006) draw upon the UNRISD work as well as ideas from other global think tanks.

While the Bank sponsored the GDN and the UN system sponsored the Social Policy in a Development Context Programme, the OECD:DAC sponsors a rather different network, POVNET (www.webdomino1.oecd.org/COMNET/DCD/Povnet.nsf). POVNET was born out of the concern on the part of some country members of the OECD Development Assistance Committee that development assistance from OECD countries was not sufficiently focused upon poverty alleviation. The informal network of bilateral donor poverty experts was formed in 1998 and undertook a 'scoping study' of current donor policies and practices for reducing poverty. This survey included the World Bank, IMF and UNDP approaches as well as that of the bilateral donors. Out of this work came the DAC *Guidelines on Development Cooperation and Poverty Reduction* (OECD, 2001b) and many other papers dealing with ODA and social protection. This network of social protection and social development advisors drawn from donor governments and others sources produced an *Over-arching Paper* on *Pro-poor Growth* (OECD, 2006b) designed to convince economists of the need to focus on ways of ensuring that growth does touch the poor. Not all members of the POVNET were happy with the tone of this report, however, arguing that by bending over backwards to talk to economists the self-censorship approach loaded the text with economistic attitudes and ignored the bread and butter of social protection as an essential element of pro-poor growth (Voipio, 2006). However, in November 2005, POVNET generated the Task Team on Risk, Vulnerability, Social Protection and Human Security under the convenorship of Timo Voipio of the Finnish Foreign Ministry, which will generate interesting outputs in due course.

In the wings but playing a part on the side of those who would want social policy within poorer countries to challenge the power and institutional obstacles to poverty alleviation, and who would want globalisation to be reformed with due attention to its social dimension, are other global knowledge networks. I would be doing myself an injustice if I did not mention in this context the Finnish-funded programme that I ran from 1997, the Globalism and Social Policy Programme (GASPP), that networks internationally through its journal *Global Social Policy*. It has made a contribution both to the analysis of the impact of globalisation upon the capacity of countries to make social policy and to conceptualising a social reformist globalisation. Its most recent policy brief argues:

> The time is now ripe for the UN system to promote and seek to secure effective social policies at national, regional and global levels to hasten the advancement of the meeting of the Copenhagen Commitments and the MDGs ... Global, regional and national social policies are needed to secure the 'three Rs' of redistribution, regulation and rights which are fundamental to our wider social vision. (GASPP, 2005: 4)

Additionally, the Comparative Research Programme on Poverty (CROP) initiated by the International Social Science Council that is closely linked to and housed in UNESCO now networks several hundred poverty researchers, the majority of whom are in developing countries. Of significance is also the network of progressive economists under the unbrella of www.ideaswebsite. org.

UNESCO has more recently become involved in networking poverty and social policy researchers globally. In 2006, with the support of the government of Argentina, it made a determined effort to contribute to the global dialogue about desirable social policies in the context of globalisation by convening the International Forum on the Social Sciences-Policy Nexus. The programme in February 2006 brought together social policy and/or globalisation-related workshops convened by UNRISD, UNDP, ILO, World Bank, CROP and many southern networks. It was also linked to networks of social development ministers across Latin America and Southern Africa, and grew out of UNESCO's Management of Social Transformation Programme (MOST). The event brought together the critical social development thinkers in the World Bank (see Chapter 2), UNRISD and UNDESA, enabling background conversations about the upcoming UN social policy guidance notes to take place.

The above review of contending and overlapping knowledge networks in the field of poverty, social policy and development could be repeated in the field of health policy. Here a dominant player is the Global Forum for Health Research (www.globalforumhealth.org), created in 1998 to challenge the 10/90 gap that referred to the fact that less than 10 per cent of health research is devoted to the diseases that affect 90 per cent of the world's population. It is funded by the World Bank, the WHO, the Rockefeller Foundation, the Bill and Melinda Gates Foundation and several northern governments. Its Council's Chair is Richard Feacham who, as we saw in Chapters 2, moved from the Bank to the WHO to the Global Fund to Fight AIDS, TB and Malaria. Its focus therefore is how to shift health research funding and how to strengthen the research capacity of developing countries. More focused upon the issue of health service delivery is the International Society for Equity in Health (www.iseqh.org), formed in 2000 and concerned to 'promote equity in health and services internationally through education, research, publication, communication and charitable support'. It has strong membership in Southern Africa, where EQUINET is one of its partners.

INGOs and consulting companies

A conceptual framework of actors

INGOs such as Oxfam, Christian Aid and Care International have come to assume importance within the global social policy-making process both in the sense of being policy advocates, often on the side of the angels arguing for improved international and national commitments to welfare, and in the sense paradoxically of being

Table 5.1   **The global welfare mix: the intermediate sphere**

	Domestic	Supranational
State	Domestic government	International organisations
Market	Domestic markets	Global markets, TNCs
Intermediate	National service NGOs and consulting companies	INGOs and ICCs
Community	Local social movements	Global social movements
Household	Households	International household strategies

Source: Stubbs (2003: 323).

agents for the delivery of aid and hence often substituting for government welfare provision. Paul Stubbs (2003) has described these actors as intermediate organisations falling between genuine civil society organisations (which we examine in a later section of this chapter) and formal intergovernmental organisations (the subject of Chapters 2, 3 and 4). They are important not only for their **policy influence and service provision,** but also because their presence in a country can distort the actual delivery of welfare in unintended ways. The higher pay of the INGO workers distorts the local labour market and undermines lower-paid public civil servants. INGOs are then part of the welfare mix that makes up the agents of welfare provision and policy in many countries in the context of globalisation.

Stubbs (2003: 135) refined the international welfare mix tabulation provided by Gough and Woods (2004) (see Chapter 1) and suggests a distinction between an international civil society or social movement component and the larger, more formal INGO sector which he combines with the International Consulting Companies (ICCs). These two components could be aggregated as a kind of global intermediate category. At the global level they are the correlates of those national actors which are neither fully public (as is the state) nor fully private (as is the household). This is represented in Table 5.1.

The paradox of development INGOs as service providers and policy advocates

Biekhart (1999: 73) traces four factors associated with the 'golden age' for European and Canadian non-state development actors in the 1970s and 1980s: a massive increase in funding from Ministries of Overseas Development, many of whom were formed in the 1960s; a more pronounced domestic profile, aided by the revolution in communications; a polarised global climate in the aftermath of decolonisation; and the massive growth of southern NGOs and social movements. Taken together, these provided a clear space for non-state actors to work as intermediaries in development contexts, as on the one hand a potential 'countervailing power' constructing 'chains of solidarity' opposed to the promotion in the 1980s and 1990s of a 'neo-liberal' policy agenda and, paradoxically, as agents to provide services on a sub-contracted basis in this new climate. INGOs had to grapple much more than ever before with the contradiction between their broad motivation for social change and social justice and the organisational requirements of securing a lucrative aid contract (Stubbs, 2003: 141), or what Michael Edwards termed the tension between 'developmental' and 'institutional' imperatives. Some managed the contradiction better than others, using a proportion of aid contract funds to cover the costs of research and policy departments that became the 'value added' contribution of INGOs in terms of development policy debates. Biekhart's conclusion (1999: 74) that, in the 1990s, 'it was now a matter of institutional survival to behave as "for profits" in a non-profit environment' represents one way out of this, as many INGOs pursued a much more instrumentalist path than previously. At this point, some of the research and policy development departments noted earlier lost ground to, or transformed into, public relations departments concerned much more with 'marketing', even 'branding', INGOs. That having been said, Oxfam and other major INGOs continue to provide regular critical appraisals of the latest move by the World Bank or UN or donors to attempt to meet the MDGs.

Self-interested International Consulting Companies

This fundamental reorganisation of many leading INGOs, introducing 'modern methods' evolved by 'management consultants' in the private sector itself, led to points of joint interest and approach with a new generation of emerging development ICCs. In any case, argues Stubbs (2003: 141), the massive increase in funds to respond to complex humanitarian emergencies from the mid-1980s also fuelled short-termism, projectisation, and intense competition within the aid market, and detracted from wider development thinking and action. Unlike western INGOs, development ICCs have gone from strength to strength, and become increasingly important in this environment. This can be linked to the broad upsurge in conditions for consultancy noted earlier. Above all, the increasing emphasis on particular business principles in aid and development creates a niche for a range of development consultancy companies, some of which have this aspect as a new or expanding arm of their work, and others of which are newly formed. A push to increase the contribution of ICCs in this aid market was provided by the collapse of the communist project in Eastern Europe and the Soviet Union in 1989–90. As Stubbs (2003) points out, Janine Wedel's highly influential study of western aid to Eastern Europe in the early 1990s, notes the role of the 'Big Six' western accountancy firms who 'with contracts from USAID, the EU PHARE program, the British Know How Fund, the World Bank, the EBRD, and others, ... began to establish offices in Central and Eastern Europe and to launch commercial activities' (1998: 51). Wedel goes on to show how these organisation and people in them sometimes acted as policy advisors, sometimes as service providers and sometimes as government agents. She termed them 'flexi-organisations'. The value base of this group differs substantially from those studied by Biekhart, of course, but they are also service contractors and, as such, need to be studied as international non-state actors in social development. The fact that PricewaterhouseCoopers, a major accountancy firm, itself formed from the merger of two of the 'Big Six' companies, employs a social policy co-ordinator in view of its increasing work in this field alerts us to the increasing importance, massively underresearched, of this group in global social development policy.

Implications for social development policy

Given this paradoxical position of INGOs as both policy advocates and contract winners, and given this juxaposition of INGOs and ICCs, can we discern the content of any policy advocacy about national social policy in a development or post-Communist transition context emerging from such players? In Deacon (1997), it was concluded on the basis of our study of the role of INGOs in the fomer Yugoslavia that 'In alliance with social development NGOs who are being given a part to play especially in zones of instability, a social safety net future is being constructed. This NGO support ... is challenging powerfully those defenders of universalist and social security-based welfare states to be found in the EU [and] ILO' (1997: 197). Certainly INGOs have elsewhere also been uncritically involved in the operation of targeted forms of poverty alleviation, such as social funds, and have been instrumental in setting up forms of service provision parallel to impoverished state services that has had the effect of further undermining public provision. In the case of ICCs, it is even clearer that the contract culture has brought private consulting agencies into the formulation of development policy, with the unsurprising outcome that privatising police is advocated. In particular, the UK government has been shown to channel large sums of money through its development ministry to private consulting companies, first to argue for and then drive forward the privatisation of public services in developing countries. Indeed, War on Want's new research publication *Profiting from Poverty: Privatisation Consultants, DFID and Public Services* (2005) examines the UK government's role in promoting privatisation in developing countries. The United Kingdom's Department for International Development (DFID) channels large sums of the UK aid budget every year to privatisation consultants such as PricewaterhouseCoopers, KPMG and Deloitte Touche in order to drive forward the privatisation of public services in developing countries. The UK government also actively promotes British expertise in the field of privatisation in order to win overseas contracts for its own companies. This includes a team within the government's export promotion arm UK Trade & Investment, which is dedicated to advising British companies on how to win contracts from the UK's own aid budget through what the government terms 'aid-funded business' (Hilary, 2005).

Changes are afoot, which leads to some uncertainty about the continuation of these trends. The aid regime now being encouraged by donors (for example, OECD, 2001b) is more concerned to provide budget support to governments, to ensure effective sector co-ordination of aid supplies, to focus help on achieving the MDGs which include provison of public services albeit at a basic level in education and health, and to ensure that development policies are owned by developing country governments and that more credence is given to and resources allocated to developing country expertise in the aid process. This might have several consequences for the development INGOs. It might lead to a greater role for INGOs in service performance evaluation or in 'training' local experts. It might not be too fanciful to conclude that a new focus on the public service element of the MDGs might enable a raprochment to be made between the more social democratic outlook of the campaigning face of many INGOs and their involvement in service delivery.

The global business view on social policy

Globalisation enables a push to privatisation

If any aspect of neoliberal globalisation in the last years of the twentieth century became the object of criticism of the anti-globalisation movement, it was international finance and international business. Multinational or transnational corporations (TNCs) were seen as the enemy. TNCs could now, it was argued, shift capital and production around the globe and consequently drive down wage rates, labour rights and social security entitlements. Taxation and social responsibilities could be avoided. Moreover, global business was poised to take over the provision of national public sevices everwhere, whether these were in the education, health or social care sectors.

Here we are concerned with what actually are the views of global business about national social policy issues. Do they campaign for tax cuts, for social security reductions, for private health care, for a safety net future? How does global business respond to the critics of TNC irresponsibility? Farnsworth (2005) sets the context by arguing that globalisation has indeed stengthened the hand of capital over that of labour in terms of the global class struggle. Four reasons are advanced for this:

- capital is able to exercise structural power where labour cannot;
- capital is better able to organise and take opportunities to engage in global policy debates with IOs than labour;
- IOs have gone out of their way to incorporate business interests within various committees and decision-making bodies, whereas labour has not been afforded the same advantage; and
- labour has a greater dependency on capital than the other way round and can always be accused of standing in the way of profitability and global poverty alleviation (Farnsworth, 2005: 218).

Farnsworths's analysis of the global business view about social policy is based upon a consultation exercise that was held by the OECD with international business; in this case it is the Business and Industry Advisory Council (BIAC) in the context of two ministerial meetings on social policy in 1981 and 1998. Farnsworth concludes that 'the bottom line for international capital is that state provision is justified only if it contributes directly to economic growth or at least does not undermine it, and is affordable only if it exists in an environment populated by profitable and successful firms' (2005: 209–210). Given this, the BIAC has urged the OECD to address impediments to job creation, including too generous social provision. Apart from education and training expenditures, with which the BIAC is more in sympathy, international business favours 'reducing expenditures and taxation (especially on corporations)' (Farnsworth, 2005: 210). The BIAC pushed for a greater role for the private sector in service delivery, and in this context pushed for the liberalisation of trade in services which it sees as a great opportunity for expansion.

High social security costs, particularly those falling on business, are opposed and in their place is favoured a more temporary and residual approach to income support. However, argues Farnsworth, global business has not pushed for the abolition of social security, rather the imposition of conditional qualifying requirements to social protection that provides for what is necessary rather than what is desirable. In terms of taxation, the BIAC prefers taxation on workers which is geared at horizontal redistrubution across a lifetime rather than vertical redistribution from richer to poorer. On pensions, business views seem to coincide with those of the Bank, favouring a basic state pension, a second occupational or private tier, and a tax-exempt optional individual savings scheme. Farnsworth concludes that:

> This hardly suggest whole hearted support for state welfare systems on the part of capital, yet neither does the above summary of its position suggest the type of rampant anti-welfare stance that business if often credited with. It is probably more accurate to describe capital's approach to social policy as pragmatic, informed more by self preservation, practical politics and the simple reality that state provision is essential to future profitability, than by a tight ideological framework. (2005: 221)

A more nuanced analysis might unpick the sectors of global business, and if this were done it is likley that among service providers there would be a greater readiness to argue for the dumping of state provision in favour of the private. Indeed, studies that have been carried out into the expansionary visions of national and international private health, social care, social protection and education providers suggests this is the case (Holden, 2002; Lethbridge, 2005; Mackintosh and Koivusalo, 2005). The USA Coaltion of Service Industries (CSI) has been particulary prominent in lobbying governments to ensure that both the WTO:GATS agreement and the World Bank's International Finance Corporation pursue vigorously activities to increase private service provision globally (Sexton, 2001).

Transnational business claims to be socially responsible

Globalisation spawned the anti-globalisation movement and hence an increased critical scrutiny of global business focused on such things as the outsourcing by large companies like Nike of their production to 'sweat shops', often employing child labour. In response and in order to protect their image and sales, Nike and other large companies claimed to have become socially responsible and began to publish reports outlining how their investment strategies were in keeping with 'world' (normally northern consumer) social and environmental concerns. Whereas in 1994 only about 100 reports had been produced, by 2003 these were numbering 1500 per year (Thompson, 2005). While large in number, 1500 reports represents only about 2.5 per cent of the total number of internationalized companies. Nonetheless, argues Thompson, 'firms that embark on this course ... demonstrate a commitment that should not be underestimated by critics ... there is nothing easy about taking CSR [corporate social reponsibility] seriously' (2005: 4).

Developments since these intitiatives have given rise to the related idea that businesses might be regarded as corporate citizens with duties and responsibilities. The World Economic Forum (WEF), which brings together the world's 1000 leading companies along with 200 smaller businesses to 'improve the state of the world', subscribes to the concept of global corporate citizenship (GCC). Its founding document on GCC states:

First and foremost, our companies' commitment to being global corporate citizens is about the way we run our own businesses. The greatest contribution we can make to development is to do business in a manner that obeys the law, produces safe and cost effective products and services, creates jobs and wealth, supports training and technology cooperation and reflects international standards and values in areas such as the environment, ethics, labour and human rights. (World Economic Forum, 2005)

Given these developments among some leading world companies, it was not suprising then that they encouraged and led the moves towards a closer relationship between global business and the UN as a way of showing how responsible they were, but also as a way of securing their business interests at that level of goverance. As Zammit comments, 'Global corporations, widely identified as the protagonists, vehicles and beneficiaries of globalisation, have become the focus of much of the public's frustration and anger. Big business can therefore be expected to welcome opportunities to associate with the UN where it could be seen to be "doing good"' (2003: 49).

The International Chamber of Commerce (ICC), comprising several thousand business associations from 100 countries, embarked upon a systematic dialogue with the UN with a view to enhancing its influence. The ICC founded the Geneva Business Partnership in 1998 to liase with the ILO and WHO about establishing global rules for an ordered liberalism (Zammit, 2003: 49). The ICC therefore welcomed the announcement in 2000 at the WEF in Davos by Kofi Annan of the Global Compact, whereby global businesses would be encouraged to sign up to nine areas of corporate social and environmental responsibility. The details and the effectiveness of this voluntary Compact will be examined in the next chapter. What is important here is that it reflects a concern on the part of a fraction of global capital to at least be seen to be socially responsible and may actually be so. Indeed, Thompson argues 'there is a "progessive capitalism" in existance, exemplified by several hundred important fims. Not all international business and transnational corporations (TNCs) are simply vicious companies out to cultivate the savage consumer. Rather it is in the interests of companies to cultivate their "reputational capital"' (2005).

Before endorsing this conclusion it is important to note some of the ways in which these global progressive leaders are acting through the WEF to advance their interests. Among the current inititiatives of the WEF is the Financing for Development Intitiative, whose key objective is 'to understand how public–private partnerships (PPPs) in the areas of water, health and education have contributed to poverty reduction. ... After finding the key to success and the key challenges for PPPs we will develop recommendations on how PPPs can improve the climate for private investment in poor countries' (WEF, 2005). A related global health initiative of the WSF aims to increase the quantity and quality of business progammes fighting HIV/AIDS, TB and Malaria.

In sum it is clear that globalisation has shifted the balance of power towards capital and away from labour in global policy-making. It has created a space for global business to exercise its voice at the global level. Its collective voice is not fundamentalist anti-welfare spending, rather it wants social spending to be undertaken only in ways which enhance profitability. A section of global business wants to be seen to be socially responsible and prefers voluntary self-regulating arrangments to this end. Perhaps of most concern to social policy analysts is the opportunity that globalisation has created for one section of global business, that engaged in the business of health and social care and education to seek and obtain a greater role for the private sector in such service delivery.

Global social movements and social policy

A conceptual framework of actors

The rise in the 1990s of an anti-globalisation movement which became symbolised by street protests at major world conferences of the WTO, the G8 and the World Bank and IMF gave rise to the idea that there was a 'globalization from below' (Falk, 1995) which needed to be studied and understood every bit as much as the TNC and G8-driven globalisation from above. If banners at these demonstrations were an indicator, then social movements both old (trade unions) and new (women's movements, movements of indigenous peoples, students) had joined hands or at least exchanged emails across borders in some kind of campaign for a civilised world that respected social, environmental and multicultural concerns. In part this conceptualisation of a civilising globalisation (Kaldor, 2003) from below was accurate, even as social scientists debated whether these movements were genuinely transnational networks operating in a deterritorialised space or alliances of nationally rooted movements still struggling to find global organisational forms that are genuinely representative, accountable and global (Mayo, 2005). Others argued about the representativeness of many of the NGOs involved in the anti-globalisation movement, while yet others argued that many actors, particularly the INGOs in this 'movement', should 'give up the pretensions, however seductive, of the ideology of global civil society and [make their] case heard on the basis of undeniable expertise and competence' (Anderson and Reiff, 2005: 38).

Mary Kaldor has provided a useful typology of global civil society actors. These range through:

- **Old social movements** from pre-1970 concerned with redistribution, employment and welfare composed of workers and intellectuals.
- **New social movements** from around 1970 and 1980 concerned with human rights, peace, women, environment and world solidarity composed of students, caring professionals, and the new information class.
- **NGOs, think tanks, commissions** of the late 1980s and 1990s concerned with human rights, development and poverty reduction, humanitarianism and conflict resolution composed of professionals and experts.
- **Transnational civic networks** from around the late 1980s and 1990s concerned with women, dams, landmines, international criminal court and climate change composed of professional, experts and activists.
- **New nationalist and fundamentalist movements** of the 1990s concerned with identity politics composed of workers, small entrepreneurs, farmers and the informal sector.
- **New anti-capitalist movements** of the late 1990s and 2000s concerned with solidarity with victims of globalisation, abolition or reform of global institutions composed of students, workers and peasants (2003: 80–1).

From all of these strands Kaldor argues the case for the concept of and existence of a global civil society:

> Global civil society includes the INGOs and the networks that are the 'tamed' successors to the new social movements of the 1970s and 1980s. It also includes the allies of transnational business who promote a market framework at the global level. It includes a new radical anti-capitalist movement ... nationalist and fundamentalist movements ... The array of organisations and groups through which individuals and groups have a voice at global levels of decision making represent a new form of global politics that parallels and supplements formal democracy at the national level ... It is the contestation between these different types of actors, as well as states, international institutions and trans-national corporations that will determine the future direction of globalisation. (2003: 107)

Chapters 7 and 8 explore these issues of global politics and global governance in the social sphere. Here we are concerned with what views and campaigns these global social movements have articulated about social policy issues within countries in the context of globalisation.

The old international trade unions and public services

The problem for the old social movement of trade unionism is that despite the rhetoric of international solidarity often articulated by its leaders, in reality in an era of neo-liberal globalisation the defence of workers' interests is often seen as, or indeed is, the defence of a particular set of northern workers' interests. Preventing jobs moving to the Global South or preventing public services in Europe being handed over to global private welfare providers can be seen as Euro-protectionist. And as we saw in the section on global business views, globalisation has tipped the balance of global forces in favour of capital (Farnsworth, 2005). Nevertheless it is possible to review the views of international trade unionism about social policy issues in this global era. Farnsworth, adopting the same method as for global business, examined submissions of the Trade Union Advisory Committee (TUAC) to the OECD. These submissions demonstrate a concern on the part of labour that the emphasis on economic growth has been to the detriment of equity, security and full employment. While accepting that there might be a mixed economy of welfare, the TUAC registered opposition to the idea that markets might dominate in welfare provision: 'Trade unions ... strongly oppose approaches to social policy which are guided by ideological or self serving thinking that "private" is better' (Farnsworth, 2005: 222). As Farnsworth concludes, 'The position of labour on social policy is again a relatively coherent one, although it often appears as a defensive one. ... Its message on the centrality of full employment and its defence of social policy as essential to future competiveness do remain constants in labour's social policy strategy' (2005: 222).

The 'social reformist' International Confederation of Free Trade Unions (ICFTU), which after the collapse of the Berlin Wall and the relative eclipse of the communist World Federation of Trade Unions (WFTU) became **the** dominant international trade union confederation, has lobbied hard on the aspects of neoliberal globalisation. It argued the case for international labour standards to accompany international free-trade and campaigned against the setting-up of export processing zones in developing countries whithin which local labour legislation is bypassed as a sweetener to foreign direct investment.

One other issue which has given rise to a significant amout of campaigning by public sector unions and their allies internationally has understandably been that of the perceived threat to public services of the growth of the global private service sector facilitated by the WTO GATS agreement (Chavez, 2006). Public Services International makes the point that:

> as an international federation of public sector trade unions, our focus is on representing, promoting and defending the needs and interests of public sector workers. Recently, this work has been dominated by the new challenges of globalisation, the threat from ideological privatisation, commercialisation and contracting out of public services, the potential offered by public sector modernisation and quality services, the attacks on services through structural adjustment policies and the intrusion of transnational corporations into public services. Most of these issues are now permeating all PSI sector work. (www.psi-int.org, accessed 1 July 2006)

In this context, and as a challenge to GATS, PSI has in 2005 launched GAPS, the General Agreement on Public Services, which aims to be an agreeement between the PSI, governments and other players that public services are an essential component of a civilised society. GAPS aims to overcome the perceived resource, accountability, equity, gender, labour, ethical, performance and sustainability gaps identified in current public service commitments and management.

The campaign for public services is, of course, constituted of others than just the trade unions representing the workers in them. Support comes from social movements of consumers and from advocacy INGOs. Mayo (2005: 153) reports and analyses the development of the Global Campaign for Education. The role of the World Bank and UNESCO in this was discussed in Chapters 2 and 4, but Mayo draws attention to the realisation on the part of some of the INGOs who had been involved in providing eductional services in poor countries that they had unwittingly substituted for what ideally should be government public free services. In consequence, Action Aid, Oxfam and others began in the 1990s the groundwork in Africa that gave rise to the formal Education for All Campaign, launched in 1999 and then adopted formally at Dakar in 2000. Celebrating the diversity of interests involved in the emergence of this campaign, Watkins says the campaign brought together 'representatives of the world-wide movement to end child labour, non governmental organisations working with landless people in Brazil, disabled people in India and rural communities in China. It includes the world's largest confederation of teachers' unions – Education International representing 23 million teachers – and international development agencies' (2000: 13).

Alongside traditional trade unions, globalisation has thrown up campaigning groups which trespass on trade union territory. The new social movements include organisations concerned with child labour and sweat shops (Silvey, 2004), with high-profile attacks on certain corporations and brands (Ghigliani, 2003). Some of these are southern-based movements such as an international networks among peasants and small farmers (Edelman, 2003). Waterman and Timms (2005: 194) suggest that the most dramatic representation of the challenge to the 'hegemony' of the northern-run traditional international trade union movement is the presence of

Southern trade unions and social movements at the World Social Forum (WSF). The WSF process has been taken to symbolise the new 'movement of movements' against and beyond neoliberal globalisation. It is significant that two Brazilian labour organisations were involved in the organising committee of the Forum held in Brazil in 2001–2003. The first was a new union, the Central Trade Union Federation (CUT), itself critical of the ICFTU. The second was the movement of landless rural workers. Nevertheless, subsequent WSF events have provided a forum for dialogue between the old and the new, between the labour and the others. One recent consequence of this was a statement emerging from a conference on the Social Dimension of Globalisation, held within the context of the WSF in January 2005 in Porto Alegre. It concludes that:

> We, the participant organisations, ICFTU, ETUC, WCL, Solidar, Social Progressive Forum, commit ourselves to take forward the debate begun by the Commission [on the Social Dimension of Globalisation] and to work to make decent work – a concept that includes worker's rights, full employment, equality between men and women, and access to quality public services for all – central to our common mission. (www.icftu.org, accessed 1 July 2005)

The global women's movement and gendered development policy

Neoliberal globalisation has shifted the balanace of power from labour to capital, and indeed this applies in general to women **as workers** too. 'Women have been identified among the most exploited labour of the sweatshops of the global factories, prime victims of the process of capitalist globalisation. And neo-liberal economic policies have been held reponsible for transforming the public policy environment in ways detrimental to women' (Mayo, 2005: 133; see also Elson, 2002). That having been said, a case can be made that globalisation has also facilitated the spread of initially northern and western feminist ideas to the Global South and East. It has facilitated the global networking of new women's movements across all continents and, in a kind of symbiotic relationship with professionals campaigning inside the UN agencies and the World Bank, contributed to what almost amounts to a mainstreaming of gender-sensitive policies in those agencies. The social policies and social development policies of such agencies has been changed in ways that favour women as a consequence.

The story of the global growth of several women's campaign groups is told by Mayo (2005). It is one of several new movements being encouraged by the existence of a global platform made available for them by the many UN conferences in the last years of the last century. The articulation of women's rights by UN agencies gives support to those articulating the case for women's rights from below. A scissor movement results, having impacts also on reluctant national governments. The UN Decade for Women from 1976 to 1985 saw the growth of the Women in Development Movement that aimed to bring women into the development planning process. Susequently a more critical approach, which came to be known as Gender and Development, emerged that wanted more significant changes to development policy. Within this context the influential Development Alternatives with Women for a New Era (DAWN) was launched by networks of southern women's groups in the context of the UN Third World Conference on Women in 1985. As Mayo explains:

> The strategy that DAWN developed from the 1990s centred upon contributing to key international events such as in the International Conference on Population and Development in Cairo in 1994, the World Summit on Social Development in Copenhagen in 1995, and the Fourth World Women's Conference in Beijing in 1995. ... DAWN has researched the impact of the debt crisis on women as well as focusing on environmental sustainability, militarism, reproductive health rights and political restructuring in the context of the increasing marketisation of goverance. (2005: 141)

What has been the impact of this and related movements and activities and campaigns on global policy, and in particular the policies of the UN and World Bank concerning social development within coutries? Sen (2004) argues that in three particular policy fields, research-based knowledge such as that generated by DAWN combined with social activism has impacted positively upon the global discourse of policy, which leads to the possibility of this impacting in some cases on policy and practice too. As she puts it, 'If knowledge is power, then changing the terrain of discourse is the first but very important step. It makes it possible to fight the opposition on the grounds of one's own choosing' (2004: 13). The three illustrative examples of policy change are: engendering macroeconomics; sexual and reproductive rights; and human rights, especially violence against women.

In the first case, the movement contributed to the mainstreaming within the World Bank of the importance of the role of women in development represented, for example, by the universal acceptance within the Bank that girls' education is a crucial element of development, as is micro-investment by women in trading and farming. This view is partly reflected in the analysis made earlier in O'Brein et al. (2000) into their examination of the impact of the international women's movement on the World Bank. In the case of sexual and reproductive rights, the movement achieved a shift in 1994 at Cairo in the global discourse about population policy from a mere Malthusian concern with over-population to 'A new framework for population-related policy ... that affirmed women's right to control their fertility and meet their needs for safe, affordable and accessible contraceptives, while recognising the social determinants, and health and rights consequences of sexual and reproductive behaviour' (Sen 2004: 7). In the final case of violence against women, Sen argues that:

> the presence of women in Vienna [International Conference on Human Rights 1993] testifying their experiences of violence – systematic rape and war crimes, genital cutting, domestic violence, dowry deaths, honour killings, sexual violence to name only a few – created a climate that made it possible for violence against women to be placed for the first time on a major human rights conference. (2004: 8)

Globalisation and the emergence of ethnic and religious-based claims to welfare

The social division of ethnicity (and related identity issues) represents a third case for globalisation's impact upon the capacity of social groups to make welfare claims. If labour's capacity for solidarity was reduced but women's capacity for solidaristic claims increased, then in this third case globalisation has enabled or driven the emergence of claims for welfare based entirely upon membership of an ethnicity or a religious group with, in some cases, damaging consequences for human solidarity. Globalisation, with its associated modernist drive to spread a western-style culture and politics internationally, has contributed to the rise of identity movements and religious movements which celebrate difference, and in some cases non-modernity. At the same time movements of workers across borders, many illegally, have led to an increase in transborder identification with homeland or else with a scattered diaspora. The increase in the identification of recent and even second- and third-generation migrants with an imagined homeland or a global religion leads in turn to nationalist reaction on the part of their host society (Castles and Davidson, 2000). The within-one-country strategy of social policy designed to cement a social contract of all citizens becomes challenged. Munck puts it rather dramatically:

> The notion of the indivisible and sovereign state is called into question by globalization … but also by social divisions based on race, ethnicity, language and religion. With the collapse of the master narrative of modernity, various groups have emerged demanding recognition and representation in society. Ethnic minorities, aboriginal and indigenous people, and the illegal immigrants have forcefully erupted on the political scene and ruptured the false unity of the nation-state. The nation-state of modernity is decentred, and a plurality of voices is now heard. (2005: 116)

Amy Chau (2003) goes even further and argues that the global spread of free market economies, coupled with the export at the behest of the USA of western notions of instant democracy, has unleashed ethnic hatred in many countries where economic power happened to be held by an ethnic minority. The Chinese in Indonesia, the whites in Zimbabwe, the Jews in Russia, those of European descent in parts of Latin America have suffered as a consequence. Ethnic resentment, she argues, has been intensified by globalisation and, moreover, Americans are hated everywhere.

While her view might be put dramatically, it is certainly the case that among the plurality of voices referred to by Munck are those speaking for organisations that do not have allegiance to one country. In the case, for example, of the The Platform of Filipno Migrant Organisations in Europe, it demands equality of rights within Europe as well as a right to participate in development in the Phillipines. In the case of some Muslims, the allegiance is to a global 'uma'. The heart of the problem for welfare state analysts and social policy projects is that these developments call into question the historic link between citizenship (including social citizenship) claims and the state. Mobile peoples with ethnic, religious and/or transborder identities and allegiances make claims above and below the state and to international non-state actors. Delanty argues, 'The state no longer dominates the discourse of political citizenship, whose components are being taken up by a broad spectrum of social actors' (2000: 134).

There is, to my knowledge, no systematic examination of what this might mean for social polices or for the social policy demands that might be being made by groups who hold primarily a sense of transborder or religious or ethnic identity. For indigenous peoples who have recently claimed the right to speak, the issue is simpler: reclaiming access to resources stolen from them and for participation, if not actual takeover, of the running of these resources/countries (witness

Venuzueala, Bolivia, Peru). For the others the possible emerging options are divided into two groups. On the one hand we might expect to see:

- expectations that religious organisations (or countries identifying with them) will resource welfare services (witness Saudi Arabia building schools/mosques/health systems in Bosnia);
- diaspora funding of homeland welfare systems; and
- remittances playing a part in homeland reconstruction.

On the other hand we might expect to see:

- demands for dual citizenship; and
- demands for supranational forms of citizenship at regional or global level.

The second group of these developments suggest movements which are for me, and others (Held, 2004; Falk, 1995) the welcome unfolding of a global modernist project with issues of citizenship and human rights now being taken up and in due course resourced at a cosmopolitan supranational level. The first group suggest a far more challenging scenario of exclusive forms of cross-border entitlements to welfare based on religious affiliation, ethnicity and identity.

The World Social Forum: beyond the global fragments?

Within the radical left politics of the UK (and elsewhere in Europe) in the 1970s when the traditional labour movement had been joined by those of women, ethnicity and sexuality, there was a concern to reunite these fragments into a coherent movement that might articulate social demands which recognised both what was common between these fragments and what was particular to each. Was it possible to make claims that acknowledged universality in a context of difference? The same kind of question might reasonably be asked of the varieties of 'global' social movements that formed and lined up behind the WSF. Is this forum and the several annual 'conferences' that it has now held in Brazil and India and elsewhere a site of a concerted set of 'demands' concerning social policies? Here we are primarily concerned with views about social policy and social development within one country.

Alas no! It is the general agreement of those who have attempted to make sense of the WSF process (Hardt, 2002; Sen et al., 2004) that beyond the founding principles which assert that the forum is a **space** within which movements opposed to neoliberalism and imperialism might come together to discuss the proposition that an 'alternative world is possible', the Forum has not begun to attempt to fashion any **common** or **collective** view about what that alternative at national or global level might look like. Hilary Wainwright (2005a), herself active in the 1970s 'beyond the fragments' movement, argues that the WSF has achieved four things:

- strengthened the transformative power of civil society;
- enabled this power to be asserted to call governments to account for their part in undesirable international treaties and activities;

- helped produce a radical shift in the relationship between civil society and political parties; and
- facilitated a plural horizontal networking of active campaigns.

These are process achievements of value, but tell us little about any common views of the WSF about any specific social or other policy. Patomaki and Teivainen conclude that 'despite various references to the necessity of imagining and constructing a different world, the issue of global democracy has not had a very high priority on the agenda of the fora ... more explicit debates between different perspectives would seem to be necessary for democratic will-formation' (2004: 124–5). Wallerstein has suggested that 'The WSF is not a movement. It is not even a movement of movements. It is more properly conceived as a family of movements' (2004: 634). He usefully suggests that here are three types of criticism of the WSF. The world centrists (or, in my terms, global social reformists) feel that the WSF is not practical or concrete in its orientation; the heirs of the Old Left regard its loose formulation that an alternative world is possible as no substitute for claims that world socialism **is** that alternative, and from within the WSF itself there are charges that decision-making processes are not transparent. Wallerstein reports that the International Council in April 2004 resolved to try to ensure that the 2005 forum facilitated more interlinkages and common action among the different participants by arranging a number of thematic terrains.

This shift to thematic terrains did not seem to have the desired affect of facilitating common action. Wainwright reports (2005b) that in practice the methodolgy to ensure these thematic meetings produced any common output was only partly implemented; the electronic connections promised by the local web were not possible and the facilitators were not very active. Callinicos and Nineham (2005) report that the effect of the physical separation of the thematic terrains was to undermine the unity of the event. In any event, the self-denying principle of the forum forbade the WSF to come up with any common articulation of a political position. Patomaki and Teivainen (2005) and Glasius et al. (2006: 84) report, however, that at the 2005 event a "manifesto" signed by 19 intellectuals was produced which restated familiar demands of the anti-globalisation movement (debt cancellation, adoption of currency transaction tax, dismantling of tax havens, promotion of equitable trade including excluding health, education and services from the GATS, permitting countries to develop their own food policy, the establishment of a universal right to social protection and a pension, protection of the environment, enforcing anti-discrimination conventions and the democratisation of international organisations including the physical relocation of UN to the South) caused concern among the WSF organisers. One way in which something approaching a declaration has emerged from the 2005 event, and indeed earlier ones, was the organisation within the framework of the WSF of an Assembly of Social Movement Organisations. In 2005 this Assembly of diverse social movemenst did agree a declaration (www.mocsoc.org), not given prominence on the WSF website, that called for social movements world-wide to work for certain ends and activities. Among the 20 to 30 calls are ones in the social policy field which are opposed to the privatisation of water, of health services and of education.

Further Reading

On think tanks and knowledge networks: Stone, D. and Maxwell, S. (2005) *Global Knowledge Networks and International Development*. London: Routledge.

On global business: Farnsworth, K. (2004) *Corporate Power and Social Policy in a Global Economy*. Bristol: Policy .

On global civil society: Mayo, M. (2005) *Global Citizens*: *Social Movements and the Challenge of Globalization*. London: Zed Press; and Glasius, M., Kaldor, M. and Anheier, H. (2006) *Global Civil Society 2005/6*. London: Sage.

Related Websites

www.ideaswebsite. org
www.unrisd.org
www.crop.org
www.gaspp.org
www.globalforumhealth.org

6

Global Redistribution, Regulation and Rights

This chapter

- Reviews progress towards the development and acceptance of the concept of a supranational 'global social policy'
- Reviews developments of a global redistribution system enabling North–South transfers to pay for MDGs and global public goods
- Reviews developments to regulate ILO-designed labour standards, TNC codes of conduct taxes and the global health and welfare market
- Reviews the development within the UN system of a set of global social rights and moves to make them more enforceable

The rise of global social policy

In this chapter we turn to the question of global social policy understood as supra-or trans-national policy. Is the case for a **global** social policy of redistribution, regulation and rights across borders being put by scholars and listened to by policy advocates within and around international organisations? In 1997 I asserted: 'There is now a global social policy, constituted of global redistributive mechanisms, global regulatory mechanism, elements of global provision and empowerment' (Deacon, 1997). Given this, I went to on to argue a preference for:

> a global social reformist project which would call for more rather than less redistribution of resources between states, for more rather than less global social and labour regulation as a framework for the operation of corporations, for more rather than less authority to be given to supranational bodies to intervene in the affairs of states where those states fail their citizens. (1997: 213)

The argument continues by insisting on the linkages between the elements:

> There should be no free trade without global social regulation. There should be no global social regulation without global redistribution. To ensure citizens (and not their governments) benefit there should be no global social redistribution without the empowerment of citizens before a global court of social rights. Trade, regulation, redistribution and empowerment go hand in hand. (1997: 213)

In many ways, all that has happened since this was written in 1997 has been the unfolding of global politics of this project and its stumbling on four counts:

1 The unilateralism of the United States.
2 The social protectionism of the EU.
3 The opposition of many southern governments and voices to a northern-driven agenda, especially when the resources to fund one key element of the matrix redistribution are missing.
4 A concern that this modernist project does not respect immense cultural differences. As Yeates put it, 'It must be acknowledged that historical, cultural, ideological, religious and institutional differences render the pursuit of "universal" public goods, or an agreed global cosmopolitan form of progress particularly difficult' (2001: 169).

Nonetheless, others within academia continued to develop the idea of a global social policy. Townsend and Gordon acknowledge that 'what remains is perhaps the most difficult: to bring about extensive redistribution of resources between and within countries to eradicate poverty and establish decent human rights' (2002: 421). But they argue that this objective 'is more plausible to world opinion than it was even five years ago'. George and Wilding devote a whole chapter to 'The Future of Global Social Policy'. They argue for seven major roles for social policy at a global level:

1 The promotion and establishment of basic human rights at an international level.
2 To supplement and complement national social policy (because of cross-border social issues: drugs, AIDS, crime, migration).
3 To create an international level playing field.
4 To raise standards internationally by action at the global level.
5 To reduce poverty and inequalities and to provide a safety net for global capitalism.
6 To provide the services which global capitalism needs to survive and prosper (environmental law, employment law, and migration regulation).
7 To promote a sense of one inextricably linked global world (bringing into being the emergent ideas of global citizenship and global responsibility) (2002: 187–90).

To achieve all of this, they argue, 'global social policy will be multi dimensional – a mix of regulation, redistribution, provision of services and guaranteeing of basic rights' (2002: 192). They conclude that the bringing into being of such a comprehensive global social policy will require 'creative thinking about ... a radically new approach to global governance' (2002: 210).

Global redistribution

The term 'global redistribution' is not normally part of the global discourse on issues of world poverty alleviation. For it to become part of that discourse would itself be a step towards the eventual construction of a supranational governance mechanism to bring systematic global redistribution about. Hurrell and Woods note that 'Today justice-claims based on the inequality of resources among states have all but disappeared ... By the 1990s just one kind of inequality remained prominent on the political agenda (both domestic and international), and that was and still is, poverty' (1999: 16). The rally cry at the Gleneagles G8 summit in 2005 was 'make poverty history', not 'reduce global inequity'. However, a more positive note is struck by Linklater (1999: 474) who, referring to among others Onora O'Neill's (1991) work, notes that 'Justice considerations have moved to the centre of the discipline [of international relations]' (1999: 474). In this part of the chapter we will describe briefly how the situation developed whereby poverty replaced inequity in the 1970s and 1980s in the context of the debt crisis of poorer countries and the practice of aid agencies. We will notice that by the time of writing the fault-lines in this architecture of poverty-focused aid were beginning to be exposed, leading to the consideration of some form of international taxation to better enable the meeting of the MDG targets. We then consider what sums of money are actually needed to meet these goals and review some of the possible sources of funds that could be used for that purpose. One step towards taking global responsibility for meeting global social needs is the discussion about global public goods. Balanced somewhere between traditional donor-driven poverty-focused aid and systematic global levies and taxes for funding global public goods are global funds (for health, education and social protection) contributed to by governments, philanthropists, business and individuals. The workings of these new and emerging funds will be examined. Finally, this section of the chapter notes the continuing perverse redistribution that takes place whereby rich northern countries benefit from resources flows from the South to the North.

Aid, debt relief and the international finance facility

From the time of the inception of the Marshall Plan in 1948 – a mechanism for financial assistance from the USA to post-war Europe, through the initiative of the Colombo Plan by the Commonwealth in 1951 to help countries in Asia, to the flowering of overseas development co-operation in the 1960s and 1970s following the independence of countries from colonialism – the dominant form of 'foreign aid' from the richer North to the poorer South – has been grants or concessional loans (loans made at less than market rates) made either by bilateral donors (two-thirds of all aid) or multi-lateral institutions (one-third of all aid) such as the World Bank's International Development Association (IDA). Overseas Development Co-operation (ODC) is a broader concept, involving non-concessional loans by countries and the non-IDA parts of the Bank and so on. The OECD:DAC includes in its count of 'foreign aid' or official development assistance (ODA), assistance that has a grant element of at least 25 per cent and be aimed at economic development or social welfare. The UN had developed a target in 1970 for bilateral ODA of 0.7 per cent of GNP but only Denmark, The Netherlands,

Sweden, Norway and Luxembourg currently meet it. The USA gives only 0.1 per cent and most European countries around 0.3 per cent. Several EU countries have recently resolved to meet the 0.7 per cent target within a few years. Much ODA is provided indirectly through subcontracts to INGOs, and of course other INGO support and global philanthropy needs to be added to North–South aid flows.

To summarise the salient aspects of a very long and complex story (George and Wilding, 2002; German and Randel, 2002; Hall and Midgley, 2004; UNDP, 2005), the following points may be made:

1   Aid had risen during the last century, peaking at $63.7 billion in 1992, and began to decline in the 1990s but some signs of recovery are now evident.

2   Most aid is not actually spent in the poorest countries but in middle-income countries serving a geo-political or commercial purpose. Often aid is 'tied aid', made conditional upon countries spending it on contracts with donor country firms, in effect reducing the amount of money actually transferred. By 1998 the 43 least-developed countries received only 21 per cent of official aid.

3   Very little aid is actually spent on basic services such as education and health. About 10 per cent of bilateral aid in 1990 was spent on education with, only 1 per cent being on basic education. The 20:20 initiative developed by UNICEF that called for 20 per cent of aid to be spent by donors on social services with a commitment by recipient governments to spend 20 per cent of their funds on the same remains largely a dead letter, although the OECD calculates that in 1999–2000 bilateral commitments for education, health and population stood at 15 per cent of aid budgets (OECD 2002a).

4   Much aid is tied aid, having to be spent on services provided by the donors. The Reality of Aid (in Africa) Project concluded that only 37 per cent of development assistance in 1997 was available for developing countries-own spending. Of the remainder, 34 per cent, for example, was spent on donor-controlled technical assistance (German and Randell, 2002; AFRODAD, 2005).

5   At the same time, the cost of repaying concessional and non-concessional loans escalated in the 1970s and 1980s such that several poor countries were owing and paying more in debt repayments to the North than their entire GNP. Eight of the eleven countries with debts greater that their GNP in 1997 were Sub-Saharan countries, and 20 of the 40 countries with debts above 50 per cent of their GNPs were also from this region. Such countries were forced to divert resources that should have been spent on education and health to debt payments.

6   In this context, much ODA then became distributed through aid agencies (INGOs and consulting companies) rather than through governments' non-existent budgets. Much ODA became very project-based and ill co-ordinated.

7   To remedy this situation attempts were made in the 1990s to co-ordinate the efforts of donors through sector-wide initiatives whereby all donor aid to, say, the education sector in one country was dispersed after donors had agreed a master plan, often under the direction of the World Bank. Increasingly in this context attempts were made to get ODA back into government budgets, but often to decentralised regions and localities that were thought to be more responsive to people's needs.

These features of foreign aid led the UK (UK DFID, 2000b) to argue within OECD:DAC that much more aid needed to be targeted upon poorer countries and within them to poorer people. Hence a radical move to challenge some of the worst aspects of the aid system added a further twist in support of the idea that social policy in a development context should be about targeted poverty alleviation through social funds and the like. Indebtedness and the call to relieve countries of their debt, spearheaded by the Jubilee 2000 campaign, gave rise to the heavily indebted poor countries initiative (HIPC) and the Enhanced HIPC2. As we saw in Chapter 2, the PRSP process was launched to ensure that countries seeking debt relief under HIPC would have poverty alleviation policies in place, and often improvements in their form of governance and the privatisation of some public services in train as a condition for receiving debt relief. This added a further push towards a targeted poverty alleviation policy focus.

The Millennium Project Task Force (UN Millennium Project, 2005b) concluded that there were many shortcomings to the existing ODA system, including that it was not sufficiently geared to meeting the MDGs. The report concluded among other things that ODA (UN Millennium Project, 2005b: 36–40) a) lacked an MDG focus, b) was often short term, c) was ill co-ordinated and d) was of poor quality because among other things it was unpredictable, targeted at emergency aid and not long-term investment, tied to contractors from developing countries and driven by donor objectives. The UNDP Human Development Report for 2005 (UNDP, 2005: 9) also reviewed the amount, quality and effectiveness of aid and recommended that at the upcoming UN World Summit countries:

- set a schedule for reaching 0.7 per cent Gross National Income (GNI) by 2015 and stick to it;
- tackle unsustainable debt;
- provide predictable multi-year financing through governments programmes;
- streamline conditionality; and
- end tied aid in 2006.

These shortcomings in the aid system, the commitments made by the UN system and the World Bank and the IMF in 2000 to meet the MDGs, and the global 'celebrity led' campaign in 2005 to 'make poverty history' conspired to create a headache for donor governments before, at and after the Gleneagles 2005 G8 summit. How could these MDG goals possibly be achieved, and how could world poverty possibly be made history using the same creaking institutional architecture of ODA? The UK government made much in this period of its occupying the Presidency of the EU from July 2005 and its holding the chair of the G8 at the same time. In the run-up to 2005, Tony Blair also launched the Commission for Africa which highlighted the issue of poverty in that world region and increased expectations that northern governments would achieve a sea-change in policy towards the South. Over a longer period, Gordon Brown, the UK Chancellor of the Exchequer who also held at this time the post of Chair of the Management Committee of the IMF, made a number of important speeches at international gatherings on the topic (Brown, 2001). All of these UK government pronouncements had been preceded by its White Paper (UKDFID, 2000b), *Making Globalisation Work for the Poor,* one point of which had been to argue that development assistance must be used more effectively.

Gordon Brown's approach to *Tackling World Poverty: A Global New Deal* had four components: a) improved terms under which poorer countries engage in the global economy, b) adoption by international business of high corporate standards, c) an improved trade regime, and d) 'A substantial transfer of additional resources from the richest to the poorest countries in the form of investment for development. Here the focus must not be on aid to compensate the poor for their poverty, but investment that builds new capacity to compete and addresses the long term causes of poverty' (2001: 7). What specific changes in rich country donor policy and what specific ideas for this huge increase in North–South transfers materialised in practice during this period around the 2005 G8 summit? Actually, despite its critics, quite a lot:

1   **The cancelling of the debts** worth about $40–£55 billion of the poorest countries owed to the World Bank, IMF and Africa Development Bank. Of the debt owed by 18 countries that had already completed the HIPC initiative, 100 per cent was cancelled immediately. Another nine countries were thought to be able to benefit within 12 to 18 months. Arguments continued, however, around the conditions to be met for such debt relief, the Germans and French in particular looking for evidence of the end of corruption, and the Bank wondering whether it would be funded by donors to compensate for lost debt income.

2   **The doubling of ODA by 2010** by the EU's richest countries and the **increase** in ODA from all donor countries by around $50 billion by 2010 (which compares with the $63.7 billion peak of 1992 and the actual total of $57 billion in 2002). Half of this increase, $25 billion, will be for Africa. A doubling of ODA by all countries was not possible because of reluctance on the part of the USA to increase substantially its share. The EU, prior to the Gleneagles meeting, had announced that the richest EU countries would aim to reach the UN target of 0.7 per cent of GDP by 2015 and that the new members, hitherto often recipients of ODA, would aim to reach 0.33 per cent of GDP by 2015.

3   **The development of an International Finance Facility (IFF)** to bring forward funds for initially the advance purchase on behalf of poor countries of vaccines. Gordon Brown had long argued for the setting-up of an IFF whereby governments would issue development bonds that would enable them to bring forward future ODA payments. While the idea was not supported by the USA at the G8 meeting, an experimental version of it is to go ahead called the International Finance Facility for Immunisation (IFFIm). France, Sweden, Spain, Italy and the UK will issue such bonds and give the funds to the Global Alliance for Vaccination and Immunisation (GAVI).

4   The agreement even by the UK to consider the French–German proposal for a **tax on air traffic** to fund specific development projects. Following Gleneagles, the French government wrote to 145 world leaders asking for support for a tax on airport take-offs to increase funds for ODA.

5   Moves by all G8 countries to '**enhance efforts to untie aid**' to purchases from donor countries and on the part of the UK government a decision to stop making aid conditional upon the Washington Consensus package of 'privatisation and market opening'. Hilary Benn, UK Minister for Development announced at the OECD:DAC a new UKDFID (UK Department for International Development) policy paper that argued that donors should focus more on outcomes of policies in poorer countries, such as the number of children in school, rather than the specific policy means to achieve these ends.

All of these developments are significant. The 25-year story of poor country indebtedness entered its last chapter. There was even talk at the G8 of global taxation and global funds for use in the South. On the other hand, there will continue to be arguments about how far some of the new ODA money will actually be merely replenishments to the Bank for debts written off, meaning that the claim that the North decided **both** to increase aid and to write off debt is false (Curtis, 2005). Also, while the move within rich EU countries to reach the 0.7 per cent of GNP target was welcomed by global poverty campaigners, the USA typically struck a discordant note in its attempted revisions of the statement being planned to be made at the end of the September 2005 UN Millennium Progress Summit. Its proposed amendment would have *deleted* the following sentence from the final declaration: 'We welcome the establishment of time-tables by many countries to achieve the 0.7% of gross national product for official development assistance and to reach at least 0.5 per cent by 2009 and urge those developed countries that have not yet done so to make concrete efforts towards allocating 0.7 per cent of their GNP for ODA' (GSP Digest 5.3, 2005; see also Borger 2005). At the same time, most of the discussion around the issue of aid is still couched in terms of donors and recipients. Little of it engages seriously with the alternative language of global taxation on global capital or the global rich to fund systematically global public goods. How exactly all of this new money is to be spent remains unclear. We will consider these issues in more detail later in this chapter and the next.

Following the Gleneagles G8 meeting of July 2005 was the much-heralded UN Millennium plus 5 World Summit. Among other reasons for it being convened was a stock-take of progress towards meeting the MDGs. The UN had been hopeful that it would build upon Gleneagles and push the USA, for example, to also commit to increase its ODA. As indicated earlier, it appeared that this aspect of the Summit agenda would end in failure when the newly appointed USA ambassador to the UN, John Bolton, tabled hundreds of amendments to the almost agreed draft outcome document. In particular, as we noted earlier, he wanted deleted all reference to the MDGs and the promised increases in ODA (GSP Digest 6.1, 2006b). In this he was defeated and the Summit did restate the commitment of donors to an increase in ODA by $50 billion by 2010. While welcoming the moves towards the 0.7 per cent level of ODA by some countries, the Summit did not reaffirm the commitment of others to reach this target, leaving the USA free to continue to fail significantly to do so. Developing countries agreed to adopt MDG plans by 2006. The initiative of some countries to go ahead with a limited form of the IFF for immunisation was endorsed (UN, 2005a). Indeed, 66 countries committed themselves to international levies, including taxes on air travel to boost aid flows (Elliott, 2005).

Subsequently, the International Finance Facility for Immunisation (IFFIm) was launched in September 2005 with British, French, Italian, Spanish and Swedish support. Norway later added its support. The first bonds were issued in April 2006. The French airline ticket solidarity tax was launched on 1 July 2006. The proposals for a broader IFF and for a wider commitment to the airline ticket tax were subsequently discussed at a major international conference on Innovative Sources of Financing for Development hosted by France between 28 February and 1 March 2006 (www.diplomatie.gouv.fr/en/). The French are proposing an International Drug Purchasing Facility (IDPF) to provide a reliable source of funds over the long term for drugs to complement the Global Fund to Fight AIDS, Tuberculosis and Malaria.

A joint UK–French working group to 'pursue further work on innovative financing mechanisms' has been established and will report to the September 2006 IMF/World Bank Annual Meeting. The conference, attended by 90 countries and 60 NGOs, marked a breakthrough from theory to practice, with 11 additional countries agreeing to raise an airline ticket tax in the near future following the decision of France and Chile to do this. A larger group of 38 countries established a 'pilot group for solidarity contributions for development'. The significance of these moves should not be underestimated. As Wahl comments in a Friedrich Ebert Stiftung Briefing, 'In adopting the air-ticket tax, France, Brazil, Chile and others, have dared to take a step into an entirely new paradigm' (2006: 8).

How much money for the MDGs?

How do the sums mentioned earlier, an increase of ODA by $50 billion by 2010, compare with what is actually needed? What would it cost to meet the MDGs? It had become common to estimate this figure as only $50 billion per year. The UN Secretary-General convened a High-Level Panel on Financing for Development that reported as the Zedillo Report in 2001 (UN, 2001). This panel agreed this conservative estimate that was later used by the United Nations Human Development Report (UNHDR) for 2003 (UNDP, 2003) as the basis for its argument that ODA needed to be 'doubled' to a total of $100 billions per year, or about 0.5 per cent of total rich country GDP. However, the Millennium Project Task Force (UN Millennium Project, 2005b: 55–9) made more detailed estimates of the cost of meeting the MDGs in all countries by first calculating the costs in a selection of typical countries and estimating the additional tax and other national resources that could be drawn upon by those countries, including the resources made available by virtue of the ending of debt payments. A MDG financing gap was then calculated, which would need to be filled by ODA (or in principle other forms of international taxation). For an average low-income country, external finance of between 10 and 20 per cent of GDP would be needed to fill the gap. For middle-income countries, the external support would be a smaller percentage of GDP. The report concluded that the cost of meeting the MDGs in all countries would be $121 billion in 2006, rising through $143 billion in 2010 to $189 billion in 2015. Estimates were then made of increases needed in ODA, making assumptions about the amount of ODA that would continue not to be focused on the MDGs (about $34 billion of the current 2002 level of ODA) and the number of countries that would not be eligible for extra ODA because of not meeting good governance criteria. Thus a total ODA need of about $154 billion in 2006, $177 billion in 2010 and £223 billion in 2015 was estimated. An absolute increase in ODA would be needed of $70 billion annually by 2006 (current $50 billion plus new $70 billion makes $120 billion), rising to an additional $87 billion in 2010 and an additional $130 billion by 2015.

Oxfam (2005) compared the G8 2005 Gleneagles commitments with previous donor pledges to work out the actual amount of new money on offer, and then compared these commitments to the projected costs of the MDGs up till 2010. They made slightly different estimates from the Millennium Report of the needs (Table 6.1).

Thus the G8 outcome that total ODA in USA dollars will be $95 billion in 2006 and $127 billion in 2010 (0.36 per cent GNI) compared to the estimated of the cost

Table 6.1 Cost of meeting the MDGs and current ODA projections (US $)

	2004	2006	2006	2006	2010	2010	2010	2010
		Overall aid level	Increase on 2004	Amount of new money	Overall aid level	Increase on 2004	Amount of new money	% GNI in 2010
Pre-Gleneagles commitments	79	91	12	0	111	32	0	0.31
G8 outcomes	–	95	16	4	127	48	16	0.36
UN MDG requirements	–	151	72	60	170	91	59	0.46
0.7 % GNI by 2010	–	144	65	53	248	169	137	0.7

Source: Oxfam (2005).

of meeting the MDGs of $151 billion in 2006 and $170 billion in 2010 (0. 46 per cent GNI). By way of comparison, rich country agricultural subsidy is currently about $300 billion annually, and about $600 billion annually is spent on defence.

The finance gap for meeting the minimum MDGs could be more or less filled by ODA **only** if the USA were to commit itself to the 0.7 per cent GNP target which is politically most unlikely. In the absence of that, the world will need to look to other forms of development finance. This is contrary to the conclusion of Atkinson, based on the more conservative $50 billion extra when he asserted that 'The funding of the MDGs could be achieved solely by increased ODA' (2005: 4).

New sources of finance for development?

How could, in principle, the world raise additional revenues to pay for the investment in education, health and social protection in poorer countries? To what extent have these alternative sources of finance been given serious consideration by the 'international community'? Valuable overviews of alternative sources of finance have been provided by Atkinson (2005), Clunies-Ross (2004) and Aziz (2005). Atkinson (2005) reviewed:

- **Global environmental taxes** including taxes on goods generating environmental externalities such as a tax on use of hydrocarbon fuels (for example, Cooper, 1998).
- **Tax on currency flows** such as a tax on foreign currency transactions (Tobin Tax) (for example, Patomaki and Denys, 2002).
- **Creation of new Special Drawing Rights (SDRs)** whereby donor countries would make their IMF share of drawing (borrowing) rights that they don't use available for development (Soros, 2002).
- **International Finance Facility (IFF)** bringing forward future ODA commitments by means of bonds issued for development. Donors would in effect borrow future ODA monies on capital market so it could be spent now.
- **Increased private donations** by individuals and firms, often linked to new UN global 'health' funds or UNICEF-type appeals.
- **Global lottery and Premium Bond** with proceeds shared between countries and a UN fund (Ahde et al., 2002).
- **Increased remittances from emigrants** by encouraging repatriation of funds by reducing transaction costs and richer countries raising taxes only on citizens, not residents (for example, Bhagwati and Hanada, 1982; Solimano, 2001).

To this list Clunies–Ross (2004) added:

- arms trade tax;
- tax on resource rent of deep-ocean minerals;
- tax on international air transport; and
- resources available from commercial enterprises.

Atkinson (2005) reviewed all of the taxes against several criteria. First was its potential to raise only the earlier conservative MDG finance gap of $50 billion per year, not the extra $130 billion per year needed by 2015 according to the Millennium Development Task Force. Second was whether there were other benefits associated with the source of funds. Third was the disadvantage of the source. Finally, the main obstacles to its introduction were noted. Table 6.2 is based on Atkinson (2005: 240–1) and Clunies-Ross (2004: 202–13).

Clunies-Ross's (2004) assessment of the other taxes he considered concluded that an arms trade tax would fall on poorer countries and generate only $5 billion annually, that deep-sea mineral extraction does not yet exist to be taxed, that a maximum feasible air transport tax might generate $20 billion, and that subsidies from commercial enterprises such as drug companies selling at cost in poorer countries could contribute a little to global redistribution.

To summarise, estimates of revenue from some of the global taxes considered by Atkins and Clunies-Ross are disputed, but a general conclusion might be drawn here that they would provide the most sustainable source of finance for development. Special drawing rights (SDRs) are worth considering. The IFF does not seem to be a long-term solution but might be useful now. Philanthropy has its place if linked to specific global funds and might increase (but see section on global funds later). Lotteries tax the poor and there is a moral issue expecting often poor migrants to fund development in their country of origin, which somehow lets the richer citizens of richer countries who often depend on such migrant labour off the hook.

To what extent has the formal process of the inter-governmental system considered or endorsed any of these ideas? The UN organised the Monterrey Conference on Finance for Development in 2001 in the wake of its Millennium Pledge to meet the MDGs by 2015. The High Level Panel on Financing for Development chaired by Ernesto Zedillo prepared a report for this conference (UN, 2001) that made a number of recommendations related to these issues:

- 'The FFD conference to obtain a commitment by industrial countries to implement the target of providing ODA equal to 0.7 per cent of their GNP' (United Nations, 2001). In the event no such commitment was at that time forthcoming, although the EU then committed itself to raise ODA to 0.39 per cent. Subsequently, as we have seen, the richer countries of the EU made the 0.70 per cent commitment at the Gleneagles 2005 G8 meeting.
- 'The FFD conference should explore the desirability of securing an adequate international tax resource to finance the supply of global public goods. It has been suggested that a currency transaction tax might provide such a source, but the Panel concluded that further rigorous study would be needed to resolve the doubts about the feasibility of such a tax. A better possibility would be for all countries to agree to impose a minimum level of taxation on consumption of fossil fuels (a carbon tax) as away of combating global warming' (United Nations, 2001). The careful wording here reflects an attempt to keep on board the USA who have a long-standing objection to the UN even considering the idea of global taxes as an independent source of funding for UN purposes. In the event, no agreement to any kind of international tax was secured at the FFD conference. Subsequently, as we have seen, there has been a commitment to an air-ticket tax by some countries.
- 'The IMF should recommence SDR allocations' (United Nations, 2001). This has not yet been implemented.

Table 6.2   Alternative forms of international taxation and revenue raising

Source	Potential funds	Other benefit	Disadvantages	Obstacles
Global environmental	Tax on rich countries could raise $50 billion.	Environmental gain	Distributional effect on households. Admin costs	Requires all high-income countries to agree
Currency transaction	Tax of 0.1 % could generate $15–28 billion (Clunies-Ross gives estimates on a 0.25 % tax of $172 billion in 2000)	Reduce foreign currency speculation	Distributional effect unclear. Admin costs	Requires general agreement
Special Drawing Rights	Allocation of $25–30 billion possible	Positive effects on global macroeconomy	Impact not clear	Has to be ratified by 100 members with 85% voting power
International Finance Facility	Could achieve $50 billion for 2010–2015 but then falling off to zero	Positive effects on global macroeconomy	Costs of new institution. What happens after 2020?	Requires sufficient donor countries to sign up
Private donations	Presently marginal but could increase. Estimated as $17 billion in 2001. Ted Turner UN endowment is $1 billion	Benefits both donors and receivers	Little	Only individual action needed
Remittances from emigrants	Large and relatively stable. $80 billion received by developing world in 2002	Benefit donors and receivers	Link to development uncertain	Money laundering and counter-terrorism legislation might be obstacle
Global Lottery	$6 billion?	–	Burden born by low-income groups	Competition with national lottery
Global Premium Bond	Hard to estimate		Admin cost. Crowding-out of other government debt	Competition with other borrowing

Source: Atkinson (2004: 202–3); Clunies-Ross (2005: 240–1). By permission of Oxford University Press.

Global public goods: breakthrough or contest of definitions?

One of the issues linked to the question of global taxation and redistribution is that of global public goods. What are they, and how should they be paid for? How do global public goods relate to development assistance? First, what are public goods? Here we are using the economist definition of public goods derived from David Humes's and Adam Smith's work. These are goods that benefit all but which are not particularly in the interests of any one person to make and sell or any one consumer to buy. Strictly, such goods are non-rivalrous and non-excludable in their consumption. If one person benefits from its provision, it does not stop another doing so. A classic example is a lighthouse; once built and operating, it is impossible to exclude ships from using it; nor is my consumption of the lighthouse's services diminished by your use of it. A safely regulated traffic scheme in a town is also a public good from which all benefit. Public goods are often connected to market failure. Public goods do not have to be manufactured by the state, but they are typically financed by the state. They serve a common purpose that benefits all.

Global public goods are therefore goods that it would benefit the whole world to provide but which no one country might be inclined to finance. Among the global public goods argued for initially by Inge Kaul et al. (1999) of the UNDP were:

- international equity and distributive justice (to secure a more stable world);
- international financial stability;
- health and global epidemiological surveillance; and
- global communications networks, peace and security.

The idea that ensuring the health of the world's population might be something that is in the general interest but that no particular national or private agency might see it as their business has a long history. Surveillance of infectious diseases that has been undertaken by the WHO for a considerable time may be regarded as a public good in the strict economists' use of the term. It is non-divisible in that it is all benefit and non-excludable, and nobody can be prevented from benefiting. Globalisation has increased the movements of people and has made this even more apparent. The 2003 SARS epidemic which spread quickly from the East to Canada brought this home.

Chen et al. make the case that the global control of tobacco consumption and illicit drugs is a public good, as are policies to prevent the depletion of the ozone layer or otherwise stop environmentally and therefore health-damaging processes:

> In sum, due in part to globalisation, health is becoming more of a global public good through two forces. First, enhanced international linkages in trade, migration and information flows have accelerated the cross-border transmission of diseases and the international transfer of behavioural and environmental health risks. Second, intensified pressures on common-pool global resources of air and water have generated shared environmental threats. (1999: 289)

If the health of everybody globally is regarded as a public good from which we all benefit, rather than a purely national or private matter which is the outcome of private behavioural choices and national government expenditures, then issues of equitable access to services and prevention become a matter for global health policy. Buse et al. argue that:

> Global health means that the health of the poorest and most vulnerable has direct relevance for all populations because of the many interconnectivities that bring us together ... At a minimum, targeted investment to provide for the basic needs of clean water and sanitation, housing, food and health care are the building blocks at the local level towards an essential infrastructure through which better health for all is achievable ... Failure to address these basic needs raises the prospect that health problems (e.g. antibiotic resistance, multi-drug tuberculosis, contaminated drinking water) and other types of risk (e.g. political and economic instability) may impact on other population groups. (2002: 277)

In sum we can say that there are three distinct components to the case that many aspects of health should be regarded as a global public good: a) because of transmission across borders, to which globalisation is contributing; b) because the cause of much disease is ultimately environmental, and at least some environmental problems themselves have international public goods dimensions; and c) because there are issues of international regulation of health care services and delivery.

The World Bank's initial exploration of the concept of global public goods argued that external benefits across borders to countries other than that where the funds are spent might be a working definition of global public goods. Thus 'global public goods are commodities, resources, services, and also systems of rules or policy regimes with substantial cross-border externalities that are important for development and poverty-reduction, and that can be produced in sufficient supply only through cooperation and collective action be developing and developed countries' (World Bank, 2000: 2). This enabled the Bank to assert contentiously that this excluded universal primary education as 'for the most part benefits of education confer locally, and produce no significant cross border externalities' (2000: 4). On the other hand, it included expenditure on communicable diseases. Choices between competing claims to considered global public goods and to have money spent on them would then have to be made, and for the Bank its priorities areas would be:

- promoting improved economic governance;
- increasing trade integration;
- eradicating communicable diseases;
- protecting the global environmental commons; and
- providing information and knowledge. (2000: 5–8)

The Zedillo report adopted a rather conservative view of global public goods, defining them as 'including peacekeeping; prevention of contagious diseases; research into tropical medicines, vaccines, and agricultural crops; the prevention of CFC emissions; limitation of carbon emissions; and preservation of biodiversity. No individual country has an incentive to pay for these goods and thus collective action is needed if they are to be supplied in sufficient quantity' (UN, 2001: 8).

Further work being undertaken by Inge Kaul and her colleagues is now shaping a conception of global public goods within the UN system that goes beyond the mere formal economist's criteria of goods which are technically non-excludable and non-rival in their consumption (for example, world peace) to embrace goods such as basic education and health care which are (or should be) 'socially determined public goods', that is, goods which might be considered rival and excludable but which by political decision could be regarded as non-exclusive (2003: 83). Political decisions about this could reflect the list of global social rights embodied within the 1967 United Nations Covenant on Economic, Cultural and Social Rights. Another approach would be to regard as socially determined global public goods those goods listed within the internationally agreed MDGs being progressed through the UN Millennium Project Task Force.

Kaul and her colleagues also make a useful distinction between development assistance and global public goods (Kaul et al., 2003: 358). Development assistance might continue in the context of progressive globalisation and could be provided with additional funds from some form of global taxation, as we have seen. Countries receiving ODA should then be allowed to use this for development purposes. Additionally, mechanisms need to be set up to manage the provision of genuinely global public goods and diminish the existence of global public bads. An international governance and spending system is needed for global public goods that are not specific to particular countries (2003: 395).

Arguing for global public goods does not mean they will be provided. Kaul et al. (1999) note three reasons why such good may not be so readily provided as might be suggested. They refer to these as the:

- **Jurisdictional gap**   The mismatch between law making being still a national business when policy issues have become internationalised.
- **Participation gap**   Those who might articulate the case for a global public good are excluded from intergovernmental process of decision making.
- **Incentive gap**   No country has the incentive to provide. Costs still fall on an outdated country-based aid system instead of a new international form of finance.

Thus, if global social policies are to be advanced that enable the provision of more global public goods to meet cross-border needs in a globalised world, then the existing institutions of global governance may need reform.

The global funds: progress to meeting MDGs or sidestepping the UN?

In recent years a number of new global funds for specific purposes have been established. They can be seen as an attempt by the UN, in particular the Secretary-General, to speed up the process of meeting some of the MDGs. These funds combine a number of different sources of finance: traditional donations from rich countries in response to UN appeals, large charitable donations from global philanthropists, and other sources. The current list includes:

- **The Global Fund to Fight AIDS, TB and Malaria** (the Global Fund) established in 2002 as a public–private partnership with a Secretariat housed in the WHO but with the World Bank managing the funds as a trustee. Initially it aimed to raise $7–10 billions annually but by 2003 had raised total pledges of only $2.1 billion, $2 billion of which had come from bilateral aid and $0.1 billion from the Bill and Melinda Gates Foundation (Ollila, 2003). This $2.1 billion was distributed to 224 programmes in 121 countries (Global Fund, 2003). By 2005, total pledges of $4.6 billion had been made, covering a spending period from 2001–2005, 6, 7 or 8 depending on the donor. The USA has pledged $1.623 million by 2008 and France $628 million by 2006 (Global Fund, 2005).

- **The Global Alliance for Vaccination and Immunization (GAVI)** was launched at the World Economic Forum in 2000, with an initial donation of $750 million to be spent over five years by the Bill and Melinda Gates Foundation. By 2002 an additional $339 million had been raised from government donors. The GAVI Board include the WHO, UNICEF, the World Bank, the Gates Foundation, rotating members from the OECD and developing countries and two research institutes. It is housed in UNICEF in Geneva (Ollila, 2003).

- **The Education for All (EFA) Fast Track Initiative (FTI) Catalytic Fund**. This Fast Track Initiative is provided with administrative support by the Bank but is chaired by a rotating G8 donor and non-G8 donor. It aims to achieve sustained increases in aid for education. In order to bridge the funding gap, the FTI established in 2003 the FTI Catalytic Fund as a multi-donor trust fund. At April 2004 the EFA-FTI Catalytic Fund had attracted only US$236 million from four donors, which 'is not enough even for the immediate needs of the first countries to join the FTI' (UNESCO, 2004: 34). Government plans are reviewed by the FTI Secretariat in conjunction with UNESCO. An annual FTI meeting takes place in the margins of the annual UNESCO High Level Group monitoring the achievement of the EFA initiative.

The Global Fund might be taken as an example of how global innovative redistribution mechanisms are being established. It uses a combination of criteria and mechanisms to allocate resources where they are needed most in the world. Using the World Banks' categorisation of countries into low and middle income, the Global Fund first distinguishes between low-income countries which are fully eligible for monies and lower-middle-income countries which must match international funds with national funds, and focus activities on the poor and vulnerable and aim to be self-sufficient over time. A few upper-middle-income countries are also eligible in much the same way as lower-middle-income countries if they have exceptional need based on disease burden indicators.

The procedure used for allocating funds within the constraints above is based on a competition between bids from Country Coordinating Mechanisms (CCMs) within each eligible country. A partnership is aimed at between the Global Fund and national political effort that also embraces, through the CCMs, national partners drawn from the private sector, the professions and users groups. Where governments are non-functioning, the applications can be made for non-governmental organisations. A board of internationally appointed technical experts adjudicate between competing applications using the following list of criteria: epidemiological and socioeconomic criteria, political commitment (of recipient governments), complementarities (to national effort), absorptive capacity (of governance mechanisms), soundness of project approach, feasibility, potential for sustainability, and evaluations and analysis mechanism in place. There are arguments for and against this responsive mode of resource allocation. Such an approach might miss the neediest that are unable to bid, but it does involve a partnership between national and global effort. At the same time, there is room for debate about the implicit conditionality built into the allocation mechanism. Good national governance is likely to be rewarded (except where it is recognised that no effective government exists). On the other hand, a global fund that simply poured money into the coffers of a corrupt national government is likely to be criticised.

One positive spin-off of the emergence of global funds for the purchase of drugs has been to put pressure upon pharmaceutical companies to reduce the price of drugs to be made available for use in poorer countries. It has been reported that the Clinton Foundation's HIV/AIDS Initiative managed to broker a price of 36 cents per day for treatment by the three anti-retroviral drugs used to treat thousands of African patients. GlaxoSmithKline is among the companies cutting prices, with the expectation of further bulk orders arising from the projected International Finance Facility for Immunisation that will fill the coffers of GAVI.

Critics (Ollila, 2003) have, however, pointed to a worrying aspect of the Global Fund and other initiatives, such as GAVI. The concern is that such funds lack democratic accountability and detract from more systematic processes of global health funding which could be developed under the auspices of the WHO (Ollila, 2003: 53). These criticisms stem from a wider concern that partnerships between multilateral agencies and corporate interests, such as those involved in some of the ad hoc health funds, may erode the existing government-based multilateral system rather than lead to its strengthening and democratisation (Martens, 2003). A further criticism of the Global Fund and the parallel World Bank HIV/AIDS Programme emerging from the Global Health Policy Research Network of the Centre for Global Development (www.cgdev.org) is that such separate and often overlapping funds create an implementation crisis within countries which has lead to:

> poor coordination and duplication, high transaction costs, variable degrees of country ownership, and lack of alignment with country systems, the cumulative effect of which is to risk undermining the sustainability of national development plans, distorting national priorities, diverting scarce human resources and/or establishing uncoordinated service delivery structures. (Shakow, 2006: 3)

My point would be that some of the technical allocation mechanisms used by the Global Fund might be built upon by a democratised and strengthened global social governance system within the context of the sustainable resources available from a global levy based on global taxation with funds flowing through normal government budgets.

An idea on the drawing board and approved by the ILO's governing body and ready to be experimented with is that of the Global Social Trust Network (Cichon et al., 2003). It builds on the idea and practice of social partnerships that fund social protection in many richer countries, seeking to extend this to international social partnerships between people in richer countries and those needing social protection in poorer countries. It will involve resources voluntarily committed (at the suggested level of €5 a month or 0.2 per cent of monthly income) by individuals in OECD countries via the agency of social partner organisations such as Trade Unions or National Social Security funds. National Social Trust Organisations would then be established in both donor countries and recipient countries and transfers would be organised through a Global Board with technical assistance provided, in this case by the ILO. Monies would then be spent by the National Social Trust Organisations, with poorer countries in partnership with embryonic social protection mechanisms at the local level. One suggestion is that the Global Social Trust Network would finance universal pensions at the level of US$1 a day. Pensions are recognised as being a very good cash benefit that actually meets the needs of whole families within extended family networks in poorer countries. The Director of the Social Protection Network of the World Bank has commented favourably upon the ideas so long as the payments are linked to its Poverty Reduction Strategy Papers process (Cichon et al., 2003). There is room for discussion as to whether the priority for international social protection expenditure should be old-age pensions or, as favoured by Townsend and Gordon (2002: 368), universal child benefits. Indeed, the proposal also suggests that social protection to be funded under this Trust should be conceived as wider than cash benefits. A 'basic family protection triangle' is envisaged, whereby family units would be protected by basic income security, essential health services and basic education. It is estimated that if between 5 and 10 per cent of employees of the OECD countries were to contribute an average of €5 per month, then the trust would collect between €1 million and €2 million a year.

The total funds managed by these global funds are small, the combined funds spending only about $2–3 billion annually compared to current ODA of $57 billion. However, as the tension develops between new ODA funds being seen as just more of the same development assistance to countries and the emerging conceptualisation of them as being to secure **globally** agreed MDGSs which have **cross-border spin-offs**, the case for them might grow.

Adverse redistribution: poaching from the South

Before there is a temptation to become too optimistic that the world is stumbling towards a more systematic process of increasing funds for development and global public goods and creating therefore a progressive process of resource redistribution between the Global North and the Global South, we need to remind ourselves that resources still often flow in the opposite way. This applies in the case of those debt payments that have not yet been written off, in terms of low commodity prices and in other ways. Of special interest in terms of global social policy is the process of rich countries having their doctors, nurses and teachers trained for them by poor countries and then poaching them at no cost.

Sanjoy Nayak (2003) has recently reminded us that although there has been an increased consensus that health and knowledge about health should be regarded as a global public good, there has been a silence about the fact that developing countries who contribute to paying for global public goods by training physicians and health workers and medical scientists are not benefiting from them. He suggests that flows of health workers from the Indian sub-continent continue at the fast rates established in the 1970s. He estimates that recipient countries have gained $12.0 to $16.0 billions alone from India due to emigration of physicians. This is far greater than all the global health funds put together. To take the example of the UK in 2002/2003, 5593 nurses trained in the Phillipines registered in the UK together with 1830 from India, 1368 from South Africa, and almost 1000 from Nigeria and Zimbabwe combined.

There have been proposals to counteract this regressive redistribution by taxing migrant physicians and sending the proceeds back to the country that trained the doctor to cover part of the cost of their education, but this has not been implemented. The Commonwealth agreed a package of measures in 2004 to end the organised targeting of poor countries by richer ones seeking teaching staff. In a similar vein, the

UK government had established a code of practice whereby its NHS Trusts should not go poaching in poor countries for nurses. However, Trusts were circumventing this by using agency nurses, as agencies were not subject to the code. This loophole is now closed, but at the same time the UK government did not agree to sign a Commonwealth Code of Practice that covered nurses. The wider ramifications of this global mobility of professional labour in terms of what reforms it suggests are needed in the global governance of migration will be addressed in the next chapter.

Global regulation

The globalisation of business activity and the globalisation of markets give rise to the globalisation of regulations. As Braithwaite and Drahos remind us, 'most of the significant globalization of rules occurred in the twentieth century, particulary since 1970' (2000: 3). Within the field of social policy, regulations concerned with internationalising labour and social standards are perhaps the most important and most controversial. Other areas of concern include those related to food standards, standards of medicines, standards of international health and welfare service providers, and the standardisation of tax regimes. The policy debate has centred around two issues: between those wanting enforceable global regulation and those preferring voluntary codes of conduct; and northern and southern perception of the need for such globalised regulation.

Global labour standards: core labour standards as global progress or setback?

Braithwaite and Drahos remind us that:

> most of the great social movements of the last two centuries have been involved in the globalisation of labour standards; the anti-slavery movement, the labour movement and the Socialist International, the women's movement, the black civil rights movement and the human rights movement generally ... For all this labour standards is not an area where global standards have been ratcheted-up in recent decades ... the combination of international competition in low labour costs, and labour market deregulation to increase the flexibility of response to it, has undermined the labour standards in many places. (2000: 252–3)

The ILO and its role throughout the twentieth century in attempting to improve labour and social standards have been caught in the cross-fire of two of the wars of globalisation: that of capital and labour and the North and the South. Progress in these areas in many, especially developed, countries had been achieved initially in the early years of the last century and then again in the 1950s, 1960s and early 1970s. By 1994 the average number of ratifications of ILO standards per country had reached 41. More conventions were ratified by developed countries (average of 52 in Europe, 42 in the Americas, 27 in Africa and 21 in Asia), although this did not mean ILO influence in developing countries was minimal (Strang and Chang, 1993). Global competition from the 1980s onwards raised the question as to whether there should be a link established between global trade and global labour standards legally in terms of writing into the emerging WTO organisation rules that ensured all members of the WTO should conform to certain labour standards. This came to be known, as we discussed in detail in Chapter 3, as the proposal to insert a 'social clause' into the WTO rulebook. As we saw then, many southern countries were against arguing that to impose such conditions would exclude them from trading globally, and such conditions could not be met by less-developed countries. The case for pressing labour standards on developing countries has been carried largely by labour unions in the advanced industrial states because of concerns about imports from low-wage countries and concerns that such pressures would influence social policy at home. As Singh and Zammit (2000) pointed out, these concerns had arisen against a backdrop of real wages in the USA being stagnant and job creation in Europe being sluggish.

The response of developing countries, and their allies in the advanced industrial states, to these claims was threefold (Singh and Zammit, 2000). The first was to question motives. A central fear of developing countries is that the concern with labour standards is disingenuous and is nothing more than a disguised form of protection and unilateralism. Second was the argument that most trade in manufactures is North–North and only workers in certain sectors may be adversely affected by the rapid growth in North–South trade in certain products, such as textiles and apparel, and anyway trade is only one possible explanation for the problems facing northern workers as technological change is also putting strong pressure on the wages and unemployment opportunities of unskilled workers in the North. Finally, developing countries pointed out that imposition of trade sanctions would have costs for workers in the South. Moreover, the advancement of labour rights is not something to be imposed from above but itself a function of economic development. In the event, the southern (and global business) arguments prevailed and the northern (and trade union) case for the social clause was lost.

It fell then to the ILO to redouble efforts on this issue. Its response was to take one step back and one forward. The step back was to retreat from any position that assumed there could be rapid progress in the futher advancement of **all** of its global standards by more developing countries **voluntarily** signing up to them. The step forward was to focus on **core labour standards** and **impose** these on all countries as a condition of membership of the ILO. This process culminated in the 1998 Declaration of the International Labour Organisation on Fundamental Principles and Rights at Work. That declaration strengthens the nature of obligations towards these core rights:

> All members, even if they have not ratified the Conventions in question, have an obligation, arising from the very fact of membership in the Organisation, to respect, to promote, and to realize, in good faith and in accordance with the Constitution, the principles governing the fundamental rights which are the subject of those Conventions. (Böhning, 2005)

The core labour standards are reduced to four: a) The elimination of discrimination in respect of employment and occupation; b) the elimination of all forms of forced or compulsory labour; c) the elimination of the 'worst forms' of child labour; and d) the right of all workers to form and join organisations of their own choosing without prior authorisation. Now armed with these new core standards, which are seen to be less a matter of choice by countries, the ILO has the capacity to act more forcibly. In 1999 it took the highly unusual step of excluding Myanmar from its proceedings, due to its persistent use of forced labour. In 2000, the ILO called upon its members to review their economic relations with Myanmar to assure that they were not complicit in the use of forced labour. Time will tell how this retreat to an enforceable list of core standards will be regarded.

Voluntary codes and the UN Global Compact: enhancing regulation or enhancing images?

Awareness of the poor conditions in which workers in many developing countries in the South laboured grew in the 1980s and 1990s among those who consumed the products of their labour in the North. Outcomes of this increased awareness were calls for corporations to ensure that their goods were sourced from companies who respected certain labour standards. Although individual companies such as Levi Strauss pioneered corporate codes in the early 1990s, the social accountability and anti-sweatshop movements gained momentum, particularly in the USA and Europe after several scandals in the clothing sector. Students were particularly important players in the development of the American movement, founding United Students Against Sweatshops in 1997. Local branches of the organisation pressured university administrations about the conditions under which clothing such as college sweatshirts were manufactured. They called on suppliers to join the Workers' Rights Consortium, a group established in 2000 to assure independent monitoring of factories and, with support from some unions, thus built bridges to labour organisations in developing countries. The movement spread to Europe, where human rights leaders, trade unions and religious groups formed a loose alliance called the Clean Clothes Campaign. European activists have targeted Adidas, Hennes & Mauritz, the Benetton Group and other European companies.

Three main approaches emerged from the anti-sweatshop movement and the broader push for social accountability in manufacturing: corporate codes of conduct, certification mechanisms, and compliance labelling. The first of these rests on the significance of reputation. Large corporations involved in design, manufacturing or retail sales continually invest in establishing and expanding their name brand recognition: through advertising, promotions, product endorsements, PR and other means. At a minimum, such companies want to avoid adverse publicity. At a maximum, they believe that a positive corporate image, including a reputation for social responsibility, contributes to sales and is demanded by the marketplace. Pearson and Seyfang (2001) summarised the arguments for and against such voluntary codes of conduct. Because these codes are voluntary, coverage of firms is uneven and the content of the codes varies. The firms adopting them do so more in response to northern consumer perceptions rather than southern workers' concerns. Attention is focused upon a few sectors: garments, sportwear, food, toys. The worst factories not connected to such global product marketing are missed. Furthermore, if global corporations drop certain suppliers from their supply chain in response to these concerns, there is then no focus of attention on the conditions in those factories, which may then worsen. Telling against such voluntary codes was a survey undertaken recently which revealed how little note was actually taken by boards of companies who had such codes in their social accounting reports (Zammit, 2003: 147–51). Codes, it seemed, were for external presentation purposes.

The limitations of voluntary codes have been met by collective efforts of various sorts to outline common principles within an industry, to certify firms for their compliance with such a code, or to 'brand' firms adhering to existing standards. An early example of a certification effort was the rugmark foundation, established in 1994 (www.rugmark.org) by a coalition of Indian industry groups and NGOs. The group's members commit to a common code of conduct with respect to child labour. Firms in the industry pay a fee to the Rugmark Foundation to affix the Rugmark trademark, but only if the firm passes inspections organised by independent auditors hired by the foundation. Key to the credibility of this assessment effort is the independence of the inspectors. Several organisations provide opportunities for firms to identify themselves with ethical practices. One example is the Ethical Trading Initiative (ETI) in Britain (www.ethicaltrading.org), which includes firms, unions and NGOs. The ETI is not an accreditation agency, nor does it perform audits: it emphasises sharing of best practice. Its members commit to a list of nine core labour standards (the ETI Base Code). Although drawn broadly from existing ILO norms, the Base Code goes well beyond it in important respects, such as the commitment to a living wage and regular employment. Companies applying the ETI Base Code are expected to comply with national and other applicable law. A review of this initiative (Ferguson, 1998b: 1) concluded that 'the evolution in code content stands as testament to the commitment of some companies to improvement in the labour conditions of their employees', but the review also pointed out that outsourced homeworkers were often excluded from such codes and needed to be included. In the USA, the Council for Economic Priorities (renamed Social Accountability International [SAI] in 2000, www.cepaa.org) has undertaken an initiative that mirrors the establishment of various industrial standards through the International Standards Organisation (such as ISO 9000 quality standard). Social Accountability 8000 (SA8000) was launched in 1997 with a board of directors drawn from business, labour and NGOs. As with Rugmark and the ISO standards in the industrial sector, the effort rests on the assumption that firms will see certification status as a kind of branding: a reputational device that signals intention and effort to the market. SA8000 rests on compliance with measurable standards based on UN and ILO conventions, and has the interesting feature of allowing workers as well as outside parties to initiate confidential challenges to the SA8000 rating. Accreditation can also be accompanied by product labelling that identifies the product in question as manufactured in accordance with given standards. For example, USA Fair Labor Association members can sew the Fair Labor Association 'FLA' label into their clothing. A potential drawback to such labelling is that the cost of counterfeiting labels is low, and although to date there is no evidence that this constitutes a serious problem, it could if social accountability gains in popularity. The Clean Clothes Campaign recently reviewed the social auditing industry and estimated that £50 million is spent annually auditing about one-tenth of the world's clothes factories. Among the leading companies now in this business of social auditing are CSCC used by Tesco, Internek who 'clean' M&S, Wal Mart and Nike, and Société Générale de Surveillance. The report concludes that such audits do have some postive impact upon the reduction of forced labour, child labour, working hours and health and safety standards, but no impact upon freedom of association, non-discrimination, employment relations and abuse at work.

Where do the international organisations fit in to the regulation of standards? We examined the role of the ILO and the WTO in the previous section, but what is the role of the UN and the OECD in this? The OECD drafted as far back as 1976 Guidelines for Multinational Enterprises, a set of guidelines addressed to OECD companies outlining the principles of acceptable behaviour by TNCs operating in and out of OECD countries. They apply to investments in the developing world by TNCs located in the OECD and in those other nine non-OECD countries adhering to them. They were revised in 2000, and 2001 saw the first report on their operation (OECD, 2001a). In terms of social and labour standards issues, sections IV and V apply. Here the guidelines call for adherence to the core labour standards concerned with the right to organise, with child labour, forced labour, and employment discrimination, but expand these to include concerns with health and safety standards at work. Since 2000, OECD countries are asked to establish national contact points to monitor adherance to the guidelines. Some of these offices are merely a government officer. In others, notably Finland, the contact point is a quadripartite mechanism involving business, government, trade unions and NGOs (OCED, 2001a). The key shortcoming of the guidelines is that they are voluntary, and there is no sanction that the OECD or members countries can bring to bear on non-compliance unless, of course, there is also national legislation that covers the same points.

Before the high moment of neoliberal globalisation and the construction of the WTO, the UN had been a significant player in aspects of international trade and investment. The United Nations Conference on Trade and Development (UNCTAD), established in 1964 at the behest of G77, concerned itself with these matters. It still does, but its views and activities have been sidelined by the WTO and OECD (Braithwaite and Drahos, 2000: 193–5). The UNCTAD had drafted a Set of Multilaterally Agreed Equitable Principles and Rules for the Control of Restrictive Business Practice, but did not follow through with any effective monitoring. UNCTAD lobbying also gave rise to the short-lived UN Commission and UN Centre on Transnational Corporations in New York. This centre operated from 1975 until USA and business lobbying killed it in the mid-1990s. During its existance it tried but failed to 'build consensus for a UN Code of Conduct for Transnational Corporations covering a broad range of abuses of power concerning labour, consumers, women, the environment, corruption and restrictive business practces' (Braithwaite and Drahos, 2000: 192). It fell next to the UN Secretary-General Kofi Annan to revive a role for the UN in this field (Kell and Levin, 2002; Zammit, 2003). The Global Compact was launched by Annan at the Davos World Economic Forum in 1999 and formally established in 2000 and works with five UN agencies: ILO, UNDP, United Nations Environment Programme (UNEP), United Nations International Development Office (UNIDO) and the Office of the UN High Commissioner for Human Rights (OHCHR) (www.globalcompact.org). There are three principle elements to the compact: a) the promotion of greater corporate social responsibility (CSR) in relation to ten principles; b) the forming of partnerships between the UN and the private sector to benefit developing countries; and c) the engagement of business in policy dialogue with civil society. The ten principles are derived from existing UN conventions and international commitments: the Universal Declaration of Human Rights (UDHR), the Rio Declaration arising from the United Nations Conference on Environment and Development (UNCED), the four core labour standards and the UN convention against corruption. Thus businesses should:

1   Support and respect the protection of internationally proclaimed human rights.
2   Make sure not to be complicit in human rights abuses.

3 Uphold the freedom of association and effective recognition of the right to collective bargaining.
4 Ensure the elimination of all forms of forced and compulsory labour.
5 Promote effective abolition of child labour.
6 Encourage elimination of discrimination in respect of employment and occupation.
7 Support a precautionary approach to environmental challenges.
8 Undertake initiatives to promote greater environmental responsibility.
9 Encourage the development and diffusion of environmentally friendly technologies.
10 (Added in 2004) Work against all forms of corruption, including extortion and bribery.

Business is encouraged to show its CSR credentials by signing up to its support for the Compact and to show in reports that it it is working to achieve at least **one** of the principles. More than 2000 companies and other stakeholders from more than 80 countries are participants. Criticism of the Compact (Zammit, 2003; Richter, 2004b) has centred upon the voluntary nature of the Compact, on the limited commitments that business has to demonstrate to claim it adheres to the principles, to the absence of any systematic reporting mechanisms, and to the absence of any sanctions. As Zammit comments, 'as things stand at the moment it seems that the monitoring of companies' corporate statements to assess the extent to which their apparent commitments to observance of the nine principles is matched in practice will fall largely to civil society organisations' (2003: 85). At the same time, Richter (2004b) has argued that instead of seeing this development as a step in the right direction which will lead to a more legal basis for global business regulation, its existence stands in the way of such a development. Global businesses use the existence of the Compact to argue against a proposal from the UN Human Rights Commission to establish a more binding framework on business practice and human rights. A Global Compact Counter-Summit (Global Policy Forum, 2004) was convened in 2004 to set out the objections to the way the Compact was, in the view of one participant, Daniel Mittler, 'allowing corporations to use their participation as a substitute for real progress, distracting the public from ther continued violation of human rights, labour rights or environmental standards' (Global Policy Forum, 2004). Defending the Compact, John Ruggie, one of its architects, argued that global corporations had power and therefore had to be brought into the fold of a strengthened UN. He pointed out that the McKinsey assessment of the Compact demonstrated that 50 per cent of the companies signing up were from the developing world, that two-thirds of the contracts of signed up companies were in the developing world, and that 50 per cent of the signed up companies had changed internal procedures since signing.

The OECD Secretariat and the Global Compact Office recently reviewed the complementarities and distinctiveness of the two approaches. They concluded 'that the initiatives have mutually reinforcing missions. The government-backed OECD Guidelines uses an inter-government process to promote the positive contribution that multinational enterprises can make to economic, environmental and social progress. The Global Compact seeks to advance responsible corporate citizenship by inspiring voluntary action in support of universally agreed principles. Opportunities for mutual advocacy and promotion will be explored.' (OECD, 2005c: 7)

Global tax regulation

Central to any discussion of social policy in a globalising world must be the question of taxation. Can national sources of tax revenue be sustained in an era of global competition? Is there a need to agree a tax harmonisation between jurisdictions? Is there a need for a global tax authority? Here we focus solely on moves towards tax harmonisation and the eradication of tax havens.

The issue of taxation in a global economy points straight to the heart of the problem of trying to manage a global economy within the confines of the concept of national sovereignty. Braithwaite and Drahos show how the preferred method of national states to engage in a complex series of bilateral tax treaties, whereby they try to agree between them the sharing of cross-border corporate taxes, created the perfect situation in which TNCs could use transfer pricing and other tax arbitrage methods to reveal only profits in low-tax regimes: 'In the contest between states and corporations over the payment of taxes, the objective of corporations was to shift profits to low-tax jurisdictions and losses to high-tax jurisdictions … The mono-centric complexity of corporations meant that a co-ordinated strategy could be developed against states which were locked into polycentric diversity' (2000: 107). Companies could outwit behind a cloak of secrecy the published policies of tax authorities.

Tax competition might involve a number of practices designed to reduce tax rates to attract Foreign Direct Investment (FDI) such as the creation of tax-free zones and giving tax holidays. At the same time, 'offshore' tax havens are designed to attract capital holdings rather than capital for investment in that haven. Recent data suggest (Campell, 2004) that tax havens contain only 1.2 per cent of the world's population, 3 per cent of the worlds GDP, but 26 per cent of the assets, and allow the declaration within their borders of 31 per cent of the profits of USA companies. As War on Want (2004), notes: 'While trans-national corporations endeavour to hold on to cash by shoring it up in tax havens, millions are lost that could have been used in the fight against poverty'. A recent Oxfam report on tax havens suggested that the amount secreted in tax havens was equivalent to six times the estimated annual cost of universal primary education and almost three times the cost of universal primary health care.

The OECD first approached this issue in its *Harmful Tax Competition: An Emerging Issue* (OECD, 1998a). However, it is essential to note that the definition of harmful tax practices used by the OECD focuses primarily upon the failure of tax havens to **report** their activities in such a way that countries can be sure to raise legitimate taxes from their citizens and companies operating through tax havens. As the first OECD report of its work stated clearly, 'It is important to note at the outset that the project is not primarily about collecting taxes and is not intended to promote the harmonisation of income taxes or tax structures generally within or outside the OECD, nor is it about dictating to any country what should be the appropriate level of tax rates' (OECD, 2000: 5). Indeed, the later report of 2004 goes on to assert 'The adoption of low or zero tax rates is *never* by itself sufficient to identify a jurisdiction as a tax haven or a preferential tax regime as *harmful*' (OECD, 2004: 5, emphasis added). To be harmful the haven must also lack transparency and refuse to exchange information with other countries. Thus it was that in 2000 the OECD identified 47 potentially harmful preferential tax regimes in OECD countries. By its report in 2004 (OECD, 2004c), 18 of these had been abolished, 14 had amended their rules so they were no longer regarded as harmful, and 13 were found not to be harmful anyway. Only two regimes required further discussion: the Luxembourg Holding Company and the Swiss 50/50 practice. The OECD sought to extend its work to include non-OECD countries and by 2004, 33 such countries were co-operating in the elimination of harmful tax practices. However, this leaves a number of high-profile non-OECD tax havens not co-operating with the attempt to end their harmful practices, such as Hong Kong and Singapore. Thus, while on the face of it the OECD initiative might be thought to be about tax harmonisation and a step on the road to an international tax authority, it is no such thing. At its heart is a state-centric view to promote transparency and international co-operation as a means of ensuring that national laws are not violated so as to protect the integrity of national tax systems.

The ending of what many would regard as harmful tax practices, that is, the lowering of taxes in competition with another country, will require a different approach and a different authority to take the lead.

Global private health and welfare regulations

The more that goods and services are traded across borders, the more the question becomes whether and how is it possible either to lay down internationally agreed standards for those goods and services, or to ensure that national regulations of such standards are not eroded in the context of global economic competition. In the first part of this section we will take the example of health services to illustrate the global regulatory issues that arise. The same or similar issues arise with regard to education and social protection. It is increasingly the case that governments ensure the health of their citizens not only by directly providing public services, but also by buying in those services from the profit or not-for-profit sectors. It is by means of **regulating** the access to, quality of, cost of and possibility of user influence of the services provided privately that governments ensure their health policy goals are met. As Saltman and Buse argue:

> precisely because the state is now expected to 'row less but steer more', its role in driving the health sector forward has in practice had to increase in scale, scope and sophistication … the concept of stewardship obliges the state to steer overall health system activity in an ethically grounded as well as a financially efficient manner … failing to regulate entrepreneurialism adequately in the health sector would be a serious breach of the state's role as a responsible steward. (2002: 6)

Holden (2006), Sexton (2001) and Pollock and Price (2000) explore the implications for the regulation of health services of the increased international trade encouraged by the WTO's GATS agreements discussed in Chapter 3. In so far as GATS will increase the amount of trade in health services across borders, it raises regulatory issues. In general terms, the tension between regulation and trade exists because article VI.4 of the GATS requires the removal of prejudicial barriers to trade in domestic regulation including qualification requirements, technical standards and licensing conditions. These regulations should 'not be more burdensome than necessary to ensure the quality of the service'. The test of burdensomeness is to be made by trade lawyers. Holden (2006) explores the regulation implications of each of the four modes of trade. In terms of cross-border supply of, for example, diagnostic services the problem is that the regulatory policies in a consumer country may have no jurisdiction over the supplier's country. Consumption abroad leaves the consumer in the hands of the providing country's regulations and not his or her own. Portable health insurance companies may have preferred providers as a way of reducing the risk of poor-quality provision. Commercial presence provides perhaps the most challenging in terms of ensuring access to the services provided by foreign companies. It has been suggested that that such providers of hospitals must, through regulation, reserve certain beds for the poor, but in the cases of India and Indonesia, Chanda (2001: 24) reports attempts to do this as being ineffective. The movement of practitioners raises the issue of the recognition of qualifications and the loss of education investment in exporting countries. As Holden notes, 'regulation meeting the needs of exporting and importing countries would require enforceable bilateral or multilateral agreements between the relevant countries' (2006). Overall, in terms of the capacity of domestic regulatory capacity, Woodward concludes:

> Most of the proposals for GATS-consistent domestic regulation to off-set the adverse effects of trade in health services are untested, unrealistic, impracticable, ineffectual and/or have limitations or potentially important adverse side-effects which are not recognised by their proponents. All would further tax the administrative capacity of the health sector, which is already critically weak in most cases, particularly in low-income countries. (2005: 526)

And of course the alternative international regulations are almost completely absent. Only in areas such as drug and food standards are there effective health-related regulations at global or regional (for example, EU) level, but even here there is often perceived to be a tension between maintaining higher standards in one country and increasing global trade. EU food standards have been accused of being responsible for cutting out African suppliers.

Much the same issues apply in the education sector. For these reasons, as we saw in Chapter 3, campaign groups such as Education International argue against the inclusion of education services in the GATS (Education International, 2006). However, given that among the modes of trade cross-border supply through distance learning and consumption abroad through student mobility in higher education is expanding, the **international** regulation of its quality has been the subject of a working party of the UNESCO set up in 2003 leading to the publication of its *Guidelines for Quality Provision in Cross-Border Higher Education* (UNESCO, 2005). The non-binding guidelines are to 'protect students and other stakeholders from low-quality provision and disreputable providers as well as to encourage the development of quality cross-border higher education that meets human, social, economic and cultural needs' (2005: 7). Their focus is to strengthen national regulatory capacity and make recommendations to governments, higher education providers, student bodies, quality assurance agencies, academic recognition bodies and professional associations. They do not in themselves provide for any capacity or role for UNESCO to set standards or vet quality. They have been published as a Secretariat document rather than as a UNESCO convention after USA objection. USA objection also ensured that the guidelines were non-binding (Jobbins, 2005).

Global social rights

The third of the three Rs of social policy is rights, in particular social rights. Indeed, for many in the world development movement, social rights underpin and provide the need for the regulation of business activity to ensure that business does not trample on rights and the need for redistribution of resources from the rich North to the poor South to enable these rights to be realised in practice. The particular character of social rights as distinct from civil rights (equality before the law) and political rights (equality of political participation) is that resources are required for them to be met. Indeed, it is this aspect of social rights that led Mishra to be pessimistic about their realisation in a neoliberal global context: 'While civil and political rights of citizenship are not a matter of contention and are being extended world-wide, social rights are on the defensive, if not in decline' (1999: 117). This view was further justified in Mishra's account because of the argument that the notion of **individuals** claiming social rights off the state was a peculiarly western conception which had no place in, for example, East Asia where 'social rights of citizenship means very little' (1999: 117). Mishra went on to argue instead for the usefulness world-wide of the conception of **community-based or collective** social standards relative to the economic development level of any particular country. Rich countries should aspire to decent welfare states so that laggard countries such as the USA should catch up. At the poorest level of economic development 'primary health care, sanitation, safe drinking water, adequate nutrition and the like may constitute basic social standards' (1999: 120). Indeed, the subsequent articulation of the MDGS might be seen as reflecting this conception of a basic set of social standards that should apply even in the poorest countries. We will return to this idea of universal minimum social standards later, when we discuss the initiative of the UK government in 1999 to argue for a set of basic **social policy principles** for the world. In the sections that follow we report the various ways in which the UN and other agencies have actually been attempting to strengthen and give practical meaning to the conception of universal social rights, the pessimism of Mishra notwithstanding.

UN economic and social rights: fine words, no teeth?

Felice's (1999) review of the viability of the UN's approach to economic and social rights is a useful starting point. He argues that despite the continued global controversy about aspects of social rights, the conflict between the North and the South regarding the social clause and labour standards, and the refusal of the US to ratify the International Covenant on Economic and Social and Cultural Rights (ICESCR), there is a corpus of international conventions and treaties addressing economic and social rights which do have meaning and impact. The ILO's raft of conventions that countries are encouraged to ratify together with its 'new' set of core labour standards, which all countries that are members of the ILO are presumed to accept, has already been discussed. In addition, in terms of economic and social rights, are the Universal Declaration of Human Rights (UDHR), the ICESR and the more recent Convention on the Rights of the Child (CRC).

Drawing upon the work of the UN Committee on Economic Social and Cultural Rights (CESCR) and the 1993 UN Vienna World Conference on Human Rights, the Maastricht Guidelines on Violations of Economic, Social and Cultural Rights have been drawn up by international human rights lawyers and represent the standing of economic and social rights in international law (Felice, 1999: 567). These guidelines hold governments accountable for the provision of basic social services, including health, employment and education. In recognition of the different level of economic development of countries the guidelines allow states a margin of discretion, but they hold that a 'state party in which any significant number of individuals is deprived of essential foodstuffs, of essential primary health care, of basic shelter and housing or of the most basic forms of education is, prima facie, violating the Covenant' (1999: 568). It is one thing to have these legal guidelines, it is another for the UN or any agency acting on its behalf to have the power to intervene to stop such violations. Whereas civil and political rights set out in the International Covenant on Civil and Political Rights (ICCPR) are under the auspices of the legally established Human Rights Committee (HRC), now Human Rights Council and hence also the concern of UN established National Human Rights Institutions (NHRIs) (Cardenas, 2003), matters concerned with the ICESCR are handled by a sub-committee of the rather weak UN Economic and Social Council (ECOSOC). This (sub) Committee on Economic, Social and Cultural Rights (CESCR), a body of 18 independent experts, receives from participating states a report two years after ratifying the Covenant and a five-yearly report thereafter on their compliance with the Covenant. These reports are considered by the CESCR and in their reports to ECOSOC they have criticised states for violations. Chile was criticised for a sharp reduction in government low-cost housing projects, Italy for its shortage of low-income housing, the Dominican Republic, the USA and Panama for forced evictions (Felice, 1999). There is, however, no right of **individuals** to report violations of economic, social and cultural rights.

One aspect of economic and social rights is the question of how far such rights are equally accorded to women as well as men and to members of ethnic and other minorities. While the UN instruments already mentioned address these issues, additional conventions and instruments have been developed to add strength to these issues of gender and ethnic equity. The International Convention on the Elimination of all Forms of Discrimination against Women (ICEDAW) came into force in 1981. State parties to the convention are obliged to take measures, including legislation to overcome discrimination in employment, education and health care. The ICEDAW established the Committee on the Elimination of Discrimination against Women (CEDAW), an entirely female body based in Vienna. As with the ICESCR, there are no individual complaints procedures so reports to the committee and reports of the committee are the main form of international dialogue to progress these rights. The CEDAW was proactive in 1992 in recommending that the rights of women should include the right to not suffer violence in the form of forced marriages, circumcision, dowry deaths and other acts. This was agreed at the Vienna 1993 conference. However, Felice comments that 'The consequence of separating women's rights from the other mainstream human rights bodies has been the potential marginalization of the CEDAW and the neglect of women's perspectives. It is impossible for the CEDAW, in a four-week annual meeting to address the numerous patriarchal practices that globally subordinate women' (1999: 582).

The International Convention on the Elimination of all Forms of Racial Discrimination (ICERD) that came into force in 1969 similarly established the Committee on the Elimination of all Forms of Racial Discrimination (CERD). Article 5(e) of the Convention obliges governments to 'prohibit and eliminate racial discrimination in all its forms and to guarantee the right of everyone to economic and social rights including: the right to work; free choice of employment; just and favourable work conditions; protection against unemployment; equal pay for equal work; the right to housing; the right to public health; medical care and social security and social services; and the right to education and training'. As with the CEDAW, country reports are commented upon by CERD. In addition, the ICERD did establish an individual complaints system, but by 1995 only 21 of the then 143 states that were party to the ICERD had accepted the complaints system and by then only five communiqués had been received by the CERD (Felice, 1999: 585). The related covenant on the rights of the child was discussed in Chapter 4.

The value of the UN Conventions does not, however, lie primarily in the extent to which the UN is able to enforce directly social and economic rights and the rights of women and minorities. It lies rather in the weapon they provide to those who would campaign to improve the practice of governments in these areas. Rights articulated at international level enable social movements within reluctant countries to strengthen their claims for decent economic and social rights. As Stean, among others, has commented: 'Since human rights discourse enjoys a certain acceptance and legitimacy in most countries around the world, it is potentially useful to, for example, dissidents living under authoritarian regimes or marginalized peoples who are thereby furnished with a language of resistance' (2005: 11). Indeed, it is for this reason that the World Bank has yet to accept a rights-based policy for any conditions attached to its loans. The language of rights gives rise to claims that the Bank may not be able to help countries meet.

Global social policy principles: nice idea Gordon, pity about the North–South divide

The UK government around the turn of the century adopted a rights-based approach to its international development strategy (UKDFID, 2000a). It was associated with a renewed push to assert: a) the universalism of human rights; b) the social dimension of them; and c) the means by which these global social rights could be more effectively realised internationally. The backcloth to this move was the intervention by the UK's Chancellor of the Exchequer to link discussion of the need to regulate the flow of international capital with a perceived need to attend to, or rather prevent, the damaging social consequences of speculative capital flows. He argued for a global social policy code. This would be a 'code of global best practice in social policy which will apply for every country, will set minimum standards and will ensure that when IMF and World Bank help a country in trouble the agreed programme of reform will preserve investments in the social, education, and employment programmes which are essential for growth' (Brown, 1999: 6) Moreover, this code 'should not be seen in narrow terms as merely the creation of social safety nets. We should see it as creating opportunities for all by investing more not less in education, employment and vital public services' (1999: 1).

It was suggested by Brown that this code should be agreed at the meeting of the World Bank in spring 1999. The question, therefore, was posed as to whom and how would this code be devised. Some initial thinking was provided by the Social Development Section of the UK DFID. It suggested that best practice in social policy involved: a) equitable access to basic social services health, education, water and sanitation, shelter; b) social protection enabling individuals to reduce their vulnerability to shocks; and c) core labour standards. However, controversy developed concerning which international organisation should have the mandate to devise this code of global social policy, the Bank with its concern to claim global expertise on these issues, or the UN with its mandate to deal with social policy. The first version produced by the Bank as to how to handle this question (23 March 1999) suggested a twin-track approach whereby 'the detailed work on best practices for these social policy principles be done as part of a delineated work programme by the World Bank' (World Bank, 1999b), and that agreement be reached with the UN for then carrying forward this work as part of the Copenhagen plus 5 meeting in 2000. However, the next version (9 April 1999) for presentation to the Development Committee of the Bank shifted clearly the balance of responsibilities towards the UN. Its twin-track approach now asserted that 'the UN takes the lead role in development of universal principles of social policy' (World Bank, 1999c) and the Bank would help its member to implement these principles. The final communiqué from the 28 April 1999 meeting of the Development Committee noted that Ministers agreed that 'further development of the principles of good practice in social policy was best pursued within the framework of the United Nations as part of ... the follow-up on ... the World Summit on Social Development' (World Bank, 1999d).

The motives for this referral to the UN were more to do with the concern on the part of some southern governments that the IMF and Bank would use the new principles as a set of social conditions in the context of loans or debt relief than with any concern to empower the UN. While some in the UN had welcomed this move, others had suggested it lets the Bank and Fund off the hook of the global social responsibility that these principles were designed to facilitate. It was now for the UN and in particular the Preparatory Committee for the Copenhagen plus 5 meeting to do the technical work on this. The Bank in its initial deliberations bequeathed a first draft to be built upon. It suggested the principles should be based upon: a) achieving universal and equitable access to basic social services including access to quality basic education and health care; b) enabling all men and women to attain secure and sustainable livelihoods and decent working conditions; c) promoting systems of social protection; and d) fostering social inclusion. It had dropped the core labour standards element suggested by the UK government.

A background paper aimed at influencing these further deliberations was produced by staff of the UK's DFID (Ferguson, 1999). Addressing the topic of Global Social Policy and Human Rights, it argued that 'the global architecture of UN conventions, declarations, and world conference documents provide the most authoritative available source for the construction of these principles' (Ferguson, 1999: 3). In effect the UN documentation provides an internationally legitimated set of agreements on social, economic and political issues. The contribution by DFID dismissed cultural relativist arguments by reference to these international agreements. It also asserted the equal weight of social and economic rights alongside civil and political rights. The paper then proceeded to explicate from the raft of UN conventions and declarations a set of social policy principles and practices. Social policy was here defined as embracing the 'empowerment' of people, the ensuring of 'livelihood security', the 'provision of services' and efforts which 'foster social integration'. The UN conventions and the series of UN conference agreements were then reviewed to generate a set of policies which embraced: a) the security of person; b) democratic participation; c) civil society; d) minimum livelihood; e) productive employment; f) labour standards; and g) service provision.

Alas, this seemingly (to western social democratic eyes) fine initiative to help shift globalisation from a neo-liberal project to one that respected a set of core social policy principles crashed to nothing in the back rooms of the UN Copenhagen plus 5 conference. A form of words that would have asked the UN to establish a working party to consider such a set of principles was rejected by a combination of southern and some middle-income countries (India, Egypt, Indonesia, Pakistan among them) who argued that the West was being hypocritical in seeking to impose a set of principle upon the South without being willing to fund the transfers of funds to enable them to be realised in practice. Furthermore, the South's experience of the 1980s Structural Adjustment Programmes had taught them that such principles would become a new conditionality in the context of either trade negotiations or debt relief. It was also argued that what might be regarded as desirable principles in one region or country might not be so regarded in another region or country. This outcome was not unlike the outcome of the 1996 WTO meeting on labour standards. It marked a turning point in UN business. Progressive northern thinking about a socially regulated globalisation was being rejected by the South in the name of the national sovereign right of countries to shape their own economic and social policies. This North–South impasse continues to this day, as we shall see in the subsequent chapter on global social governance and in the final chapter on the politics of global social reform. However, the guidelines on social policy now being drawn up by UNDESA and UNDP in the context of the UN 2005 Summit decision that countries would make development plans to meet them may not meet such a fate. There is likely to be wider acceptance of these guidelines by the Global South because they are being driven by staff in UNDESA who have the respect of the South and they are being couched in terms of advice to sovereign governments (see Chapter 4 for more on this).

Conclusion

It may be concluded that in the first years of the twenty-first century, the world is stumbling towards articulating a global social policy of global redistribution, global social regulation and global social rights and creating the institutions necessary for the realisation of such policies in practice. More significant than the recent increase in ODA have been the birth of new global funds for health and education and social protection. Poorer countries may now access global resources on certain criteria of social need. These funds, of course, have their critics because at the same time they tend to suggest that in the case of health, for example, it can be secured through pharmaceutical and technical 'vertical' programmes rather than broad-based 'horizontal' public health programmes within countries. Their accountability is also called into question. We are also witnessing the move from purely North–South support for within-country social development to the articulation of the concept of global public goods that may need to be provided out of taxes on global processes such as air travel. Global business is being asked by the UN to act in a socially responsible way. Of course there are no teeth, and the idea of voluntary codes rather than enforceable rules prevails for now. There is no social clause in international trade deals, but there is now a global expectation on all countries who are members of the ILO that they uphold core labour standards whether they have chosen to sign up to them or not. Despite continued international controversy about aspects of global social rights, their very existence and promulgation by the

UN enables others to campaign for their realisation in countries where governments have hitherto been reluctant to concede them. Alongside these embryonic policies and practices of global redistribution, regulation and rights the international community has confirmed, despite a strong attempt by the USA to persuade it otherwise, its commitment to the MDGs that are in effect a minimum set of global social standards in education, health and poverty alleviation. Social policy guidelines are being designed to facilitate their meeting. Of course, these do not go far enough. Holden (2005b), for example, argues that these global social policy developments embody a limited move towards at best a residual global social policy. He suggests, 'Economic conditions and institutional configurations are such that GSP provisions will continue to be piece-meal, minimalist, and essentially neo-liberal for as long as effective global political movements in favour of a more extensive GSP is absent' (2005b: 15). Of course, the global institutions to ensure decent GSP are met are not strong enough; these already existing GSPs are only benchmarks around which there will be continued global social struggle. The important point is, in my view, that the language and discourse has changed from that used in the heyday of global neoliberalism. The global market left to itself will not secure the meeting of global human and social needs. Just as within one country the market has to be embedded in a set of political institutions to secure social justice, so does the global market. It is to the reform of these institutions of global social governance that we now turn.

Further Reading

On global social policies generally: George, V. and Wilding, P. (2002) *Globalization and Human Welfare*. Basingstoke: Palgrave.

On global taxes: Atkinson, A.B. (2005) *New Sources of Development Finance*. Oxford: Oxford University Press.

On global public goods: Kaul, I., Grunberg, I. and Stem, M. (1999) *Global Public Goods: International Cooperation in the 21st Century*. Oxford: Oxford University Press.

On the global compact: Zammit, A. (2003) *Development at Risk: Rethinking UN-Business Partnerships*. Geneva: South Centre-UNRISD.

On global social rights: Mertus, J. (2005) *The United Nations and Human Rights* : *A Guide for a New Era*. London: Routledge.

Global Social Policy, GSP Digest; Section on Global Redistribution, Regulation and Rights (www.gaspp.org)

Related Websites

www.theglobalfund.org
www.un.org/esa/ffd
www.undp.org/globalpublicgoods
www.unglobalcompact.org
www.ohchr.org

7

The Governance of Global and Regional Social Policy

This chapter

- Reviews the fragmentation of and competition between international institutions which constitutes the existing 'system' of global social governance
- Considers radical proposals for reform of this system
- Sets out seven possible developments in terms of strengthening the role of the UNs; policy collaboration between institutions; improved aid policy for the South; PPPs and networks; reforms of the World Bank and WTO; management of labour migration; the development of 'Constructive Regionalism'.

Institutional fragmentation and competition

An analysis of the existing structures of global social governance has to begin with an overview of the United Nations and Bretton Woods organisations and the problematic relationship between the two. Both the UN and the Bretton Woods organisations were founded after the Second World War, over 50 years ago. While the brief of the UN system and its agencies embraces security and peace, human rights, humanitarian interventions and economic and social affairs, the brief of the Bretton Woods organisations (World Bank, IMF and formerly GATT) was at least formally focused only on the management of international economic relations and the provision of loans for reconstruction, and later for development. The GATT was transformed into a new, more ambitious World Trade Organisation (WTO) in 1994 after nearly a decade of negotiations. The governance of the three sets of institutions is different for each, and all are problematic in some way.

The UN is governed on the basis of 'one country, one vote' in the General Assembly, but with security matters the responsibility of the Security Council. This has five permanent members – the so-called 'Perm Five' (USA, UK, France, China and Russia) – and an additional ten country members who participate on a rotating basis. Each of the five permanent members of the Security Council has veto power over any proposed resolution. The limitation of the General Assembly arrangement is that voting on the basis of one country, one vote regardless of size and economic strength is not appealing to the major powers. There is limited democratic accountability, although regular consultations take place with NGOs and business and other civil society organisations. At the same time, as we have seen, the UN is associated with a range of autonomous agencies, each with their own governing bodies and policies. Most important from the point of view of global social policy, as we have seen in Chapter 4, are the ILO, WHO, UNESCO, UNDP and UNICEF. The UN is entirely dependent upon contributions from its members, which are assessed on the basis of a complex formula that takes into account country size. A number of countries are in arrears to the organisation, however, the most important of which is the USA, which has effectively withheld its contribution in the past in order to force organisational changes on the UN and particular bodies.

Both the IMF and the World Bank are governed by boards of their members, but voting rights are allocated to countries on the basis of their financial contributions to the organisation. As a result of this voting structure, the USA and the EU exercise an effective veto over the activities of the two organisations, and the USA in particular wields substantial influence over policy. There is far less transparency in the deliberations of some aspects of the Bank and IMF compared to the UN agencies, as board deliberations are not open. Both the IMF and the World Bank are formally regarded as agencies of the UN family, but this is misleading as they act entirely independently of any UN policy, although they do engage in dialogue with, for example, the UN's Economic and Social Committee (ECOSOC). It is also significant that the funds available to the Bretton Woods organisations far exceed those available to the UN agencies. In this way, the Bank especially is able to project its ideas about global social policy far more effectively than the UN agencies. The Bank can also command the world's most effective researchers and policy analysts.

A direct descendant of the GATT, the WTO differs again in its form of governance. It is theoretically governed by a General Assembly of all member countries, and operates by consensus. However, power within the organisation depends on the power to structure the agenda and to make trade concessions, which means that large countries have more influence. Southern governments have been critical of the back room (green room) cabals of richer countries who tend to dominate proceedings. The relative poverty of poorer countries has also been an issue, since it means they cannot afford to employ lawyers in Geneva to defend their corner. The developing countries have become more active in the WTO over the last decade, as we saw in Chapter 3, and are now influencing the agenda and decisions of the organisation.

Thus at the global level there are a number of competing and overlapping institutions, all of which have some stake in shaping global social policy towards global social problems. This struggle for the right to shape policy and for the content of that policy is what passes for an effective system of international social governance. The fragmentation and competition may be analysed into different groupings of contestations. First, and most damagingly, the World Bank, and to a lesser extent the IMF and WTO, are in competition for influence with the rest of the UN system. The Bank's health, social protection and education policy for countries is, as we have seen, not always the same as that of the WHO, ILO, or UNESCO respectively. While the world may be said to have one emerging Ministry of Finance in the shape of the IMF (with lots of shortcoming) and one Ministry of Trade in the shape of the WTO, it has two Ministries of Health, two Ministries of Social Security and two Ministries of Education. Then again, the UN social agencies (WHO, ILO, UNICEF, UNESCO) are not always espousing the same policy as the UNDP or the UN

Department of Economic and Social Affairs. Moreover, the Secretary-General's initiatives, such as the Global Compact or the Millennium Project, may by-pass and sideline the social development policies of the UN's Department of Economic and Social affairs. The UN Chief Executive Board for Coordination brings together the Chief Executives of all the UN agencies and attempts to ensure policy coherence within the UN system, but in terms of global social policy this is frustrated by the fact that a) the World Bank, IMF and WTO are present, and that b) the five main social agencies are gathered in the company of a total of 26 agencies with very different briefs.

Quite apart from conflict between the UN and Bank and within the UN system, there is also the G8, G20 (N) and G20 (S), G77 and other groupings of countries. While the rich G8 continue to assume the right to make global policy, the newer Canadian-led meeting of Finance Ministers, the G20 (N), is struggling to forge a broader global consensus and the G77 remained, until Cancun, more a party of opposition to the northern agendas. The new G20 (S) led by Brazil, China and India may mark a break from this. Regional groupings of countries such as ASEAN then have to be brought into the picture. Interaction between all of these groupings has often led to UN international social policy-making in recent years becoming stale-mated, with the EU, G77 and USA adopting entrenched positions.

Finally, of course, we have to add to this list of actors the variety of non-governmental or non-state actors we reviewed in Chapter 5. Business, broader civil society organisations, INGOs and other private actors are increasingly involved in the processes of global social governance and global social policy determination. So for global governance more broadly conceived, we are faced with a complex archi-tecture of governance that 'is characterised by a high degree of diversity and com-plexity ... The heterogeneous and at times contradictory character of global governance presents a challenge to any attempt to understand its operation and evo-lution in theoretical terms' (Koenig-Archibugi, 2002: 62). Within the specific field of global health governance the same complexity can be noticed. Concluding a major study of global health governance undertaken within the German Overseas Institute, Hein and Kohlmorgan note: 'The new institutional setting of global health governance due to networks, partnerships, and increased private activities strength-ens social rights to health, but tend to circumvent the formal and democratically authorised UN organisations like the WHO' (2005: 35).

Radical and ambitious global social governance reform

Unsurprisingly, there have been a number of calls for global institutional reform in the sphere of social policy and provision in the past decades from international civil society and the scholarly community, and indeed from within the UN system itself. Here we note first radical and ambitious reform ideas, then the reasons why such ambitious and radical reform is unlikely, and end the chapter with more circumscribed reforms and developments in global social governance that we are more likely to witness in the coming decades.

There are movements and ideas about global governance both from the **radical liberal right, from the radical left and the radical South** that would rather tear up the existing institutions. The radical right in the USA is increasingly irritated by the need to make international policy in the shadow of the World Bank and UN, whose influence they would wish to see reduced. The USA has not supported the setting-up of the International Criminal Court, and it has withdrawn its support for the Global Warming Treaty and attempted to get reference to the MDGs removed from the outcome of the 2005 UN Summit. In this scenario, the USA becomes even more obviously the global super-power 'exercising global governance' in its own interests, unmediated by international organisations. In terms of the World Bank, the Meltzer Commission – the International Financial Institutions Advisory Commission established in 2000 by the US Congress – called for an end to Bank lending to middle-income countries to hand banking back to private lenders, and for it to become a development agency giving grants and technical assistance and so on to poor countries. Jessica Einhorn, former managing director of the World Bank, writes in *Foreign Affairs* (Einhorn 2006) that the World Bank's window for middle-income countries, the IBRD, 'seems to be a dying institution'. She proposes ways that the institution might be phased out. In an article, Martin Wolf of the *Financial Times* states: 'Let us be brutal: the IMF is on the brink not just of "obscurity" as Mr. King [Governor, Bank of England] suggests but of irrelevance' (Wolf, 2006). In another article Fritz Fischer, former executive director at the World Bank, calls for amalgamating the IMF and World Bank (see GSP Digest 6.2 for full details).

On the other hand, the '50 years is enough' movement among radical NGOs called for the abolition of the Bretton Woods organisations for different reasons. Here the wish is to strengthen the UN as **the** main agent of global social governance by raising global taxes on international currency transactions through the agency of a UN-run global tax authority and instituting an Economic Security Council mirroring the existing Security Council to oversee global policy. The UN would be made more accountable not only to national governments, but also more directly to global 'citizens' by means of a second chamber of parliamentary representatives or civil society representatives. Such ideas are to be found in Patomaki's (2001) *Democratising Globalisation* and Patomaki and Teivainen's (2004) *A Possible World: Democratic Transformation of Global Institutions*.

The idea that the the World Bank cannot be fixed and will wither is argued persuasively by Ellerman (2005a, 2005b). The Bank will fail, he argues, because it suffers from its monopolisation by economists, because of its affiliation with the USA, because money is not actually the key to development, because it works through governments which are part of the problem, and because it cannot exit from bad relationships. This sense of crisis concerning the future of the Bank and the Fund was reflected by the Institute of Policy Studies (www.ips-dc.org/overview.htm) in a strategy meeting of activists it convened in April 2005, during the spring meeting of the Bank and the Fund. The meeting drew attention to the increased disconnection of major developing countries from the two institutions, and in particular the early repayment of debts by Argentina and Brazil and the refusal of other countries (China, Thailand, Philippines, India) to take out loans which was leading to a budgetary crisis in the IMF (www.globalpolicy.org/socecon/bwi-wto/2006/0427ngoefforts.htm).

One way of imagining a radical global social governance reform is to project onto the global level those institutions and policies in the social sphere that operate at national and regional (EU) level. In Table7.1 we can see how far we are from establishing at a global level anything approaching a system of social governance

Table 7.1 **Social functions of governance at national, regional and global level**

Function/policy field	National government	EU regional government	Current global arrangements
Economic stability	Central banks	Central Bank in euro zone	IMF/ Bank of international settlements?
Revenue raising	National taxation	Customs revenues plus government 'donations' (talk of tax harmony and regional tax)	None, but mix of UN appeals, ad hoc global funds, bi- and multi-lateral ODA
Redistribution	Tax and income transfers policy plus regional funds	Structural funds on social criteria	None, but ad hoc humanitarian relief, special global funds, debt relief and differential pricing (drugs)
Social regulation (labour and social standards)	State laws and directives	EU laws and directives	Soft ILO, WHO etc. conventions. UN Conventions. Voluntary codes
Social rights (citizenship empowerment)	Court redress. Consumer charters. Tripartite governance	EU Luxembourg court redress. Tripartite governance	UN Council for Human Rights, but no legal redress. Civil society monitoring

that is already emerging at the European regional level. In Table 7.2 we can see what kind of institutional reform would be required at the global level to emulate national and European governance and policy-making.

While ambitious reformist ideas of this kind involving a global civil service made up of a merged bank and UN may be regarded as utopian at best, it is to be noted that some of these issues do surface in the 2002 Report of the Secretary-General to the 57th session of the UN entitled *Strengthening the United Nations: An Agenda for Further Change* (UN Secretary-General, 2002). We pick up this point later.

At the same time and leading in a different reform direction, there has been the growth of the civil society-influenced anti-globalisation movement in the past two decades that has begun to find political and organisational expression in the annual meetings since 2001 at Porte Alegre, Brazil, of the World Social Forum (WSF). This meeting has often been criticised for being against globalisation but not being clearly for anything. However, as we suggested in Chapter 5, it is possible to detect strands of thinking which would constitute a radical alternative to existing globalisation. The de-globalisation strand would replace long-distance trade and global markets with

Table 7.2   **Current and radically reformed institutions of global social governance**

Constituent interests	National institutions	EU regional institutions	Potential radical reformed global institutions
The electorate	Parliament	EU Parliament with fewer powers	World Peoples Assembly?
Government ministers	Cabinet etc.	Councils of ministers	Reformed UN ECOSOC?
Civil service	Ministries	EU Commission	Combination and rationalisation of overlapping functions of UNDESA, UNDP, ILO, WHO, UNESCO, UCTAD, World Bank, WTO, OECD, and a new Tax authority
Judiciary	Courts	Luxembourg Court (And CofE Strasbourg Court of Human Rights)	New International Court with human rights mandate
Capital	Central Bank	Central Bank	Central Bank
Labour (civil society)	Trade Unions and statutory consultations	TUs on Economic and Social Committee and consultations	Enhanced TU and civil society consultation mechanisms

local production for local use that would nurture local economies and sustain ecological systems. Colin Hines's (2000) *Localization: A Global Manifesto* represents such a strand. Others would see this happening on a regional scale where regional groupings of countries such as ASEAN would re-establish a degree of protection for regional production. Walden Bello's views (1998, 2000, 2004) expressed on the website of the Focus on the Global South Movement (www.focusweb.org) reflect this tendency. In Bello (2000) he went so far as to argue that 'Multilateral structures entrench the power of the Northern superpowers under the guise of creating a set of rules for all … The fewer the structures and the less clear the rules, the better for the South' (2000: 61). Rather more constructively a few years later he argues:

> In other words, what developing countries and international civil society should aim at is not to reform the TNC-driven WTO and Bretton Woods institutions, but, through a combination of passive and active measures, to either a) decommission them; b) neuter them (e.g. converting the IMF into a pure research institution monitoring exchange rates of global capital flows) or c) radically reduce their powers and turn them into just another set of actors co-existing with and being checked by other international organisations, agreements and regional groupings. This strategy would include strengthening diverse actors

and institutions such as UNCTAD, multilateral environmental agreements, the ILO and regional economic blocks … A key aspect of 'strengthening', of course, is making sure these formations evolve in a people-orientated direction and cease to remain regional elite projects. (in Bello, 2004: 116–17)

The extent to which Walden Bello and his colleagues in the Global South are committed to a very different approach to the reform of global social governance than many Northern reformist actors is exemplified by two recent *Focus-web* publications (www.focusweb.org). While many anti-neoliberal movements in the North will agree with the case for derailing the WTO and the goal of ensuring that it is 'permanently crippled as an agent of the global-neo-liberal agenda' (Focus on the Global South, 2005), many of the same northern activists and scholars who are global social reformists will not understand or be sympathetic to the arguments of *Focus-web*'s Nicola Bullard (2005) that there are four reasons why the reform of the UN is not a priority. She writes that until the imbalances between 'the USA and the rest of the world, and between globalised capitalism and citizens' are resolved, the 'United Nations will be nothing more than the ineffective "conscience" of the world' (2005: 2). She argues that there is no reason to suppose that a strengthened or reformed UN will make any difference, and asks why social movements should spend any time saving it. The focus should be instead on bottom-up campaigns 'to secure land, food, water, social security, freedom from oppression and self-determination'. She concludes that the 'task is not to "reform" the United Nations but to join arm in arm with the social movements and communities to build the political and institutional tools so that "we the peoples" can, ourselves, fulfil the promises made by the UN 60 years ago' (2005: 6). It will be argued in the final chapter that while this within-country focus should be a part of the struggle to mend the world, it should be combined with many other struggles at several levels and at several sites including those to reform the UN.

Martin Khor of the Third World Network (TWN) (www.twn.org) shares some of this view, but tends to put more importance in the strengthening of the UN as a whole. He emphasises the need for a South–South policy dialogue and co-ordination linked to joint work to strengthen the UN (Khor, 2000, 2001). These views of Khor and fellow 'eminent personalities' such as Roberto Bissio of Social Watch, Deepak Nyyar, Chavravarthi Raghaven of the South–North Development Monitor and others were reflected in the *Report of* the G77's *High-Level Advisory Group of Eminent Personalities and Intellectuals on Globalization and its Impact on Developing Countries* (High Level Advisory Group, 2000). We return to an aspect of this thinking, the need for a policy space in the South, in a discussion of reforming the architecture of overseas aid below.

Others even see within the anti-globalisation movement the beginning of a genuinely anti-capitalist '5th International' that would talk again (15 years after the collapse of the Berlin Wall) about the need to replace capitalist globalisation with world socialist planning. This Marxist anti-capitalist position is exemplified by Callinicos (2003) and sometimes alluded to by Sklair (2002). Discussion of this strand of anlysis and politics will be reserved for the last chapter.

A position somewhat between these de-globalisation or anti-globalisation positions and what we called 'radical reformism' is the recent work of George Monbiot (2003), within which he argues cogently for:

- The replacement of the World Bank and IMF with a new International Clearing Union (ICU) with its own currency upon which countries could draw to a limit of half the value of its trade over the past five years.
- The replacement of the WTO by a Fair Trade Organisation (FTO) that would permit developing countries to defend infant businesses and which would ensure that foreign investors would leave more wealth behind in a country than they extract.
- A revised UN assembly with a population-weighted voting system adjusted for the degree of democracy exercised in the home country.

His strategy for forcing compliance by the rich North to these plans that are in the interests of the poor South is that the South's debt to the North, which is worth twice the reserves of the world's central banks, would not be repaid unless the reforms were forthcoming.

Viable and likely developments in global social governance

These radical (right, left and South) reform ideas to abolish the World Bank, the radical de-globalisation ideas, the anti-capitalist ideas and the Monbiot radical institutional reform plan in the interests of the global South are of interest, and support may grow for them. However, we turn now to proposals to modify in less dramatic ways the way the global governance system works given the realities of a still Northern-dominated global capitalist system. Even so the ideas below still constitute an ambitious reform agenda.

Strengthening the UN's role in economic and social policy: the ECOSOC saga, the moves to 'one' UN and the new social policy guidelines

The tension and sometimes policy conflict between the World Bank and the UN agencies on matters of national and global social policy was a thread that dominated the reviews of these actors in Chapters 2 and 4. The relation between the two agencies is at the core of the problem besetting global social governance. The fact that the World Bank has hugely more resources to propagate highly questionable privatising and targeting social policies while the UN is left to argue for more public and universalistic approaches on the sidelines with little clout is **the** matter of most concern. Interestingly, a major Nordic review of the World Bank and the UN, *Dinosaurs or Dynamos?* by Bergesen and Lundel (1999), concluded that the UN should retreat to fulfilling a normative function, setting guidelines and rules, and doing this well and leaving the Bank to implement development in practice. Alternatively, it suggested the Bank could be the global repository of knowledge on development questions. In my view, either approach would perpetuate the UN–Bank tension where both are competing to define good policy and practice.

Any desirable reform must involve strengthening the UN in this struggle for influence. The Report of the Secretary-General to the 57th session of the UN in 2002, *Strengthening of the United Nations: An Agenda for Further Change* (UN Secretary General, 2002), recognised (para. 19) the growing role of the UN in helping to forge consensus on globally important social and economic issues and called for the corresponding strengthening of the principal organ concerned with those issues, namely the Economic and Social Council (ECOSOC). It stressed the need for improved agendas and streamlined business. At the same time, the report (para. 130) said the Department of Economic and Social Affairs will be strengthened with the appointment of a new Assistant General Secretary and the creation of a policy-planning unit within it. Indeed, this has now been undertaken with the appointment of Jomo K.S. as Assistant Secretary-General, who is well known as a critic of the application of neo-liberal economics in East Asia (Jomo, K.S 1998), to work with the new UN Under Secretary-General for Economic and Social Affairs, Jose Antonio Ocampo. The policy-planning unit has now assumed importance in collaborating with the Division of Social Policy and Development in drafting the Social Policy guidance notes to enable countries to plan to meet the MDG targets. Hitherto getting a coherent global economic and social policy within the Executive of the UN had been problematic. For example, the Department of Social Policy Development did not collaborate with the upstairs Division for Public Economics and Public Administration on its volume on *The World Public Sector Report: Globalization and the State* (UNDESA, 2001). This in-house fragmentation had contributed to the tendency for the Secretary-General to, in effect, create his own UN Economic and Social Policy that emerged in practice through the networked processes of the Global Compact and the Millennium Project and bypassed those charged within UNDESA to fashion such a policy in dialogue with country delegates in ECOSOC and the Commission for Social Development.

The attempt to make the ECOSOC an effective body that would be taken seriously by the Bank and the US government might be harder than the UN Secretary-General imagines. Only the high-level segment of ECOSOC brings together ministers who might have these issues as their brief. More often, lower-level meetings are bedevilled by the basic problem that besets most UN meetings – the inability of the country delegate to address the substantive issues at hand. Ill-worked out country positions on social and economic agenda items are conveyed by civil servants whose expertise is not in this area. While countries do not have a coherent and joined-up policy towards global economic and social issues such that each Ministry, and hence each UN delegate, speaks to the same brief, it is impossible to expect ECOSOC to evolve through debate a coherent global economic and social policy. This matter of country coherence on globalisation issues we will return to in the last chapter. At the same time, ECOSOC is structured such that most delegates are those who attend the UN General Assembly's Second Committee that considers economic matters. General Assembly Third Committee delegates who consider social matters are normally absent (Scholvinck, 2004: 10), thus further preventing the development of a coherent UN economic and social policy.

Some people (Haq, 1998; Falk, 2002; Nayyar, 2002; Dervis, 2005) have argued that the role of the UN in the management of the world's economic and social affairs would be strengthened by the creation of an Economic Security Council (ESC), rather like a reformed Security Council with a few members who could better direct global economic and social matters. Mahbub Haq (1998: 228) argues the case for such a body by returning to the fundamental argument that globalisation has created a set of global social problems which only strong global leadership can solve: global poverty, narcotics control, population growth, ecological security, international migration and spread of diseases. In his view, the ESC 'will be an apex body that will supervise the policy directions of all multilateral institutions including the Bretton Woods's system and UN development agencies' (1998: 243). Most recently, and in terms of political impact the most important, is the contribution of Kemal Dervis, recently appointed Director of the UNDP, in his book written for the Washington-based think tank the Centre for Global Development. In *A Better Globalization: Legitimacy, Governance and Reform* (Dervis, 2005), he argues for a UNESC with six permanent members (EU, USA, Japan, China, India, Russian Federation) with eight others, two each from a) Asia, b) Latin America, Canada, the Caribbean, c) the Arab League, d) Africa and the Other Europe. Voting would be weighted by population, GDP and financial contribution made towards global public goods. It would be the strategic governance umbrella for the World Bank, IMF, WTO and the UN system.

The role and function of Johan Scholvinck, the director of the Division for Social Policy and Development within the UN Department of Economic and Social Affairs, see this as an unlikely development and argues that it is better to concentrate reform efforts upon ECOSOC, although even this will not be easy (Scholvinck, 2004). The report of the World Commission on the Social Dimension of Globalisation (ILO, 2004c) addressed this issue and seemed to back two horses. It argued both that 'There should be serious consideration of existing proposals to create an economic and social security council' (2004c: 530–1) and that 'ECOSOC's capacity to coordinate global polices in the economic and social fields should be strengthened by upgrading its level of representation, including an executive committee at ministerial level and inter-ministerial interaction on key global policy issues, and the adoption of new forms of functioning' (2004c: 533–4). Scholvinck (2004: 10) is sceptical, noting that ECOSOC is based in New York which means its natural constituents are mainly the Ministries of Foreign Affairs and to some extent Ministries of Development Co-operation. He goes on: 'Ministers of Finance never attend ECOSOC except the rather uneventful gathering after the Spring Meetings of the Bretton Woods Institutions. Note, by the way, the word "after". What this signifies is that ECOSOC is informed about what happens in Washington rather than the other way around' (2004: 10). And on the idea that there should be an Executive Committee, the immediate question becomes who will be on it, because 'the moment it is transformed into a decision-making body the interest on serving on it will increase exponentially' (2004: 10). Scholvinck favours putting more emphasis upon the deliberations of the Commission for Social Development and ensuring its agreed outcomes are then tabled at ECOSOC and even the General Assembly. After all, the conclusions of the Commission, often radical on matters of social policy as we saw in Chapter 4, have been reached by a process of intergovernmental agreement and compromise.

The role and function of the ECOSOC was addressed in the Secretary-General's report to the UN Summit in September 2005. *In Larger Freedom: Towards Development, Security and Rights for All* (UN Secretary-General, 2005b) praised the work of ECOSOC to date and asserted that a reformed Council 'could start to assert leadership in driving a global development agenda' (para. 179). It should 'hold annual Ministerial-level assessments of progress towards agreed development goals, particularly the MDGs. These assessments could be based on peer reviews' (para. 176) and 'It should serve as a high-level development cooperation (biennial) forum' (para. 177). The final agreed outcome of the Summit (UN Secretary-General, 2005a) did indeed 'recognize the need for a more effective ECOSOC as a [not the] principal body for coordination, policy review, policy dialogue and rec-ommendations on issues of economic and social development, as well as for imple-mentation of the international development goals agreed at the major United nations summits and conferences, including the MDGs' (para. 155). It went on to endorse the specific procedural recommendations of the Secretary-General, and these changes will now take place. While all of this is to be welcomed, Jens Marten, a repected analyst of UN matters previously known for his assessment of the future of multi-lateralism, warns that while strengthening the role of ECOSOC in devel-opment issues this new emphasis risks sidelining the broader economic brief of ECOSOC and in turn the UN:

> Its areas of responsibilities would be narrowly confined to development issues. The IMF, the World Bank and the WTO would continue to decide on international eco-nomic, monetary and trade policies outside the UN . . . Thus at best ECOSOC would amount to something like an enlarged OECD's Development Assistance Committee (DAC) augmented by the developing countries. (Martens, 2005: 7)

The reform of ECOSOC was only one part of the UN reform moves being pushed by Kofi Annan in 2006. There are three other elements. In addition, the first steps were taken to rationalise some of the overlapping and competing mandates that have been given to UN agencies over the years (www.un.org/mandatereview/execu-tive.html). The inventory of mandates compiled by the Secretariat drew attention to the problems of overlap between UN organisations and gaps between mandates and resources. Also proposals are being considered to tighten up financial and adminis-trative control within UN HQ and to give the Secretary-General greater executive powers and move financial issues to a subcommittee of the General Assembly. This move was, however, strongly resisted by the G77, who wished such powers to remain with the General Assembly for fear that such moves would take power away from southern countries. A compromise was reached which gave the Secretary-General rather more limited financial powers than he wished for.

   More significant was the proposal to set up a High-level Panel on United Nations System-wide Coherence in the areas of Development, Humanitarian Assistance and the Environment (GSP6.2 Digest). Appointed by Kofi Annan on 16 February 2006 and including Gordon Brown (UK), Ruth Jacoby (Sweden), Ricardo Escobar (Chile) and the prime ministers or presidents of Pakistan, Mozambique, Tanzania and Norway, it began work on 5 April. Annan intended that this panel will report on streamlining the UN in these three fields by September 2006 (www.un.org/News/Press/docs/2006/ sgsm10406.doc.htm). Northern and EU governments have already lobbied it hard: a group of 13 donors (EU countries and Canada) wrote to the Prime Minister of Norway, in his capacity as Co-chair, proposing a rationalisation of the UN in each country so that there will be one UN team under one UN co-ordinator and one UN programme (www.globalpolicy.org/reform/docs00/0328bigchanges. htm). Hilary Benn for the UK government has added the idea of one funding stream. In terms of social policy in the context of social development, this appears to suggest that the UNDP will take on a more central role and hence upgrade its social policy analytical work in helping countries plan for the MDGs. Policy dialogue between the Bank and UNDP is well advanced to ensure the 'MDG-isation' of the PRSPs (Trogemann, 2006). The formulation by UNDESA with UNDP of the new Social Policy Guidance Notes is central to this development. Specialised agencies such as the ILO and the WHO would occupy a think tank or advisory role in this scenario. More inter-agency dialogue about social policy and social protection between the emerging lead UNDP agency and these specialised agencies would be needed. In the words of the report of the Secretary-General on this topic to the July 2006 Session of ECOSOC, the 'UN Development Group should promote multi-stakeholder policy dialogues at the national and regional level, including ministries of health, education and labour and relevant UN agencies, with the objective of building national and regional capacity to develop a multi-disciplinary approach to economic and social issue' (UN Secretary-General, 2006). This emerging scenario suggests that the UN would be strengthened in those areas where it might be said to have comparative advantage (peace, development, humanitarian, environment), leaving the fields of economics and trade to the IMF/Bank and WTO. Within the UN it would seem that the UNDP might be the winner within this reform, and to the extent that the UNDP and the Bank tend to share more common ground than the Bank and the ILO/WHO/UNESCO this might be a worrying result, the new *Social Policy Guidance Notes* (Ortiz, 2006) notwithstanding. The G77 and China initially responded negatively, warning against the UN being responsible for only niche issues and preferring instead the revamping of UNCTAD. Indeed UNCTAD published in September 2006 (UNCTAD, 2006) a report arguing that the UN should set up a new agency to channel bilateral aid to the South and act rather like the EU structural funds which requires matching funds from recipient governments Thomas Fues has argued strongly that 'while sceptical voices see this [the system wide coherence idea] as yet another ploy to bolster western dominance, sympathetic observers consider it as the final opportunity for a meaningful role for the UN in the international development architecture' (2006: 1). The panel reported in November 2006 (united Nations, 2006b) and did indeed make recommendations for UNDP working with UNDESA to lead MDG planning. It also proposed a new High Level L27: a leaders group of key countries working under ECOSOC. This report is likely to be rejected by G77 (see GSP Digest 7.107.2).

Inter-organisational co-operation, policy dialogue and synergy: the World Commission on the Social Dimension of Globalisation

Strengthening the role of the UN in international social and economic affairs by means of independent funding via global taxation and giving more clout to ECOSOC might be one way of curtailing the global influence of the World Bank and hence USA thinking on economic and social policy. Another approach is to call for inter-organisational co-operation and policy dialogue between the Bank and UN agencies. This was perhaps the most important conclusion of the ILO-sponsored World Commission on the Social Dimension of Globalisation which reported in 2004. Thus 'International organizations should launch **Policy Coherence Initiatives** in which they work together on the design of more balanced and complementary policies for achieving a fair and inclusive globalization' (ILO, 2004c: para. 608–11). The first of these, it said, should address the question of global growth, investment and employment creation (para. 611). It also proposed that 'A **Globalization Policy Forum** should be established by interested international organizations. The Forum would be a platform for regular dialogue between different points of view on the social impact of developments and policies in the global economy. Participating institutions could produce a regular "State of Globalization Report"' (ILO, 2004c para. 618–22). This Globalisation Policy Forum would address and monitor the social impact of developments and policies in the global economy and would be designed to bring about cohesion between the international institutions on social issues.

These proposals for policy dialogue between international organisations can find reflection in the initiative of the UN Secretary-General discussed in the last section to win agreement at the September 2005 UN Summit for ECOSOC to hold a biennial global policy forum on development issues, and in the report of the High Level panel. At the same time, the ILO itself is pursuing 'its' reports recommendations by attempting to secure a dialogue with the World Bank and other actors on its chosen priority field, that of 'growth, investment and employment', by means of a 'multi-disciplinary task force composed of staff of the participating agencies working with leading economists and other professionals from business, labour and the academic world' (ILO, 2004b: 31). The more detailed specifications of the proposed work suggest that the task force 'would look at macro-economic, financial, trade, investment, labour market and related social policies among others, to achieve higher and more stable growth and higher levels of employment'(2004b: 31). This feels like a project doomed to failure; shutting away in a back room for a lengthy time old-style Keynesian reformists of the ILO with new-style liberal economists from the Bank engaged in a titanic struggle of the economic dinosaurs, while the real innovations in global education, health and social protection policies are made elsewhere. Coherence and convergence between the social policies of the Bank, the ILO, the WHO, the UNDP are actually taking place, as we saw in Chapters 2 and 4. The movement of Bank professionals towards the recognition that inequity is bad for growth (World Bank, 2005a) and that services for poor people are poor services (World Bank, 2003c) are indictors of this. Policy dialogue is taking place effectively between the global social policy epistemic community in conferences, workshops, journal articles and joint action, all under the eye of critical INGOs. It is unlikely to be better advanced through formal working parties charged with forcing the pace.

Progress towards a more formal collaboration between the World Bank, the OECD, the UN ECOSOC and other agencies is also more likely to develop around joint monitoring of progress towards meeting the MDGs. As long ago as 2001, the joint Development Committee of the Bank and IMF issued a communiqué asserting that 'Dialogue among the ECOSOC and the Bretton Woods Institutions offers unrealised potential . . . a combined effort by the Bretton Woods institutions and the United nations, along with the OECD, to check periodically on progress towards the MDGs, would provide an efficient and practical approach to improved cooperation' (World Bank, 2001). Indeed, in April 2002 the Development Committee agreed that the World Bank in 'collaboration with staff of partner agencies' would produce an annual Global Monitoring Report on progress towards meting the MDGs. The first report appeared in 2004, with the second appearing in September 2005 (World Bank, 2005c). The report, published by the Bank in glossy format, claims that its partner agencies include the UNDP, UNDESA and ECOSOC. This has not, however, prevented the UNDESA's statistical division from producing in 2005 its *Progress Towards the Millennium Development Goals 1999–2005* (UNDESA, 2005d) and UN ECOSOC preparing in September 2005 its publication *Achieving the Internationally Agreed Development Goals: Dialogues at the ECOSOC* (UN Economic and Security Council, 2005). So it is still the case that the two protagonists in Washington and New York compete for the quality of publication (the Bank wins hands down), of statistical presentation (again the Bank wins) and the visibility of the policy message. In the case of the World Bank's *Monitoring Report*, the Executive Summary contains a sharp five-point message:

- anchor action to achieve the MDGs in country-led development strategies;
- improve the environment for stronger private sector-led economic growth; scale up human development services;
- dismantle trade barriers; and
- substantially increase the level and effectiveness of aid (World Bank, 2006c).

The Executive Summary of the UN report contains no such clarity of message, although buried in the small text of the report on goal 8 are calls to 'create decent and productive employment opportunities', and calls for an 'increase in development assistance and wider and deeper debt relief'(UNDESA, 2005d). Even the common project of the MDGs agreed by the Bank and the UN and the OECD sometimes does not seem enough to generate a truly common endeavour, even at the level of reporting progress.

Changes in the architecture of aid: a policy space for the South?

One thing is sure: the continued commitment of the world to meeting the MDGs and the real increases in ODA that have come in the wake of this presents a challenge to the existing architecture for delivering aid to developing countries. Because the increases in ODA announced in 2005 are substantial, choices in effect present themselves. Most of this increased ODA is from bilateral donors and could imply a retreat to more bilateral relationships rather than increased flows and collaboration through multilateral organisations. On the other hand, the limitations and failures of co-ordination associated with the bilateral system might imply a greater use of the emerging global funds, such the Fund for AIDS, TB and Malaria or the Fast Track Initiative for Education. A third scenario currently, at the time of writing, being developed for Africa is to consolidate all ODA monies into a single Action Plan to be formulated by April 2006 and reviewed annually. What role the African Union (AU) as a regional player might have in this is interesting, and hints at a theme we take up later regarding strengthening the social dimension of regionalism as a global social governance reform strategy.

The problem of aid co-ordination is not new. The OECD:DAC formulated the Paris Declaration on Aid Effectiveness in March 2005. Donors (OECD, 2005e) agreed then to: a) align aid flows with recipient government priorities; b) increase the amount of aid flowing through government budgets to 25 per cent; c) reduce the number of overlapping missions to countries; d) increasingly use recipient government procurement mechanisms in the aid process; e) increase the predictability of aid flows; and

f) make aid more transparent. However, some of these aims have not been realised and some are now regarded as woefully inadequate. The *2005 UNDP Human Development Report* signals that international co-operation is at a cross-roads:

> International aid is one of the most powerful weapons in the war against poverty. Today, that weapon is underused and badly targeted. There is too little aid and too much of what is provided is weakly linked to human development. Fixing the international aid system is one of the most urgent priorities facing governments at the start of the 10-year countdown to 2015. (UNDP, 2005: 75)

The message is clear. More aid is needed, as we have discussed in earlier chapters, but moreover, 'More aid delivered through current aid structures will yield suboptimal results . . . it means ending tied aid, reducing the volatility and unpredictability of aid flows and rethinking the scope of conditionality' (UNDP, 2005: 76). Spelling out the continuing problems in more detail, the report goes on to enumerate them:

- **Volatility of aid**: Aid is 40 times more volatile than recipient government's other sources of revenue, and the gap between promises and disbursements can be 2 per cent of government GNI.
- **Conditionality:** The World Bank has tried to shift to process conditionality, but aid still comes with conditions. Benin, for example, under its Poverty Reduction and Growth Facility and associated Bank Poverty Reduction and Support Credit, is subject to 90 actions to be monitored.
- **Donor non-coordination:** The Ethiopian government in 2003 received aid from 37 countries, all operating with dozens of projects. Even where a sector-wide co-ordination is in place, as in education in Zambia, this only covers 50 per cent of educational aid.
- **Tied aid:** The tying of aid to the condition that countries must buy donor country products with the aid still continues in some case raising the price of goods and services by up to 40 per cent.
- **Project, not budget support:** A large amount of aid continues off-budget, weakening public finance management. The share of aid through budgets is now about 53 per cent. In the view of the UNDP report, it should aim to be 100 per cent. (UNDP, 2005)

If the lessons of the UNDP *Human Development Report* were taken to heart, then we might look forward to a situation within which all donors pool their funds, sometimes made possible via taxes on transborder financial or travel activities, through a common fund managed by one global agent to recipient government budgets with a minimum of conditions attached. In this scenario much of the focus of this book would become redundant in future years! We would no longer be concerned with whether the USA or the EU was shaping the World Bank's policy-lending conditions. The global discourse within and between international organisations would begin to assume less importance. We would equally be less concerned to ensure the World Bank and IMF was accountable to recipient governments through changing board membership and voting patterns and so on. It might just be that the moves to one the UN initiative discussed earlier represent such a development.

The reclaiming by the Global South of the right to make social policy and social development policy choices is thus a movement that is beginning to have impetus and impact on the global aid process. This became most evident in the context of global trade issues. First in Singapore, then in Seattle, then Doha and Cancun, an increasingly articulate southern voice challenged some of the northern priorities at these meetings of the WTO. Global labour standards were not to be imposed as a part of trade deal; the disadvantages to the South of the TRIPs agreement, particularly as it effected drug prices, became apparent and northern agricultural subsidies were challenged. This challenge in the context of the WTO is not surprising as the WTO, which the North had thought it had shaped in its image, had marginalised the UNCTAD as a forum for trade and development talks where the southern voice was more readily heard. The UNCTAD had, and still does, provide one forum where some southern governments have been able to debate an alternative developmental path from the export-orientated and privatising path laid down by the Washington Consensus. According to Charles Gore (2000), work within UNCTAD combined with thinking within at least two of the UN Regional Economic Commissions (ECLAC in Latin America and ESCAP in East Asia) and echoing some of the analysis of the UNDP HDR Office and UNICEF, has generated a 'southern consensus' or a 'coming paradigm shift'. In broad terms, this implies an approach to development that involves: a) strategic integration of a country's economy into the international economy with appropriate sequencing and sector-only opening; b) not only macro-economic policy but also a productive development policy focusing on areas of comparative advantage; c) building or retaining a pragmatic developmental state; and d) the management of the distributional consequences of development 'primarily through a production-orientated approach rather than redistributive transfers' (Gore, 2000: 98). These ideas now find an echo in the UNDESA with the appointment of Ocampo, late of ECLAC, as Under-Secretary General and his deputy, late of the ESCAP region. He comments (Ocampo, 2006) that the UN is now well placed to reassert its role at a time when neoliberalism shows signs of crisis. Strengthening local southern capacity, policy ownership and alternative knowledge systems requires, he argues, a context that favours intellectual pluralism and a reinvigorated state sector such as within the UN. This, he says, contrasts with the Bretton Woods organisations' way of doing things that favour the top-down imposition of ideas.

More global public–private partnerships, task forces, networks and ad hoc initiatives

Because significant global institutional reform such as the merging of the UN and Bank's social policy and social development functions seems unlikely and major global social policy change towards, for example, a more substantial international redistribution financed through global taxation is difficult to achieve, and because there are now so many loci of action and initiatives on global social issues, we may be witnessing a shift in the **locus** and **content** of policy debate and activity from those more formally located within the official UN and Bank policy-making arenas to a set of practices around networks, public–private partnerships and projects which, in some ways, by-pass these institutions and debates and present new possibilities for actually making global change in particular social policy arenas. Ngaire Woods, in a chapter in Held and McGrew's (2002) *Governing Globalisation*, argued that: 'The global governance debate is focused heavily on the reform and creation of international institutions ... yet global governance is increasingly being undertaken by a variety of networks, coalitions and informal arrangements which lie a little further beyond the public gaze and the direct control of governments' (2002: 42). Among examples of these networks, partnerships and projects are:

- the UN Secretary-General's Millennium Project involving ten task forces to consider the implementation of the MDGs;
- the Global Alliance for Vaccination and Immunisation (GAVI), established in 2000 with a major donation from the Bill and Melinda Gates Foundation, to encourage other public and private donations to achieve the goal of increased vaccination against preventable diseases in developing countries; and
- the UN Secretary-General's Global Compact with Business.

The essence of this emerging networking and partnership form of policy development and practice-shifting through a focus on specific projects is the collaboration between stakeholders in international organisations, the global corporate sector, international NGOs and civil society organisations. Such a shift in the locus and substance of global policy-making and practice has received support recently from commentators coming from very different institutional positions. Rischard (2002), the World Bank's vice president for Europe, in *High Noon: 20 Global Issues and 20 Years to Solve Them,* argues that global multilateral institutions are not able to handle global issues on their own, that treaties and conventions are too slow for burning issues, that intergovernmental conferences do not have adequate follow-up mechanisms and that the G7/8 type groupings are too exclusive. Instead, what is needed are Global Issues Networks (GINs) involving governments, civil society and business facilitated by a leading multilateral organisation, which create a rough consensus about the problem to be solved and the task to be achieved, the norms to be established and the practice recommendations, and which then report on failing governments and encourage good practice through knowledge exchange and a global observatory which feeds a name-and-shame approach. Charlotte Streck (2002) in *Global Environmental Governance: Options and Opportunities* argues for Global Public Policy Networks (GPPNs) that bring together governments, the private sector and civil society organisations. She insists that recent trends in international governance indicate that the focus has shifted from intergovernmental activity to multi-sector initiatives, from a largely formal legalistic approach to a less formal participatory and integrated approach. Such GPPNs can agenda-set, standard-set, generate and disseminate knowledge and bolster institutional effectiveness. Streck is building here on the work of Witte et al. (2000), who argued that international organisations had a particular role they could play in GPPNs as convenor, platform, net-worker and sometimes partial financier. The Global Public Policy Institute (www.globalpublicpolicy.net) under Reinicke's directorship and with luminaries such as Ralf Dahrendorf, Kermal Dervis, Mark Balloch Brown and Mary Robinson, has been formed to 'explore and support innovative approaches to effective and accountable governance'.

There is clearly something in these accounts of the way policy-making has become projectised and task-centred and based on networks and alliances. A key question is how intervention in these tasks and projects and networks might be anything other than opportunistic or self-interested or pragmatic. Because so much of this kind of work is subcontracted in terms of its intellectual and policy content and in terms of implementation, principles that guide these actors become important. This raises the question again of how these principles are to come into being. There is a case, therefore, for not only the networks and partnerships focused on short-term projects and tasks, but also for longer-term **global political alliances** that might fashion sets of principles and steer members of the task forces. If intervention to mend neoliberal globalisation is project-based, then the actors in those projects need a solid ethical reference point and set of policy principles against which they can assess their proposals for action. We are back to global social policy, but not a policy to be debated and won in the chambers of the UN or won in intellectual dialogue with Bank experts (though these activities need to continue); instead, a policy implemented in practice by those who find themselves on such projects. We return to this issue of constructing global political alliances in the last chapter.

The 'Report of the World Commission on the Social Dimension of Globalisation' (ILO, 2004c) noted this approach to global problem-solving and policy-making, commenting that 'Several advantages have been claimed for these new mechanisms: the benefit of rapid and non-bureaucratic action; the ability to mobilize diverse actors and skills' but counselled that 'this approach restricts participation to a select number of actors, raises questions of accountability and representation of all interested parties, and runs the risk of being technocratic' (para. 581). Nonetheless, 'Global networks are likely to multiply as a result of globalisation itself and we need to look to these for new and promising forms of governance' (para. 582).

A major concern of critics (Martens, 2003; Ollila, 2003; Richter, 2004b) of these developments, and especially of the public–private partnerships, has been that the corporate sector might start dictating UN policy and that the ad hoc processes and mechanisms are not accountable to UN democratic processes. Such partnerships can, in their view, distort UN/WHO health policy towards measures such as drug and other technical-fix interventions rather than broader public health approaches. Richter (2004b: 85) calls for more open debate within the UN and WHO on the risks of such partnerships and for safeguard practices to be established to prevent undisclosed interests shaping policy. Boas and McNeill (2003: 146) articulate three concerns about the new partnerships with business: will they lead to the fragmentation of the multilateral institutions just at the point when progress is being made towards co-ordination between agencies? Will such partnerships lead to a lack of policy coherence just when policy coherence and convergence is on the agenda? Will 'privatisation' of the UN lead to the distortion of polices? Martens argues that 'the creation of more satellite funds outside the UN system may not only end up weakening the United Nations, it may at the same time impeded cross-sectoral development strategies aimed at implementing the MDGs'(2003: 25).

Reforms of the World Bank and WTO

The question of the accountability of the World Bank and the IMF not only to their share holding governments but also to their customers has been a long-standing concern to elements of global civil society. The concerns (Christian Aid, 2003a, 2003b; Martens, 2003) relates to three areas: the apportionment of voting rights; the composition of the executive boards; and the selection of organisation staff. Voting rights currently largely reflect the principle of 'one dollar, one vote' rather than 'one county, one vote' so that countries with more GNI and trade flows and currency reserves get a bigger say. Reforms would centre on reducing the weight attributed to economic size and give a greater weight to the 'one country, one vote' principle. Alternatively, GNI could be counted in purchasing power parity terms that would benefit countries like Brazil, China and India. In terms of the executive boards, industrialised countries presently have an absolute majority. The EU in particular is over-represented, with EU countries currently appointing to the IMF 7 out of the 24 executive directors, while all the Asian countries have 4 and the African, Latin American and Arab groups appoint 2 each. It has been proposed, therefore, that the EU should appoint three at most to even-up the membership. It is one thing to change the membership of the Board of the Bank, but quite another to change bank policy. Those more progressive ideas about social policy and social development now emerging in the Bank do eventually have to be endorsed by the Board. This requires that the Finance Ministers sent there are amenable to such ideas. The struggle within donor countries to ensure that they articulate progressive social policies at Bank board meetings is addressed in the last chapter. The same point applies when the Bank is seeking to replenish its funds. Here donors have a chance to shape policy.

In terms of staff selection there are a number of concerns. One is the appointment of the president of the Bank and the managing director of the IMF that is carved up between the USA and Europe. Another is the proportion of senior officials who are northern. But perhaps more telling in the long-term, given the focus of this book, are the economic and social policy ideas promulgated by all staff at the Bank and the IMF. Here the domination of both institutions by a) economics and b) USA economics is the issue. At present 90 per cent of the IMF staff members who have a PhD have been trained at USA or Canadian universities. Perhaps the new work reviewed in Chapter 2 on political and institutional obstacles to equity being undertaken within the Bank will lead to it recruiting more political and social scientists.

The WTO is by contrast, at least on paper, an organisation that gives greater weight to the Global South in terms of all countries who are signed up to the WTO having one vote. It is for this reason, of course, that the USA and Europe have not had it all their own way at WTO ministerial meetings. In practice, however, critics (Khor, 2001; Martens, 2003; Bello, 2004) have pointed to the closed 'green room' deals that are struck by richer countries and then presented as resolutions to the rest, who feel obliged to sign up for fear of trade sanctions or other financial bullying by the USA. Martin Khor (2001) has called for all WTO members to have access to all negotiations, that all country standpoints should be given equal consideration, that no pressures should be put on governments to sign up to deals and that all countries should have time to consider proposals. One element of this equalisation of inputs is the extra resources that would be needed by some southern governments to enable them to appoint adequately informed trade lawyers to challenge the hundreds of USA lawyers on hand. Technical assistance from the North to the South to help this situation should, and is likely to, increase. Calls have been made by elements of global civil society to open up more of the deliberations of the WTO to civil society scrutiny and engagement. The 1996 WTO *Guidelines for Arrangements on Relations with Non-Governmental Organisation* state simply, 'There is currently a broadly held view that it would not be possible for NGOs to be directly involved in the work of the WTO or its meetings' (Martens, 2003: 42). In 2003, WTO Director General Panitchpakdi did, however, set up two consultative bodies, one for business and one for NGOs and trade unions. It is not only NGOs who have complained at the WTO secrecy, but parliaments also who have felt that their members could not hold their governments properly to account in, for example, the current GATS negotiations (Martens, 2003: 41).

The better management of global labour migrations

The UN Summit in 2005 (UN, 2005a) made brief reference to the need to protect the human rights of migrant workers (para. 61) and for policies to be developed to reduce the cost of transferring remittances (para. 63). The small amout of space given to this issue was due in part to the UN awaiting the final report of the Global Commission on International Migration that did report in October 2005. The report (UN, 2006a) argued that six principles (paraphrased below) should underpin reforms to the management of international migration:

- **Migration should be chosen** and not forced. People should be able to realise their potential within their country of birth but if they chose to migrate they should do so because their skills are needed elsewhere and to do so in a regulated way.
- The **contribution of migrants to promoting development** in their country of origin and their country of destination should be recognised and reinforced.

Within this context the report and some of its commissioned research papers (Holzmann et al., 2005) review the problems associated with the non-portability of pensions and health care entitlements. It notes that less than 25 per cent of international migrants work in countries with bilateral or multilateral social security agreements, and often such agreements do not cover health care entitlement. Temporary migrants who are expected to pay into social security schemes but cannot benefit from them when they return home have a strong incentive both to work in the informal economy and not go home afterwards. More inter-governmental agreements on portabilty of benefits and access to benefits in destination countries is needed. At the same time, more discussion as argued for by some developing countries is needed within the context of the GATS to explore the options within the mode 4 concerning the movement of natural persons to liberalise the global labour market in service personnel in ways that provide for their international entitlement to social benefits:

- In **stemming irregular migration** states should co-operate with each other to ensure their efforts do not jeopardize human rights including the right of asylum.
- Migrants and citizens of destination countries should [ensure] a **mutual process of adapation and integration** that accomodates cultural diversity and foster social cohesion.
- The **legal and normative framwork** affecting international migrants should be strengthened [so as to] protect the human rights and labour standards of migrant men and women.
- The **governance of international migration** should be enhanced by improved coherence and strengthened capacity at the national level; greater consultation and

cooperation between states at the region level, and more effective dialogue and cooperation among governments and between international organisations at the global level. Such efforts must be based on a better appreciation of the close linkages that exist between international migration and development and other key policy issues, including trade, aid, state security, human security and human rights.

Within the context of the last principle concerning international governance, the report recommended to the UN Secretary-General the 'immediate establishment of a high-level inter-institutional group to define the functions and modalities of, and to pave the way for, an Inter-agency Global Migration Facility. This Facility should ensure a more effective institutional response to the opportunities and challenges presented by international migration'(UN, 2006). This recommendation reflected the concern of the Commisssion that in this field of migration, just as we noted earlier, as is the case in the fields of social policy and health policy, the institutional architecture at global level is characterised by a lack of inter-agency co-operation and co-ordination and the absence of one overarching authority on migration. Drawing heavily upon a paper submitted to the Commission by the Migration Policy Institute (Newland, 2005), the report notes that within the UN family there is the ILO, OHCHR, UNDESA, UNFPA and UNHCR, 'the mandates of which have evolved in specific historical, geographical and thematic contexts' (UN, 2006: 73). The Iinternational Organisation on Migration(IOM) operates outside the UN. Recently the World Bank, UNCTAD, UNDP and WTO have assumed a greater role in this policy area. Incoherence between these organisations often reflects the incoherence of governments in relation to them. The representative sent to the ILO will not be the same as the one sent to the IOM. Bringing all of these issues under one authority would, in the thinking of the report, ensure **efficiency, policy coherence and the pooling of expertise** (UN, 2006: 74). Several options for creating an overarching UN authority on migration are considered by the report, reflecting the calls for such an agency by Newland (2005), Bhagwati (2003) and Helton (2003) among others. It acknowledged that the UN High Commission for Refugees(UNHCR) might need to continue to deal with forced migration and refugees. It concludes that the IOM might be best suited to become **the** UN Agency for Economic Migration working closely with the ILO.

Subsequently, UNDESA's Population Division's *Compendium of Recommendations on International Migration and Development: The United Nations Development Agenda and the Global Commission on International Migration Compared* (www.un.org/esa/population/publications/UN_GCIM/UN_GCIM_ITTMIG.pdf) was published. The Population Division of the Department of Economic and Social Affairs is responsible for the substantive preparation of a high-level dialogue on international migration and development that the General Assembly was due to conduct in September 2006. In the United Nations, a series of inter-governmental conferences and summits convened mostly since 1990 have made a number of commitments and recommendations related to international migration. This report provides the complete set of texts relating to international migration, extracted from the outcome documents of the UN's conferences and summits. Consequently, this compilation permits an assessment of where there is already consensus regarding measures that can improve the benefits of international migration and address its drawbacks. In addition, this report presents a comparison of the recommendations emanating from the UN's conferences and summits with the recommendations made by the Global Commission on International Migration (GCIM). These recommendations are one of the inputs to the high-level dialogue that the General Assembly will conduct in September 2006. Meanwhile, Secretary-General Kofi Annan appointed Peter Sutherland, an international businessman who headed the WTO, to serve as his Special Representative for Migration! In his new role, Mr Sutherland will help the Secretary-General prepare for the General Assembly's high-level dialogue on international migration and development. The new envoy will also be engaged in preparing an overview of migration and development issues requested by the General Assembly that will cover a range of issues, including migration's impact on development and the movements by highly skilled and educated migrant workers. Subsequent developments in the reforms can be tracked either via UN reform pages or the GSP Digest 6.3 and 7.1.

Moves to constructive regionalism with a social policy dimension: a global federalism alternative?

It is worth being reminded at this point that some in the Global South (Bello, 2004) regard this focus by largely northern and European scholars and civil society activists on reforming the existing institutions of global social governance as mistaken. The point is not so much to reform and strengthen institutions that operate in the interests of the North (except perhaps parts of the UN), but to undermine and outflank them by creating new countervailing sources of power serving the interests of the Global South. This is where the construction and strengthening of regional organisations of countries that have a partly southern protectionist purpose enter the picture. Rather than seeking to develop, as this book has done, a case for a **global social policy of redistribution, regulation and rights** that must also imply a strengthening of northern-based institutions, the focus should perhaps be on building several **regional social policies of redistribution, regulation and rights.** Equally, rather than seek to win the Bank over to a European progressive perspective on social policy so that the Bank and the UN concur on the advice to national governments about the best social policy, the point should be to **liberate a policy space whether southern governments and civil society can construct their own policy choices.** Reforming global social governance should perhaps imply building a world federation of regions, each with competence in their own locations. The Transnational Institute's project on alternative regionalisms puts it like this:

> As the crisis of neo-liberalism deepens, there is an urgent need for the articulation of alternatives. The TNI Alternative Regionalisms programme aims to address the question of development alternatives from the perspectives of social movements in Africa, Asia and Latin America and seeks to effectively influence the shape and substance of regional governance in the South, as key lynchpins in a more pluralistic, flexible and fairer system of global governance. (2004: 2)

In fact, of course, several emerging trading blocks and other regional associations of countries in the South are beginning to confront in practice the issues of the relationship between trade and labour, social and health standards and the issue of how to maintain levels of taxation in the face of competition to attract capital. In this context the potential advantage for developing countries of building a social dimension to regional groupings of countries have been commented upon by policy analysts (Deacon, 2001a; Room, 2004; Yeates, 2005b) and is being acted upon within several world regions. Such advantages may be summarised as having an external and internal dimension.

In relation to the rest of the world, such an approach affords protection from global market forces that might erode national social entitlements and can create the possibility of such grouped countries having a louder voice in the global discourse on economic and social policy in UN and other fora. Thus Falk argued, 'from a world order perspective the role of regionalism is to help create a new equilibrium in politics that balances the protection of the vulnerable and the interests of humanity as a whole against the integrative, technological dynamic associated with globalism' (1995: 245).

Internally through intergovernmental agreement, regionalism would make possible the development of:

- Regional social **redistribution** mechanisms: these can take several forms, ranging from regionally financed funds to target particularly depressed localities, or to tackle particularly significant health or food shortage issues to funds to stimulate cross-border-cooperation. Capacity-building of weaker governments by stronger ones is another approach. If such mechanisms are in place, then North–South transfers funded either by ODA or global taxes could be transmitted to specific localities via the regional structure.
- Regional social and labour **regulations**: these can include standardised health and safety regulations to combat a within-region race to the bottom. Food production and handling standards could be included. Agreements on the equal treatment of women, minorities and indigenous groups could be included.
- Regional social empowerment mechanisms that give citizens a voice to challenge their governments in terms of regional supranational social **rights**. Principles of social policy and levels of social provision could be articulated and used as benchmarks for countries to aspire to. In the long-term, following the example of the Council of Europe's (not the EU) Court of Human Rights, citizens can be empowered to challenge perceived failures to fulfil such rights.
- Regional **intergovernmental co-operation** in social policy in terms of regional health specialisation, regional education co-operation, regional food and livelihood co-operation and regional recognition of social security entitlements. The possibilities for the sharing of specialist health services are countless. Cross-border agreements on education mobility can foster regional identity. Cross-border labour mobility issue can be managed more effectively and with greater justice if there are social security mobility rights.
- Regional regulation of the de-facto **private regional** social policies of health, education, utilities and social protection companies. Regional formations may be, in principle, in a stronger position concerning private suppliers to lay down and police effectively cross-border rules regarding, for example, access rights of the poor to private services.

Of course, the European Union in the Global North represents the most advanced form of such regional integration. In terms of supranational social policy, it can be said that the EU has an embryonic social policy in all the three fields of social redistribution, social regulation and social rights. The structural fund of the EU is the mechanism whereby the union funds (which are contributed to approximately according to country GNP and population size) are allocated to the development of impoverished or economically under-developed areas within the union. There are social regulations in the fields of health and safety, equal opportunities, labour law, co-ordination of social security schemes, labelling of tobacco products and social dialogue mechanisms that apply to all countries, including those that are about to join (Threlfall, 2002). In terms of regional social rights, there was established at an earlier stage the Community Charter of Fundamental Social Rights of Workers. This was added to in 2000 with the adoption of the Charter of Fundamental Rights. The proposed future constitution of an enlarged union that could have made these rights enforceable has not, however, been ratified.

In terms of the EU attempting to influence and guide member states' social policy, the story is one of only a gradual shift over the past decades from one in which the principle of subsidiarity initially characterised the approach. By this was meant that policy decisions should be taken at the lowest level that was appropriate. This was interpreted in the social policy field as being at country level or lower, even though one could advance the argument that it is most appropriate in an era of competition between countries to decide certain social policies such as tax rates at a higher level, as lower-level decision-making would be bound to ensure tax cutting. Gradually the idea that the EU Commission should have more competence in the social field gained ground. It is helpful to think in terms of the EU social policy towards country policy as being made up of the hard or legally enforceable **acquis communautaire** and the softer **acquis**, which emerge in the context of structured dialogue between countries and between them and the Commission's Directorate of Social Affairs. This softer approach to co-ordinated social policy-making is now institutionalised in the OMC or Open Method of Co-ordination (de la Porte and Pochet, 2002). The OMC in the fight against social exclusion was introduced in March 2000; in the area of pensions it was introduced in March 2001; and in the area of health care it was introduced in June 2001. Assessed as a mechanism for wide public participation and dilalogue, the OMC has been found wanting but seen as a mechanism whereby national civil servants are encouraged to ratchet-up their polices against agreed benchmarks, and through policy learning it has its champions (Chalmers and Lodge, 2003; de la Porte and Nanz, 2004).

There are signs of such a regional approach to social policy emerging in the Global South. MERCOSUR has developed regional labour and social security regulations, and has a mutual recognition of educational qualifications. SADC has approached health issue on a regional basis, and its gender unit has made progress in mainstreaming these issues across the region. ASEAN has declared that ones of its purposes is to facilitate the development of caring societies, and has a university scholarships and exchange programme. SAARC has included social issues on the agendas of its summits, and in 2002 signed a regional convention for the promotion of child welfare and a regional convention on the prevention of trafficking of women and children for prostitution. At its summit in November 2005 it resolved upon a Decade of Poverty Alleviation, a regional food bank and a Poverty Alleviation Fund. The Andean Community (CAN) agreed in 2004 a regional Integral Plan for Social Development that involves technical co-operation on social policy among Andean countries, including the exchange of good practice, regional monitoring of the MDGs and a number of regional social projects. Some similar developments are emerging at the level of the African Union and in regional groupings of countries in West and East Africa.

While an adequate assessment of the significance of the social dimension of southern regionalism will have to wait upon further research and the passage of time, it can be concluded on an interim basis that:

- There is a social dimension to several regional groupings. These range from the least developed in ASEAN to the most developed in MERCOSUR.
- Regional think tanks, regional NGOs and to some extent the regional secretariats are more focused on advancing this dimension than national governments.
- Emerging social problems with a regional dimension may stimulate further intergovernmental co-operation. These include cross-border labour migration, cross-border AIDS infection, cross-border drug running.
- The imminent advancing of free trade arrangements within some regions will either lead to increased concern with differential labour standards and other aspects of regional social policy, or to the beginning of the erosion of the trading bloc.
- In all regions, the political choice between either strengthening the existing regions, together with their emerging social dimension, or dissolving the existing regions in favour entering neoliberal inspired wider trading blocs, will need to be faced soon.

Progress will be influenced by two kinds of global dialogues, one a North–South and the other a South–South. The North–South dialogue has two strands: one is the USA–South 'dialogue' which is being driven by the USA to open up all world regions to either broader trading blocs that involve the USA (Asian Pacific Economic Co-operator or APEC and Free Trade Area of the American or FTAA), bilateral trade deals with the USA. This way spells disaster for regional social protectionism in the South. The other is the EU–Southern Regionalism dialogue that is a little more complex. On the one hand it contains features as in the USA–South dialogue where a southern regionalism is being encouraged to open up trade links with the EU to its advantage (Keet and Bello, 2004), and the other involves an inter-regional policy dialogue that seems to be motivated to spread the message of the importance of developing a social dimension to regional trading arrangements. For example, the Asia–Europe Meeting Trust Fund (ASEM) established with EU and Asian funding was conceived to expand the dialogue between these two regions. Curiously, the World Bank became the agent for this fund, although it retained its autonomy from the bank. Within the context of this programme, a series of social policy conferences were convened involving European and Asian scholars and policy-makers. The volume arising from this series, edited by Marshall and Butzbach (2003), concludes that there is a case for inter-regional understanding on the importance of implementing social standards in the context of globalisation. Similarly, the EU missions inside SADC and MERCOSUR do have a capacity-building and training element to them that does not seem primarily motivated by protecting the trading interests of the EU (Farrell, 2004).

This brings us back again to the importance of a South–South policy space and dialogue, this time on southern regionalism. The Transnational Institute is currently facilitating, with the support of the Alternative Information and Development Centre (AIDC) in South Africa, Focus on the Global South in Thailand, the Brazilian Institute of Social and Economic Analyses (IBASE) and Red Mexicana de

Accion Frente al Libre Comercio (RMALC), a South–South dialogue on alternative regionalism within which transborder civil society movements are paying a significant part (Transnational Institute, 2004). At the same time, UNESCO convened in February 2006 a High-level Symposium on the Social Dimension of Regionalism in Uruguay within the context of its International Social Sciences-Policy Nexus event. At this symposium some regional secretariats engaged with scholars from the TNI programme, the United Nations University Centre for Regional Integration Studies (UNU-CRIS) and GASPP on the topic of regional social policy. The Buenos Aires Declaration resulting from the Policy Nexus 'call[ed] upon the regional organisations such as MERCOSUR and the Africa Union, in association with social scientists and civil society, to further develop the social dimension of regional integration, and call[ed] upon the United Nations to facilitate inter-regional dialogues on regional social policies' (UNESCO, 2006). It is to be hoped that this call will be heeded by UNDESA. Indeed, UNDESA is working with SADC on just such a project.

Worth considering within this context is the motivation that seems to be building up behind the campaign to change the G20 (N) meeting of finance ministers into a L20 meeting of prime ministers and to shift power from the G8 to the L20. The former Prime Minister of Canada Paul Martin, argues (Martin, 2006) that the L20 group of countries speak for 90 per cent of the world's economy, 67 per cent of its population and 80 per cent of its trade. It is a body with strong and stable regional powers. A meeting of L20 prime ministers away from the glare of publicity and freed from issuing communiqués and without initially a secretariat might enable many of the North–South tensions that are blocking progress in UN and World Bank forums to be overcome. The USA remains resistant to the idea, but China and many other G20 countries are positive. A first meeting that the USA would not be able to stay away from might take place, hosted by China within the next year or so. The German Development Institute and the Canadian Centre for International Governance Innovation have joined forces to argue that the coming into being of the L20 and the ECOSOC reforms would be 'complementary building blocks for inclusive global governance and a more effective UN' (German Development Institute, 2006). In view of the discussion about regionalism above, the case might in my view be strengthened if the regional powers such as Brazil, India and South Africa were members not, as now, because of their regional economic strength, but because they had a mandate to speak on behalf of their regional associations of countries. Germany has the leadership of G8 during 2007 and South Africa the leadership of G20 (S) at the same time, and this might provide a joint forum for the advance of the L20 idea and its link to constructive regionalism.

Interim conclusion: global governance reform and legitimacy

Proposals for the reform of global governance as a whole and global social governance in particular range therefore from the very radical involving institutional decommissioning and rebuilding, through major reform of the current architecture to minor changes to the management and priorities of particular agencies. Some reform proposals point to the importance not so much of changing institutions but to better collaboration and policy dialogue between them through networked forms of international governance, including private actors at supranational level. Others point to the unlikelihood of any significant growth in the power of international agencies given the position of the USA on such matters, and point instead to the importance of improvements in bilateral aid and its better co-ordination. Yet others standing in the Global South would want to pursue a strategy involving the pluralisation of supranational governance arrangements, including attaching a new importance to regional institutions. How to judge and how to predict? Governance arrangements can be judged against a number of criteria, including their legitimacy, transparency and accountability, their effectiveness, and their procedural soundness. These judgements become more complicated for global governance than they do for national or even regional governance because of the huge North–South differences of interest. Judging against some yardsticks is one thing. Predicting the direction that reforms in global social governance will take depends more on an assessment of the politics of the situation. The next chapter will attempt a forward-looking projection in the light of an assessment of political forces and interests and the ideas and weight of the actors, movements and lobby groups engaged in the reform struggle.

Further Reading

On global governance: Held, D. and McGrew, A. (2002) *Governing Globalization*. Cambridge: Polity.
On reforms to global social governance: ILO (2004) *A Fairer Globalization: Creating Opportunities for All*, Report of the World Commission or the Social & inclusion of Globalisation. Geneva: ILO.
On a Global South view: Bello, W. (2004) *Deglobalization: Deals for a New World Economy*. London: Zed Press.
On regionalism: Farrell, M., Hettne, B. and Van Langenhove, L. (2005) *Global Politics of Regionalism*. London: Pluto.
Global Social Policy GSP Digest Section on Global Governance (www.gaspp.org)
Global Governance

Related Websites

www.g77.org
www.southcentre.org
www.focusweb.org
www.cris.unu.edu
www.wdev.eu

8

Conclusions and Implications for the Analysis and Future of Social Policy Nationally and Globally

This chapter draws conclusions from the book about the

- Contemporary content of global social policy both as global advice to countries and as supranational social policy
- Analysis of social policy change in a global context
- Implications for a global social reformist strategy

Global social policy overview

Global Social Policy 1: global actor views about national social policy – 'safety nets' contend with a 'new universalism', but the private sector still has its powerful supporters

We have shown that the World Bank's role in shaping and damaging national social policy in a development and transition context has been very important in the 1980s and 1990s. Its insistence on user charges prevented access to education and health. Its beneficiary index demonstrating that public spending often benefited those other than the poor was used in effect to undermine the embryonic welfare states of Latin America, South Asia and Africa. The losers were the urban middle class who had depended upon state universities and hospitals and pensions. These losers are being thrown into the arms of new global private service providers, and as a consequence abandoning their historic role as state builders. Which policy is emphasised by the Bank is often sector-specific: privatisation is, according to many in the Bank, good for pensions and for tertiary education. In the health sector, a privatising strategy is questioned by some but clearly supported by the IFC. The intellectual struggle inside the Bank between those who still favour safety nets for the poor and private services for the better off, and those more attuned to the European story of cross-class alliances shaping better public service for all, does now seem to be tilting in favour of the later. Indeed, partly because of the influence of the heretic social development section of the Bank, it is true that one reading of WDR2006 (World Bank, 2005a) is that concern with the institutional and political barriers to equity are also now centre stage, even in the Bank. The problem, however, for those within the Bank who have struggled long and hard to reform its social polices in a more progressive direction, is that they are working in an institution that does not have global legitimacy. Far better that their efforts and their money had been directed to the UN social agencies whose work they have undermined.

The thrust of IMF social policy in the 1990s was also the 'safety net' comprising targeted subsidies, cash compensation in lieu of subsidies, or improved distribution of essentials such as medicine. Although criticism of the Fund's structural adjustment facility led to its replacement by its Poverty Reduction and Growth Facility, critics continue to point out the contradiction between the IMFs short-term concerns with macroeconomic stability and these longer-term poverty reduction goals. IMF fiscal targets often lead to diminished social spending. However, in terms of the IMF's own account of its social policy prescriptions for countries, there has been a significant shift from the structural adjustment days. It now cites approvingly evidence of social spending in countries that received IMF support, claiming that real spending on education and health has increased. We have seen how the WTO as the relatively new kid on the bloc of International Organisations is also impacting upon national social policies in controversial ways, particularly in terms of boosting global private service providers and in terms of the constraints of the TRIPs agreement. We have shown that the social policy advice of the OECD occupies a position somewhere between the market opening and liberalising push of the IMF and WTO on the one hand, and the concern of UN social agencies on the other to protect public services. It has argued that globalisation creates the need for more, not less social expenditure.

Although the World Bank took over the global leadership role in the 1980s and 1990s and argued for and secured the role-back of the state system of pensions in favour of privatised and individualised forms, the ILO fought long and hard to expose what it regarded as flaws in the dominant World Bank thinking on pensions by arguing that there was no demographic imperative leading to privatisation, that the European-type schemes are reformable and sustainable, and that the privatisation strategy is merely a cover to increase the share of private capital savings. Moreover, it argued that the strategy was risky in the context of unregulated capital markets and imposes a heavy burden on current workers who have to finance the existing PAYG system as well as funding their own schemes. Just as in the Bank, so in the ILO there were other tendencies. The Social and Economic Security programme had taken a broad brief to examine the policies in the twenty-first century that might contribute to universal citizen (and resident) security in the context of global labour flexibility. This programme argued for the emergence of a new universalism from below embodying, for example, universal cash income benefits conditional on a child's attendance at school or universal categorical pensions. These ideas are now largely mainstreamed within the ILO, and under the new leadership of the Social Security Department considerable effort is being made to form alliances with the EU, UNDP, WHO and others to advance this agenda.

We have shown how the shadow of the World Bank is cast over the role of the WHO as it was in the case of the ILO. So much so that the last but one Director

General Bruntland was concerned to rescue the WHO from the margins of international influence and establish it as an agency able to compete with, or at least stand alongside, the Bank as an authorative voice on global health issues and national health policies. To do this she believed it necessary to shift the WHO discourse from a purely normative one about health for all to one which engaged with economists. Health expenditures were to be encouraged not because they were morally desirable, but because they were a sound investment in human capital.

World Bank versus UN social agency issues arose also with regard to education and the role of UNESCO. Within the context of the Education for All campaign with which UNESCO is centrally connected, the big question of money was in effect left to the Bank who would mange the Fast Track Initative and the global education fund for education. Similarly, the UNDP's ownership of and responsibility for the implementation of the MDGs sits uneasily alongside the equally important role of the World Bank in a development context. First we noted that in sum these MDGs represented both progress and retrenchment. The progress was in the timelines for meeting them and for the commitment embodied in goal 8 of the development of global partnership for development. The retrenchment was in the focus on targeting the poorest of the poor and in its focus only on primary education and reproductive health. Setting this caveat aside, the main issue with regard to the realising of the MDGs was that countries would have to plan increased public expenditures. However, to have their World Bank run PRSPs approved by the Joint Staff Assessment of the World Bank and IMF, countries would actually bear in mind that these two institutions are still basically wedded to the Washington Consensus involving macroeconomic stability and privatisation. How MDG planning unfolds over the next few years is crucial. Of central importance will be whether the reinvigorated '1 UN' and the new UNDESA/UNDP social policy guidance notes combined with greater North–South transfers enable countries to challenge the remnants of Washington Consensus thinking in the Bank.

Thus the ideas about desirable national social policy carried and argued for by the international organisations surveyed in Chapters 2, 3 and 4 reveals something approaching a 'war of position' between those agencies and actors within them who have argued for a more selective, residual role for the state together with a larger role for private actors in health, social protection and education provision and those who took the opposite view. This division of opinion often reflected a disagreement as to whether the reduction of poverty was a matter of targeting specific resources on the most poor, or whether it was a matter of major social and political-institutional change involving a shift in power relations and a significant increase in redistribution from rich to poor. It does seem, in 2006, that the tide has turned against the targeting and privatising view, and the opportunity now exists for the UN working with sympathetic donors such as the Scandinavians and some other European countries to begin to undo the damage wrought by the Bank over the past decades.

At one level, things have therefore changed since I wrote *Global Social Policy: International Actors and the Future of Welfare* (Deacon, 1997). There having reviewed the intervention of international organisations in the making of social policy in Eastern Europe, I concluded that the opportunity created by the collapse of the communist project was grasped enthusiastically by the World Bank. In alliance with social development NGOs, a social safety net future was being constructed. This approach, I concluded, 'was challenging powerfully those defenders of universalist and social security based welfare states to be found in the EU and the ILO' (1997: 197). Now in 2006 I have concluded differently, that in terms of the global discourse about desirable national social policy still taking place within and between international organisations, prescriptions for national social policy involving safety nets contend with a renewed emphasis on universalism. At the level of ideas from my normative and analytical standpoint this is good news. However, now we have to contend more directly with the WTO and its alliance in effect with global business pushing the privatisation of services with the support of the hitherto unexamined International Finance Corporation of the Bank. The struggle over ideas might have been won but the structural context of the global economy and the place of global business within it may yet render that a Pyrrhic victory. In other words, despite the evidence of a more universalist approach and a renewed concern with equity inside UN agencies and even the Bank, four elements within the new global context might yet undermine a public service orientation and equity approach to social policy and social development. These tendencies are:

- The World Bank's continuing belief that in the context of development governments should really only provide basic levels of social provision and social protection, its acknowledgement of equity issues notwithstanding.
- The UN's concern with its MDG targets that may ensure a focus only on basic education and health care, despite attempts to downplay this within the new *Social Policy Guidance Notes* (Oritz, 2006).
- The NGO's and CC's continuing self-interest in winning donor contracts to substitute for government social services.
- The moves being made within the WTO to speed the global market in private health, social care, education and insurance services.

If this more pessimistic scenario turns out to be true, we know that where the state provides only minimal and basic level health and social protection services, the middle classes of developing and transition economies will be enticed into the purchase of private social security schemes, private secondary and tertiary education and private hospital level medical care that are increasingly being offered on a cross-border or foreign investment presence basis. The result is predictable. Unless the middle class is also catered for by state provision, good quality social provision can't be sustained. In this scenario, the middle classes of developing and transitional countries may give up their historic role as national (welfare) state builders that served their welfare needs and take the risk of entering an unregulated and service-delivery influenced global welfare market. As Shana Cohen summed it up, 'the political goal of the global middle class would be to obtain access to services formerly subsumed within the province of the state, that now increasingly, comes from the non-located, heterogeneous social relations that signify and support globalisation' (2004: 141). As a result, 'the social and political bond between elite and non-elite falls apart globally and locally leaving only economic benefit and exploitation' (2004: 141). And as Gould has demonstrated, the aid business has played a major part in seducing the professional and middle class of developing countries from this role they used to occupy: 'Seduced by access to the dollar economy, they prioritise acquiring skills for … the requirements of the aid cartel … at the expense of contributing to the development of domestic manufacturing and processing industries that would generate actual wealth within the national economy' (2005: 148). He continues: 'the intellectual and entrepreneurial class must choose between a self-referential and parasitic post-developmentalism, and national(ist) development projects – enhancing domestic savings and productive investment, improving the productivity of land and labour, building the revenue base of the public economy' (2005: 149). The renewed emphasis on state building within the UNDESA guidelines suggests these concerns are understood at that level.

Global Social Policy 2: a contested politics and practice of social redistribution, social regulation and social rights at global and regional level

In terms of supranational global social policy, we concluded in Chapter 6 that in the first years of the twenty-first century the world is stumbling towards articulating a global social policy of global redistribution, global social regulation and global social rights and creating the institutions necessary for the realisation of such policies in practice. More significant than the recent increase in ODA have been the birth of new global funds for health and education and social protection. Poorer countries may now access limited global resources on certain criteria of social need. These funds, of course, have their critics because they tend to suggest that in the case of health, for example, improved health can only be secured through pharmaceutical and technical 'vertical' programmes rather than also broad-based 'horizontal' public health programmes within countries. Their accountability is also called into question. We saw that we are also witnessing the move from purely North–South support for within-country social development to the articulation of the concept of global public goods that may need to be provided out of taxes on global processes such as air travel.

Global business is being asked by the UN to act in a socially responsible away. Of course there are no teeth and the idea of voluntary codes rather than enforceable rules prevails for now. There is no social clause in international trade deals, but there is now a global expectation on all countries who are members of the ILO that they uphold core labour standards whether they have chosen to sign up to them or not. Concern, however, continues to exist about the underdevelopment of global regulatory capacity in the health, education and social care markets. Despite continued international controversy about aspects of global social rights, their very existence and promulgation by the UN enables others to campaign for their realisation in countries where governments have hitherto been reluctant to concede them.

Alongside these embryonic policies and practices of global redistribution, regulation and rights the international community has confirmed, despite a strong attempt by the USA to persuade it otherwise, its commitment to the MDGs that are in effect a minimum set of global social standards in education, health and poverty alleviation. Of course as we suggested earlier, these do not go far enough. Of course as we saw in Chapter 6, the global institutions to ensure these are met are not strong enough. Of course these are only benchmarks around which there will be continued global social struggle. The important point is that the language and discourse have changed from that used in the heyday of global neoliberalism. It is no longer the dominant belief that the global market left to itself will secure the meeting of global human and social needs. Just as within one country the market has to be embedded in a set of political institutions to secure social justice, so does the meeting of global human and social needs.

But we also observed in Chapter 6 that as well as developments in **supranational global social policy** we could observe an embryonic development in some regions of **supranational regional social policy**. Indeed, we argued that intergovernmental regional agreements could make possible the development of regional social **redistribution** mechanisms, regional social and labour **regulations**, regional sector social policies in health, education and social protection, regional social empowerment mechanisms that give citizens a voice to challenge their governments in terms of regional supranational social **rights**, regional intergovernmental co-operation in social policy in terms of regional health specialisation, regional education co-operation, regional food and livelihood co-operation and regional recognition of social security entitlements, and last but not least, regional regulation of the de facto private regional social policies of health, education, utilities and social protection companies. In the future, developments at the level of regional social policies may be as important as global social polices. Regional groupings of countries could act as a conveyor-belt for global funds to poorer parts of the regions.

The analysis of social policy in a global context: beyond welfare regimes and comparative frameworks

In Chapter 1 it was suggested that our understanding of social policy-making at national and supranational level in a globalised context might be informed by the insights of certain theories of policy change at the international level. Among those suggested were the **complex multi-lateralism** approach of O'Brien et al. (2000) within which international policy is shaped not only by inter-state negotiations but also by international organisations engaging directly with international civil society, the global **policy advocacy coalitions** approach of Orenstein (2005) which focuses upon alliances formed between international organisations and others in *Global Knowledge Networks* (Stone and Maxwell, 2005) to argue for a certain policy, and the **politics of scale** approach of Stubbs (2005) which suggested that we need to pay attention to the way global actors are in the local. We also drew attention to the **world society theory** approach of Meyer et al. (1987) that based its approach on the activities within an already-existing global society that transcends borders. Cross-border professional associations act to defuse policy ideas and practices wherever there are members. Education policy and practice, health care procedures and practices become the same everywhere in conformity with professional standards according to this approach. The value of all of these approaches, but also the limitation of the Meyer approach, has been demonstrated by the findings in this book. There is no global diffusion of the best and most scientifically accepted global policy idea, rather there is continued conflict and contestation about alternative policy ideas at the global level. We can also conclude more concretely that any adequate understanding of the social policy-making process both at national and supranational level in an era of globalisation requires an analytical framework that can handle and make sense of:

- The character, role and influence of the numerous new players that are brought into the making of both national and supranational social policy. As we have seen this range is very large, extending from formal international organisations through a range of non-state global private actors. One element of this phenomenon is the **flexible and multi-faceted nature** of many of these actors: sometimes the same agency is policy advocate and service provider. Another is the **variety of the networks and alliances** struck usually temporarily between international public, international private and international civil-society actors to address particular global welfare issues. The **intersection of the global and national is the heart of the matter** in terms of analysis and understanding.

- The significance of the **global discourse about desirable national and international social policy** taking place within and between these international organisations and their associated epistemic communities. The precise ways in which the struggle over social policy ideas is played out and interpreted by policy intermediaries who are agents travelling between the national and global are central here. Individuals, think tanks and policy entrepreneurs matter in this process in the absense of a global democratic political process: they have more purchase on the global policy-making process than on the national. What is happening is not so much a gobal process of diffussion of an agreed approach, but a global contestation about that approach within which individuals often make a difference.

- The activities of **global private welfare providers,** their clients and the impact of their activities on the national cross-class social contracts necessary for the development of solidaristic national welfare states. Perhaps most relevent to future research into social policy-making in a globalising context is the role being played by the **globalised middle class** of developing and transition countries. If the new global/transnationalised middle class is forsaking the state-building projects of their parents, then the future for cross-class welfare solidarities at the national level looks bleak and so must be reconstructed at the supranational level. At the same time, the focus shifts to the currently weak supranational regulation of education, health and social protection services.

- The implications of a **global movement of peoples** that challenges territorial-based structures and assumptions of welfare obligation and entitlement and indeed politics. Forms of welfare solidarity that cross borders framed within religious, ethnic or cultural terms become part of the mosaic of a globalised social policy. Aspirations towards **supranational citizenship providing social rights at regional and global level** emerge here to accompany the earlier discourse and practice of interstate reciprocal arrangements for migrant workers.

It is the **multi-sited, multi-layered, multi-actored nature** of the social policy-making process that emerges from this study. This is not to say that states do not matter. They remain important, but some more so than others. They remain important as mediators of international influence and they in turn contribute to international policy dialogues. But state social policy choices in most countries are framed within those alternatives being canvassed by public and private international actors and are strongly influenced by loan conditionalities set by lending and donor agencies. At the same time, the embryonic forms of a truly global (in the sense of supranational) social policy of redistribution, regulation and rights affect national social policies. The priorities of spending decided upon by global health and education funds influence priorities within national health policies if funds are to be accessed. Globally determined MDGs are built into country planning mechanisms even if their realisation in practice would require more than donors are prepared to offer. Country processes for arriving at poverty reduction strategies in may countries are overseen by international actors and are likely to be drafted by international consultants and policy activists. Agreements between countries and the WTO advance the balance of the public/private welfare mix towards the private, even though the capacity to regulate the private at the national level is weak and at the international level is non-existent or blocked by the USA. And developed mature welfare states are not immune from this process, as ideas about pension reform or health care reform travel from those countries more subject to the immediate pressures of the IMF or Bank via the 'open method of co-ordination' into the European heartland. But that having been said, EU ideas about social policy at national and regional level, weaker and less cohate, do travel abroad also. The OECD is one site of contest between the liberal and social solidaristic welfare agendas.

Having argued that national social policy choices, especially but not only in conditions of post-communist transition or development, are strongly influenced by the global economic and political context, developing countries paradoxically increasingly assert that **social policies are the sovereign choice** of national goverments. As we discussed in Chapter 7 and return to later, the anachronistsic governance structure of the UN feeds this fetishism of the national in the policy-making process. These assertions are an understandable reaction to the perception that the Global North has shaped the policy choices of the Global South for too long: first through empire and colonialism, then through IMF-imposed structural adjustment, and then through ODA-driven process conditionality. Understandable as this is, it obstructs the North–South debate that would seem to be needed about desirable national and supranational social policies in an interconnected world.

If the logic of this southern 'the national-is-sovereign' position were taken to extreme, and indeed southern governments escaped the yoke of northen social policy imposition and even discourse, then much of the content of this book would be of historic interest only. It would no longer matter that the ILO and the World Bank dialogued about social protection to reach a policy convergence. It would no longer matter that the MDG objectives of the UN seemed to be at odds with the PRSP process of the Bank. One reaction by northern donors to this southern wish to get out from under the northern imposition of policies is, as we have seen, to ask only for outcome conditionality. More lending and gifts will be subject only to the achievement by developing countries of better mortality, educational attainment and poverty reduction data. We in the North would stop being global actors and become merely global monitors of progress.

Returning to the analytical level, the findings of this study of the policies of international actors must challenge quite strongly the tradition of **comparative social policy or comparative welfare state analysis**. While there is support for the view that developed welfare states are relatively immune from reforms imposed by or resulting from global economic and political pressures, this does not mean that the comparative analytical framework developed by the narrow preoccupation of welfare state scholars within rich OECD countries can be made to travel easily in a globalising world. **The welfare regime literature that divides the world into liberal, conservative corporatist, social democratic and perhaps also state-led developmental welfare states begins to unravel at the margins of these worlds.** Already Barrientos (2004) has been forced to describe national social policy in Latin America as shifting from Conservative-informal to Liberal-informal as a result of the adoption of aspects of the

Chilean pension reforms in several countries. Julia Szalai (2005) recently attempted to describe Hungary with the term 'Conservative-Liberal'.

Rather than attempting to squeeze emerging welfare states and social policy formations into the until-recently frozen Anglo-Saxon and European landscape, better to regard emerging welfare states in John Clarke's (2005) words as 'policy assemblegies'. **These policy assemblegies are products of the multi-actored and multi-layered processes** we have been trying to cast a little light on in this volume. While it might still apply that welfare reform in mature welfare states is in part path-dependent, this framework for understanding social policy reform in most countries of the world has limited value. By the same token, **expectations that emerging welfare states will follow in the path of earlier European trajectories needs to be revised.** What is resulting and will result from the complex politics of new welfare state building that transends national space and takes place at several levels and involves multiple international actors will be different. At the same time, the emerging transnational social policies of regulation, redistribution and rights will need to be understood in different terms. Rather than path-dependancy or the logic of development, it might be possible, as we suggested in Chapter 1, to continue to invoke notions of class, gender and ethnic struggles and the associated articulation of visions of work, family and nation to make sense of social policy formations and settlements, but how we use this analytical framework will need modification too in the globalised context. World interconnectedness, or at least the neoliberal form that it has taken, modifies the balance of class forces so that the global business view of desirable social policy is strengthened, enables the ideas of womens' movements to cross the globe and invade the spaces of the World Bank so that more women-friendly policies emerge, and fractures national solidarities in favour of ethnicised ones with complex social policy consequences.

Deploying an analytical framework that attempts to hold on to the idea that social policies are outcomes of the struggles and mobilisations and visions of class, gender and ethnic-based interests that have been changed in a globalised context, together with an analytical approach that also insists on the importance of international actors and transnational policy intermediaries and processes, can help us make sense of the nature of social policy at national, regional and global level. However, knowing the empirical facts upon which to build the analysis in this complexity is not easy. Indeed, Stubbs (2005) has argued that no team of researchers, however multi-disciplinary and multi-linguistic, can ever know all the acts of all the transnational actors who have helped shape a particular policy assemblage in a particular locality. Certainly, to make sense of even part of this complex reality, social policy analysts who have always been multi-diciplinary animals gleaning (and rejecting) insights from politics, economics and sociology need now to engage with the theories of international relations and deploy an arsenal of research methods appropriate to international diplomacy, business forcasting, the anthropology of the powerful and network analysis and probably much more besides.

A multi-sited, multi-actor, multi-level global social reformist strategy to make the world a fairer place

If our analysis is correct, one thing is sure about the character of the political process that will shape the social policies of the future at national, regional and global level and shape the future structures of global and regional social governance: it will be multi-sited, multi-actor and multi-levelled. To put this another way, from the normative standpoint of this volume our concern to make the world a fairer place, better able to meet the social needs of more of the world population, political struggle will need to take place at a number of sites and involve a number of different actors:

- Struggles between neoliberal and social solidarity agendas within **countries** will continue to play a part, and perhaps none more important than that is the USA.
- Debates about best social policies for countries within and between global **epistemic communities** will contribute.
- The work of **global policy advocacy organisations and international think tanks** will matter.
- The winning-over of **international corporations** to socially responsible practice will count.
- Debates within the **anti-globalisation movement** about what actually are the prospects for and actual policies of alternative globalisations will be important.
- The unsung work of **international civil servants** within the UN, EU, G8/G20 meetings struggling to keep the main lines of meeting declarations on a progressive track matter.
- **Individuals** as policy translators and intermediaries working both in and against the international organisations and in the spaces in between them count.
- But eventually success, if there is to be any, will depend on the construction of a **global political alliance** that embraces most of these actor and sites.

Making policy in the spaces between agencies and tiers: a new progressive political alliance?

That is not to suggest any neatly ordered system of multi-level governance is at work where progressive social policies simply have to be won first at the local and then at the national and then at the regional level and finally in the debating chambers of global social governance! Rather, as Clarke has put it, 'This cannot be simply grasped as multiple tiers or levels, since sovereignties overlap and collide in the same space (with jurisdictional claims being the subject of conflict and negotiations). Different polities or sovereignty-claiming agencies are constituted differently – most obviously in terms of their representative base' (2005: 413). Indeed, this has led some to argue that it is precisely in the spaces between such contending and overlapping (partial) authorities that the most effective moves to make transnational policy might take place. Thus because there are now so many loci of action and initiatives on global social issues we may, as we explained in Chapter 7, be witnessing a shift in the **locus and content** of global policy debate and activity from those more formally located within the official UN policy-making arenas (whether of ECOSOC in New York or in the councils of the ILO and WHO in Geneva) or focused on UN/Bretton Woods institutional reform, such as the establishment of an Economic Security Council to a set of practices around networks, partnerships and projects, which in some ways by-pass these institutions and debates and present new possibilities for actually making global change in particular social policy arenas.

In Chapter 7 we suggested that a key question therefore becomes how intervention in these tasks, projects and dialogues might become subject to some principles of justice and equity. There is a case, therefore, for not only the networks and partnerships focused on short-term projects and tasks, but also for longer-term **global political alliances** that might fashion sets of principles to steer members of the task forces. Perhaps rather hidden from view, these global political alliances are being shaped and active already. Perhaps the choice of experts to sit on the World Commission on the Social Dimension of Globalisation; perhaps the choice of people to serve on the Millennium Task Force; perhaps the work of the Helsinki Process (see more below), which launched three Tracks within which international dialogue between northern and southern voices took place, leading to a conference in 2005 calling for a new political will to be fashioned to better manage globalisation; perhaps the choice of membership of the High-Level Panel on UN Policy Coherence is evidence of such an implicit anti-neoliberal global political alliance within and between international actors. Perhaps the conference convened by Gordon Brown on 16 February 2004, at which the new President of Brazil and many INGOs spoke about the need to get other countries signed up to his International Finance Initiative to double overseas aid, is a sign of the emergence of a global social democratic alliance. Perhaps this is a kind of war of positions, albeit at a fairly reified level, whereby the dying global hegemony of neoliberalism is being contested and outmanoeuvred. Perhaps if countries follow the Swedish initiative and legislate to ensure that **all** government policy is subordinated to a responsible approach to globalisation (see below), progress will be made. Perhaps if countries follow the proposals of Kaul et al. (1999) to appoint issues ambassadors for global public goods issues, such as education, health and water, these ambassadors will in effect be participants in this war of positions. Perhaps the US Treasury does not have total grip anymore? Perhaps the next edition of Boas and McNeill's (2004) book will conclude that powerful states (notably the USA) contend with other powerful states (notably Europe, China and Brazil), powerful organisations (such as the IMF) contend with other powerful organisations (such as the UNDP), and powerful disciplines (notably economics) contend with other disciplines (notably social and political science) to wage a war of positions as to how the terms of debate about globalisation should be framed. To the extent that this is the case, the role of intellectuals and their ideas struggling **in and against** and **in between** the international organisations will have been important. This shift in influence of contending ideas will reflect also a shift in the balance of power whereby social movements from below will have had an impact upon national governments and international actors.

One important element in the formation of this global progressive political alliance in the field of social policy is the work going on, as I write, in the spaces between the several overlapping networks of international social policy movers and shakers. Emails are bouncing back and forth between international civil servant activists in POVNET (OECD), ILO, UNDESA, UNDP, UNRISD, the Finnish, Swedish and other donor governments to fashion agendas for an ILO–EU seminar on 'Social Protection and Inclusion: Converging Efforts from a Global Perspective', a Swedish–UNRISD seminar disseminating the results of the Social Policy in a Development Context Research Programme, a Finnish Ministry of Foreign Affairs seminar to discuss 'Appropriate Social Policies in a Globalised World', and a A side event following on from this at this at the next UN Commission for Social Development putting the case for such polices and more besides.

Northern governments: the 'globalisation policies' of the USA, the Nordics, the EU and the UK

Spaces between agencies and organisations may be places where individuals and other change agents can work their reforming paradigms, but the agencies and organisations with which they are liasing still matter. The formal winning-over of the various actors at the several levels is still important. So ironically within a book that has espoused the importance of the transnational and the global, we do need to return towards its end to the national and to the policy struggles within countries. For as several commentators on globalisation have suggested, states still matter (Weiss, 2003), and more importantly as Yeates (2001) and Boas and McNeill (2004) argued, powerful states make globalisation in their image. Of particular importance, then, is the policy of key national governments in the North to globalisation. And perhaps none is more important than the USA. When the USA initially tried but failed to denude the final text of the September 2005 UN summit of all progressive content, it did look as if there was a war of position between the USA and the rest of the world. Whether it has been the question of setting up the International Criminal Court, the Toyota Protocol on climate change, the question of innovative global taxation, the attempts by the WHO to reign in the food-processing companies in the matter of added sugars, the issue of donors providing free needles and condoms to prevent the spread of AIDS, the listing by the WHO of abortion pills as essential medicines, or attempts by southern countries to use the medical emergency exceptions to produce or import cheap drugs, the USA has been in terms of the value standpoint of this book on the wrong side of the argument (see also Sands, 2005). Without the USA and notwithstanding the southern opposition to a northern-driven globalisation, there would by now be a strengthened UN, a more effective system of international taxation and aid, and the rules of the global economy would be more socially responsible. As Sachs has said, 'The lack of US participation in multilateral initiatives has undermined global security and progress towards social justice and environmental protection … Political action within the United States and from abroad will be needed to restore its role on the road toward global peace and justice' (2005: 365). However, it must be added that individuals and corporations within the USA continue to be some of the mainsprings of global philanthropic effort. Following in the path of the Ford Foundation, Rockefeller and others, the Bill and Melinda Gates Foundation is the mainstay of the global fund for Aids, TB and malaria and other global medical initiatives.

It is beyond the scope of this book to analyse the prospects for such a change in USA policy towards these issues. Of importance, however, within this context is the burgeoning of progressive think tanks and policy advocacy networks **based** within the USA **and** concerned with US global policy. One such is the Washington-based Centre for Global Development (www.cgdev.org) presided over by Nancy Birdsall. Among the American-based scholars on the board of directors are Dani Rodrick, Jeffrey Sachs, Amartya Sen and Joseph Stiglitz. One means at its disposal to be critical of the USA is its new approach to 'ranking the rich' countries (Roodman, 2005). Its Commitment to Development Index rates countries according to:

- quantity and quality of foreign aid;
- openness to developing-country exports;
- policies that influence investment;

- migration policies;
- support for creation and dissemination of new technologies;
- security policies; and
- environment policies.

In 2005 while Denmark, the Netherlands and Sweden ranked first, second and third respectively, the USA trailed in twelfth position. The low standing of the USA was, according to the country analysis provided by the Centre, due to: the small aid volume; the large share of tide aid; the high trade barriers to textiles and apparel; restrictions on investing pension funds in emerging markets; its bearing of a small burden of refuges in humanitarian crises, the low numbers of immigrants from developing countries entering the USA; high greenhouse gas emission and many other shortcomings in this policy area; the export of arms to undemocratic governments; and its push to incorporate TRIPS-plus polices in bilateral trade deals.

Among other USA-based and targeted progressive globalisation policy advocacy centres are the Open Society Policy Centre, also in Washington, set up by George Soros (www.opensocietypolicycenter.org) and the Mikhail Gorbachev-initiated State of the World Forum (www.worldforum.org). One of the Open Society Policy Centre's initiatives is the Co-operative Global Engagement Project that generated the report on *Restoring American Leadership: Cooperative Steps to Advance Global Progress* (Open Society Institute, 2005). In terms of global social policy, the report advocates that the USA should donate $1.1 billion in 2006 to the Global Fund to Fight AIDS, TB and Malaria, exclude from any trade agreements any TRIPS-plus provision that restricts full access to generic medicines needed to fight these diseases, improve the co-ordination of the USA's own Millennium Challenge account with bilateral and multilateral donors and ratify the Convention on the Elimination of All Forms of Discrimination Against Women (2005: 57, 83, 98).

At the other end of the spectrum in terms of progressive policies towards socially responsible globalisation lie the Nordic countries, in particular Sweden and Finland. Not only do they rank highly on any index of commitment to global development, they also have advanced policy initiatives and thinking on the international stage designed to reform global social governance. A key issue for such northern governments is that of policy coherence between ministries. While a country's development policy might be laudable, its trade policies might absolutely contradict this. While its support for UN initiatives might be creditable, its voice at the World Bank Board might lend support to questionable social polices and questionable conditionality. While a country might lend and give a lot, it might insist that the loan or gift is spent on companies operating out of the donor country (tied aid). Awareness of these and related issue led the Swedish government to declare in December 1999 that it would establish a parliamentary commission of enquiry into Swedish policy for global development. Subsequently, the government resolved to formulate an integrated Swedish globalisation policy. Indeed, it was the Minister of Trade, then Leif Pagrotsky, who was assigned the task of leading a working group to secure such a policy. In his first report he stated clearly, 'it is not acceptable for the same country's politicians to sit in various international institutions and work for mutually conflicting goals' (Pagrotsky, 2001). In December 2003, the Swedish government enacted a new Policy for Global Development that declared a national commitment to allocate 1 per cent of its gross national income to ODA, declared global poverty reduction to be an overarching goal of its policy, and importantly established the principle that all government policy of all ministries would contribute to 'equitable and sustainable development'. This approach has been commended by the peer-review process of the OECD (2005d). To sustain this work requires a constant monitoring by those concerned with global social policy of the role played by their government representatives at the WTO (trade ministers) and at the World Bank Board (finance ministers). These trade and finance experts need to be provided with social policy arguments.

While Sweden focused internally on how its policies might contribute to a socially just globalisation, Finland focused externally on how it might enable a global dialogue to be advanced on these issues. Finland has always punched above its weight in global affairs. Its key location between East and West during the cold war years enabled it to contribute to an East–West dialogue. Now it saw itself as well placed to contribute to a North–South dialogue. Following on from its joint presidency with Tanzania of the ILO's World Commission on the Social Dimension of Globalisation, it established with the co-operation of the Tanzanian government the Helsinki Process on Globalisation and Democracy (www.helsinkiprocess.fi). This process included the Helsinki Group, which involved high-level government 'representatives' including Claire Short of the UK, stakeholders from business, international organisations and the scholarly community, spokespersons for international policy advocacy groups such as Ann Pettifor of the Jubilee 2000, Mary Robinson of the Ethical Globalisation Initiative, Strobe Talbot of the Brookings Institute, and importantly a significant number of contributors from the Global South such as Martin Khor of the Third World Network. This high-level group met periodically to brainstorm on global governance reform. It also set in motion three tracks: New Approaches to Global Problem Solving, Global Economic Agenda, and Human Security. The first track convened by Nitin Desai, former UN Under-Secretary-General for Economic and Social Affairs, generated a valuable report authored by John Foster (2005). It concluded that the Helsinki process had noted three deficits that needed to be overcome if global governance arrangements were to move forward. The first was a 'democracy' deficit as power is concentrated in the hands of a few governments (G8). Second was a 'coherence' deficit between ministries with government leading to conflicting international obligations and, we could add, conflicting international organisations. And third was a 'compliance' deficit, as international institutions fail to implement decisions they make. It is one thing to analyse these shortcomings, quite another to marshal progress for reform. Thus the theme of the final conference in the Helsinki process held in September 2005 and the title of the final report (Helsinki Process, 2005) was *Mobilising Political Will*. The foreword to the report by the Ministers of Foreign Affairs of Tanzania and Finland noted simply that 'we have started a process of building a group of governments which is willing and interested to work together to advance issues debated within the Helsinki Process …'. The report itself reflected the work of the Helsinki Group and deals with five issues: poverty and development, human rights, environment, peace and security and governance. On poverty and development it restates with urgency many of the reform proposals we reviewed in the last chapter: 'developed countries must live up to their commitments', 'global problems call for global financing', and 'development and combating poverty have to be central concerns in WTO negotiations'. Each of these topics will now be the subject for work by five ongoing round tables. Of significance is who is lending support to these ideas, not the ideas themselves. It remains to be seen whether the driving force created by the Helsinki Process can be sustained so that it continues to play a part in the construction of a global political alliance for global social governance reform. At the close of the conference, the co-chairs announced that the following governments regarded themselves as friends of the Helsinki Process and were committed to further-ing the multi-stakeholder approach to global problem solving: Algeria, Brazil, Canada, Egypt, Hungary, Malaysia, Mexico, South Africa, Spain, Thailand, the UK together with Finland and Tanzania. At the same time it is interesting to note that, at the time of writing, invitations are being sent out by the Finnish Ministry of Foreign Affairs for a meeting in November 2006 on 'Appropriate Social Policies in a Globalizing World'. Among the invitees are the leading progressive social policy ana-lysts from UNDESA, UNDP, ILO, UNICEF, UNRISD, OECD, POVNET, together with Ministers and scholars from the Global South (watch GSP 7.1 Digest for update).

The listing of the UK among the friends of the Helsinki Process is interesting. The policy towards global social governance of the UK is of importance for the clout that it continues to have in several international forums (G8, EU, IMF, World Bank, OECD:DAC), notwithstanding the damage done to this by its involvement in the Iraq war. Its global social policy initiatives are several, often progressive, sometimes con-tradictory and can't be ignored. Among these we may list in recent years:

- its advancing of the **goal of global of poverty reduction** as the key aim of interna-tional development (UKDFID, 2000b);
- its advancing of a **rights-based approach to social policy internationally** (Ferguson, 1999);
- the articulation by Gordon Brown of a desirable set of **global social policy princi-ples,** albeit ones that were not to be accepted by suspicious southern governments (Brown, 1999; Ferguson, 1999);
- its support for codes of **conduct for business** and ethical global trading activities (Ferguson, 1998b);
- the campaign to establish an **international finance facility** to support global funds, albeit it seemed initially at the expense of the alternative tax on air travel;
- the championing by Gordon Brown of early **multilateral debt relief** and the announcements of bilateral debt forgiveness;
- the challenge by Tony Blair to the EU to **lower the subsidies on agriculture** and reduce trade barriers;
- its recent 2005 commitment to **increase substantially its ODA** and the decision of Hilary Benn, UK Secretary of State for International Development, to end the pol-icy of requiring privatisation as a condition of such ODA (Hilary, 2005);
- it's launching of the **Commission on Africa** and not shrinking from publishing its sometimes hard-hitting report;
- its use of the G8 presidency in 2005 and its EU presidency in the same year to **advance international development causes;**
- its decision to compensate aid agencies for monies lost to them when the USA decided not to fund agencies who gave birth control advice and condoms; and
- the involvement of Tony Blair in the Progressive Governance Network convened initially in 2000 by Bill Clinton and supported by the UK-based Policy Network that organised the 2003 meeting and generated the London Communiqué that called for a global progressive agenda (www.progressive-governance.net).

Indeed, although the UK government under Tony Blair and Gordon Brown has been committed to policies that accept the inevitability of global free trade and global financial flows and adjusted its **domestic** labour market and social policies accordingly by subsidising low wages, it has argued **internationally** for policies that it perceives as being in the interests of global social justice. Admittedly the following was a speech at a Labour Party Conference, but it shows something of Blair's approach to the topic. 'The issue is not how to stop globalisation. The issue is how we combine it with justice. If globalisation works only for the benefit of the few, then it will fail and will deserve to do so ... power, wealth and opportunity must be in the hands of the many, not the few. If we make that our guiding light for the global economy, then it will be a force for good and an international movement that we should take pride in leading' (Blair, 2001). Gordon Brown has articulated this vision more clearly: 'The challenge is immense but in the spirit of the Marshall Plan the answer is not to retreat from globalisation. Instead we must advance social justice on a global scale, to the benefit of all, and to do so with more global cooperation not less and with stronger, not weaker, international institutions ... This generation has is in its power if it so chooses to finally free the world from want' (Brown, 2001a). Behind the scenes, the UK Fabian Society, which can be credited with advancing the cause of the national welfare state in the past, has been working to articulate a vision of global social responsibility in dialogue with some Labour ministers (Jacobs et al., 2003; Fabian Globalisation Group, 2005).

The UK published its new White Paper *Eliminating World Poverty: Making Governance Work for the Poor* (UKDFID, 2006a) just as this book was being finished. It is supportive of a number of progressive ideas about reforming aid and reforming governance at national and international level. It celebrates the recent ending of school and health fees in some African countries, asserts that all people have a right to education and health services and, in times of insecurity, to social security. It calls for strong developmental states, applauds the example of Malaysia, and argues the case for strengthened regional forms of governance. At the global level it repeats the call for one UN, and argues the case for the UN playing a more important role in standard-setting. It puts the case for greater developing country involvement in a more transparent World Bank and IMF.

Much of northern country globalisation policy is filtered through the European Union. Is it possible to characterise the response of the EU as a whole to the pressures of a liberalising globalisation? To what extent has the EU used its position as a global player to push for socially responsible globalisation? I have argued elsewhere (Deacon, 1999) that the response of the EU to neoliberal globalisation in terms of both its internal and external social dimension has been variable over time and between parts of the EU system. Included within this range of responses are: accommodation to the liberalising global agenda in labour markets and associated social policy; social protectionist inclinations in some of its trade dealings; expressions of global social concern for human rights in its common foreign and security policy; assertiveness at the level of discourse, if not in terms of deeds regarding the need for a social dimension to enlargement; attempts to link trade aid and standards within some of its development policy; and ineffectiveness in terms of World Bank discussions on global financial regulation, but perhaps a new assertiveness about the social dimension within the global discourse on social policy.

One explanation for the confusion in EU's role as an actor on the global stage is the issue of who it is in different situations who has the right to speak on behalf of the

EU in different global forums. Who speaks for the EU on the global stage? Who has the power to make external policy? What is the relationship between the Commission and Parliament and the Council of Ministers? How important is the EU Presidency in all of this? In other words, the synergy between the policies towards globalisation of different Ministries being developed now with one country, such as Sweden, is harder to secure in the complexity of the EU. It may be concluded that in terms of the contribution of the EU to the discourse and policies of globalisation:

- the contribution of different elements of the EU institutional structure is different;
- the European Parliament has often resolved polices which appear to go furthest in the direction of embodying the idea of a socially responsible globalisation but it is not burdened yet with the job of seeing these through;
- the Commission, divided as it is along functional lines, speaks with contradictory voices attempting to juggle the defence of Europe's particular interests with fine words about human rights;
- the Economic and Social Committee articulates concerns about globalisation but these are often tinged with a protectionist hue;
- the intergovernmental process has led to coherent EU contributions concerning the social dimension of globalisation in some forums such as the UN's Commission for Social Development; and
- the Common Foreign and Security Policy of the EU is fashioned by a dated conception of foreign policy and has not yet been able to integrate an external dimension of EU social policy as part of its brief.

This is regrettable because, as we noted in the last chapter, the EU represents in principle a model for other world regions to follow if they wish to develop a social dimension to their economic collaboration. Certainly if the EU wishes to extend its influence to help construct a world of regions with a social dimension in order to counter global neoliberalism, then it will have to put its social development policy before its trade interests and it will have to match its moralising about rights with resource transfers to enable these rights to be realised in practice. Are there signs of changes in the right direction? Certainly the EU commitment to increase the ODA of many of its members substantially at Gleneagles suggests this is the case. Indeed, on 2 March 2006 in the run-up to the UN Millennium Review Summit, the European Commission released papers focused on how to improve EU aid effectiveness to meet the challenge of the MDGs. In its Communication to the Council and Parliament on Financing for Development and Aid Effectiveness (Commission of the EU, 2006a and 2006b), it:

- reviews positively the commitments to increase ODA but urges member states to do even more;
- welcomes the two innovative sources of finance supported by some member states: the IFF for Immunisation and the Airline Solidarity Tax;
- argues for a more effective complementarity between country and EU aid packages to countries;
- reports positively the decision of Portugal to lead the way by moving to multi-annual budget support to countries with a less than annual review of conditionality;
- recommends the further untying of EU and member state ODA;

- urges the publication of the final report of the International Task Force on Global Public Goods;
- suggests further means whereby the EU members states and the Commission co-ordinate and increase the visibility of the EU presence as a block at the meetings of the IFIs; and
- calls for the implementation of an effective Aid for Trade package and improves the mainstreaming of trade into poverty reduction and development strategies.

All of these points, if acted upon, do seem to be steps in the right direction if the EU is to play the role some would wish for it on the global stage. However, Eurodad's review of these documents (2006) calls for the EU to be an even stronger global player on the innovative sources of finance agenda and to speed up its part in the debt cancellation process. The Commission has also recently (Commission of the EU, 2006c) published a new communication on *Decent Work*, which is focused both on EU countries and on developing ones, and is collaborating with the ILO to advance the Decent Work agenda through the UN system.

South–South dialogues: what do China, Brazil and India want in terms of global social governance?

Let us remind ourselves of the context and emergence of the impasse in the North–South global social policy dialogue that derailed a number of northern-driven global social reforms. The following attempts either by northern governments or northern social activists to inject a social purpose into the global economy have met with southern government or southern social movement opposition:

- the 1996 suggestion to include a social clause in trade agreements;
- the 1999 proposal for a set of global social policy principles; and
- the current and ongoing moves to incorporate support for global labour and social rights into World Bank lending practice.

It was argued sharply by a spokesperson for Focus on the Global South at a Globalism and Social Policy seminar on globalising social rights in New Delhi in 2000 that 'the South is the new Left'. At that point many global social reformers based in the North were arguing for the 'European' case for global social democracy against the 'North-Atlantic' case for global neoliberalism. The conversation that ensued was reported in the Forum section of GSP 1.2;

> it concluded: the wide-ranging discussion demonstrated that while agreement between northern and southern participants on the desirability of equity generating social policies *within* countries was possible there was much less agreement on how, if at all, globalisation could be made compatible with such an approach to social justice. The optimism of some northern contributors who believed in the possibility of combining globalisation with social protection and international justice was sharply contrasted by the assessment on the part of many southern contributors about how much more daunting were the obstacles to such changes and how much more fundamental might need to be the change in north–south power relations to ensure this had any positive impact in the south. (Deacon, 2001c: 148)

This led to the conclusion that 'The impasse in the North–South debate about global social standards can only be overcome if the North is more commited to much greater North–South Transfers and if the South begin to own for itself a set of social policy principles based on best practice appropriate to developing country conditions' (Deacon, 2001b: 69).

The starting point of governments of the Global South in this search for a southern position on global social governance appears to be the motivation not to have the comparative advantage of southern countries in global trade eroded by the imposition of 'unreasonable' standards. The continued opposition to many northern initiatives is still coloured and informed by the history of structural adjustment and the belief that the North is preaching standards without contributing the resources to help attain them. Getting out from underneath 'northern' globalisation and working for a plurality of contending agencies and locations of power has been the strategy of Walden Bello (2004) while leading the Focus on the Global South movement. Determined opposition to the self-interested polices argued for by the USA and the EU at successive WTO meetings has been one tangible outcome of this move to southern empowerment. The alliance of Brazil, India, South Africa and China together with other southern countries (the new G20) has begun to shift the global power balance. The fact that to avoid the collapse of the WTO 2005 Honk Kong talks, the G8 needed to meet at Prime Minister level with these countries plus Mexico was indicative of this. Rethinking TRIPS, rethinking GATS, rethinking Northern Social Protectionism are from the point of view of the South tangible outcomes of this new balance of power.

That having been said, it continues to be hard to discern the emergence of any sustained South–South dilaogue and view on southern social standards or any sustained South–South dialogue on reforming global social governance in the interests of the South. There are a number of sites of such an emerging dialogue. Southern-orientated think tanks and research networks such as the South Centre, the Transnational Institute, UNRISD's Social Policy in a Development Context programme and the UNDP-sponsored International Poverty Centre in Brazil are numbered among these. Certainly the UNRISD programme has been reasserting the case for a universalist approach to social service provision in the South (Mkandawire, 2004), but has had little to say on global social governance issues beyond calling for greater and more effective social regulation of global business (Utting, 2000). Southern policy advocacy networks and coalitions such as the Third World Network and the Focus on the Global South are becoming more influential, especially around WTO issues, but as we saw in Chapter 5, the umbrella World Social Forum does not see itself as advocating particular policies to better manage globalisation.

There was an initiative by the UNDP's Programme of Technical Cooperation between Developing Countries (UNDPTCDC), in 2000 to launch a South–South Dialogue on Social Policy under the programme entitled 'Managing the Risks of Globalisation: A South Exchange on the Role of Social Policies'. This was inspired by the G77's Havana Declaration of 2000 (www.G77.org) that had stressed the need for South–South Co-operation in the matter of social development. Its first seminar in Beirut in 2001 brought together 40 social policy researchers and makers from Brazil, Chile, China, Costa Rica, Egypt, India, Jordon, Korea, Lebanon, Morocco, Peru and the Phillipines. It even established a short-lived Southern Social Policy Group Network but, alas, after this one seminar and one issue of *Co-operation South*, this initiative stalled for lack of infrastructure once the person who inspired this initiative moved on in her UN career. Other UN sites and locations of fragments of the southern contribution include UNCTAD. Charles Gore (2004) of UNCTAD has drawn attention to the double-bind southern countries find themselves in when trying to meet World Bank PRSP requirements and aspire to UN MDG planning. UNCTAD is currently arguing in the context of UN reform discussion for a new UN agency to channel ODA to the South (UNCTAD, 2006). The ILO, particularly the ILO-SES programme, the UNDESA and the Commission for Social Development provide the South with a platform for exchanges of experience on social protection, as we reviewed in Chapter 4. The moves towards a new univeralism from below, including a renewed interest in categorical benefits paid conditionally upon behaviour change such as school attendance, emerged from this work. Perhaps the initiative by UNESCO to hold within the context of its International Forum on the Social Sciences Policy Nexus in February 2006 a High-Level Symposium on the Social Dimension of Regionalism (see Chapter 7) may generate a more sustained South–South dialogue on the social policy dimension of regions. Certainly the African Union with support From UNDESA is now working in this field.

One recent indication of the collective view of the Global South with regard to global social and economic policy and governance issues is provided by the proposals submitted by the G77 (actually now 132 developing countries) together with China to the draft declaration of the UN 2005 Summit on the MDGs. The submission in june 2005 which in effect represented, with China, 76 per cent of the world's population, asserted that:

- there should be no conditions attached to development assistance;
- the WTO Doha round should ensure that the interests of developing countries are fully reflected, especially with regard to TRIPS;
- the northern countries should reaffirm their committment to provide ODA at the level of 0.7 per cent of national income;
- consideration should be given to **all** innovative financing mechanisms developed by the UN Technical Group on Innovative Financing and such financing should be additional to ODA;
- developing countries should have the policy space to formulate their own development strategies; and
- there is a need for the reform of global economic governance to ensure the voice and participation of developing countries and for the UN to have a 'more decisive and central role' in international economic policy-making.

Beyond this analysis of the collective G77 view, it is not easy to say much about the policies towards the social dimension of globalisation of the key southern national players: Brazil, India, China and South Africa. Their alliance is fragile and based primarily on ensuring market opening to major agricultural producers and some other manufacturing sectors, and also on TRIPS. There is also some unanimity on resisting pressures via the GATS or other means to open further the service sector to foreign competition. India has, however, broken rank on this and is actually proposing to use to its advantage the provision within the GATS agreement regarding mode 4, the movement of natural persons, to better regulate the trade in skilled labour (Yeates, 2005: www.focusweb.org/india). It is also developing niche markets in the global market for plastic surgery. India and China have of course, in many ways, been advocates of neoliberal globalisation and opposed to global labour and social standard-setting. Brazil, under President Lula, has on the other hand been much more critical of neoliberalism and has sought the strengthening of Latin American Trading blocs as a partial defense against the USA. The Bolivian President, Evo Morales, has now supplemented this with a call for a Latin American Peoples' Trade Agreement.

Towards a global social reformist hegemony, market-induced global levelling or a federated world of regional diversity with converging social standards?

This book has argued that policy choices concerning health, education and social protection within countries and transnational social policies of redistribution, social regulation and social rights at regional and global level are being influenced within a globalising context by international actors of various kinds. While the social polices of the more developed welfare states of Europe are relatively immune from such pressures, except perhaps in the field of labour markets and some associated social security measures, this is certainly not the case in most other parts of the world. The national and transnational social policies advocated by the World Bank, the IMF and the WTO on the one hand in general contend with those advocated by the UN system, although there is much common ground. The book has examined the case for reforms to the system of global social governance, including the strengthening of the UN that might help secure better and more universally available public services for health, education and social protection even within poorer countries.

As such the book has been written through the lens of a social policy analyst even as we have strayed into much broader concerns in the last chapters. As such the book will be criticised. It will be criticised for both its preoccupation with the details of specific social policies being articulated by international civil servants working in the ILO or World Bank, as well as its concern to defend and seek to generalise the welfare state success stories of Europe to the rest of an unwilling world.

On the first point, Munck (2005), commenting on earlier writings, has asserted: 'thinkers such as Bob Deacon reflect the institutional bias of academic social policy that not only privileges state institutions but also, as Nicola Yeates notes, brings into the question only "the more institutionalised sectors of opposition movements" (Yeates, 2001: 130)'. He continues, 'there is, however, a much wider and "wilder" process of contestation going on across the globe in relation to the social impact of globalization. It is these "globalization from below initiatives" that are shaping global social policy every bit as much as the policies of enlightened reformers in the international forums, (Munck, 2005: 79). Or again, elsewhere in the same text, 'While the domain of global social policy will undoubtedly be a terrain of contestation, it has certain limitations from a transformationalist perspective. It is, first of all, a top-down perspective that tends to ignore the importance and impact of the contestation of globalisation from 'below'. Furthermore, as Nicola Yeates argues, this approach focuses on the supranational organisations such as the IMF and World Bank and 'reflects the institutional tendencies within academic social policy itself which privileges state institutions' (Yeates, 2001: 130). My defence against such an argument is two-fold. This book **has** been concerned also to examine what the social movements from below have to say about specific social policies. The conclusion was often to find them wanting in terms of specific national and transnational social policies. Organisations such as Focus on the Global South, very effective in mobilising opposition to the WTO and World Bank, tend to be bereft of specific alternatives. The World Social Forum has resolved not to fashion a manifesto, preferring instead a thousand voices to bloom. Somebody has to be concerned with the nuts and bolts of institutional social policy. At the same time this book **has** been concerned to articulate a political strategy for global social reform that **is** multi-actor, multi-sited and multi-levelled. Northern countries seeking to create the political will for change through alliances of like-minded countries, internationalised global policy advocates working in and between the spaces of often frozen institutions, and moves towards South–South dialogues both of social movements and of governments all, I contend, have a part to play in global social reform.

This debate about 'top-down' prescriptions for global social policy echoes the debate around the broader articulation of a global social democratic reformist strategy associated with David Held (2004) and his colleagues. Held restated his global social democratic agenda in summary form as:

- salvaging Doha;
- cancellation of debts;
- reform of TRIPS;
- creation of a fair regime for transnational migration;
- expand the negotiating capacity of developing countries;
- increase their participation in running the IFIs;
- establish new financial flows for investment in human capital; and
- reform of the UN.

Such an approach is dismissed unfairly from a rather different political standpoint by Meghnad Desai as a 'social democratic programme engaged in recreating the state at the global level'(2005: 69). Instead, in a variation on the Focus on the Global South approach that the people left to themselves will refashion the world, he insists:

> A new global order will eventually be recreated-but not from a statist, top-down, 'global new deal' type approach. It will be created because in the course of globalization the response of people moving to where the jobs are and of capital moving to where the profits are will erode national sovereignty. The global order will be created because multi-national corporations will demand a uniform standard of environmental or accounting practices in order to operate across the globe. Indeed such global governance from below could happen faster if individual jurisdictions did not insist on preserving their own laws (as in the European Union). It will require the erosion of state sovereignty and the strengthening of human rights independently of territorial states. (2005: 69)

I wonder, Meghnad, which international civil servants, working in which agency funded by whom and with laws enforced by what legal authority will oversee the enforcement of these human rights? These institutional details matter and are the stuff of global social policy, in this example global social rights enforcement. Such disdain for the details of social policy at national and transnational level tends to be the hallmark of those given to grand polemics against the present but who have no policy road map to chart the future.

While Desai would nowadays not write explicitly in these Marxist terms, his idea of the spontaneous emergence of a global order echoes the sentiments of the Marxists Hardt and Negri, who see globalisation as the final 'progressive' arrival of Empire within whose terrain the class struggle will finally be fought:

> Class struggle, pushing the nation state towards its abolition and thus going beyond the barriers posed by it, proposes the constitution of Empire as the site of analysis and conflict. Without that barrier, then, the situation of struggle is completely open. Capital and labour are opposed in directly antagonistic form. This is the fundamental condition of every political theory of communism. (2000: 27)

They write of the 'organisation of the multitude as a political subject, as posse, [that] thus begins to appear on the world scene' but note that 'the only event we are still awaiting is the construction or rather the insurgence of a powerful organisation ... We do not have any models to offer for this event ... only the multitude through its practical experimentation will offer the models and determine when and how the possible becomes real' (2000: 411).

So I insist again that while 'waiting' for the posse to get its act together, we should seek to reform existing neoliberal global capitalism in a global reformist direction. Indeed, in doing so, we may not be asking for anything very different from that which Hardt and Negri's 'powerful organisation' might want. After all, the first two of the three political demands of the multitude are, according to Hardt and Negri 'The general right to control its own movement (across borders) is the multitude's ultimate demand for global citizenship' and 'a social wage and a guaranteed income for all ... once citizenship is extended to all we could call this guaranteed income a citizenship income' (2000: 400–3).

In terms of the second anticipated criticism, there is one important sense in which this book may be distinguished from others (Held, 2004; Patomaki and Teivainen, 2004) that advocate some kind of global social democracy and might allow it to be redeemed in the eyes of those who would see such a project as an imposition of western policies. In the last chapter, a strong case was developed for a **regional** approach to transnational social policy. Interestingly, while on the one hand Arrighi (1993) suggested long before there was much talk of globalisation that 'the next hegemony would have to be world social democracy', Robert Cox was already suggesting instead that we depart from the search for a new progressive hegemony and suggested a search for 'a new form of world order; post hegemonic in its recognition of co-existing universalistic civilisations, post-Westphalian in its restructuring of political authority into a multi-level system and post-globalisation in its acceptance of the legitimacy of different paths towards the satisfaction of human needs'(1993: 286). Given the subsequent rise of religious identities, Scott Thomas has argued persuasively against the idea that 'religious and cultural pluralism ... must ... be overcome by an ethic of cosmopolitanism if there is to be an international order', insisting to the contrary that ways must be found of 'absorbing non-western elements in international society'(2000: 815). Rieger and Leibfried have also argued that social policy in the West is closely derivative of its religious roots and hence insist:

> We must reassess the transferability of Western institutions to countries with a different cultural foundation as well as our standards of measurement of progress in the development of a welfare state. (2003: 326)

In a footnote (172) to this section, they insist that 'the ILO is a bearer and propagandist of specifically Western norms and ideals of social policy design'. And in a comment on an article of mine (Deacon, 2005) reviewing the extent to which even the World Bank had now come to accept the worth of a universal approach to welfare provision, Rieger chastises that 'this thinking is clearly linked to notions of social policy that have a strong cultural bias' (2005: 13).

It is within this context of such challenges that the case for diverse **regional social policies** exists and has been supported in this volume. But there is also a more pragmatic case. It is arguable that because of the continued opposition by the world superpower to any kind of strengthening of the UN system and any talk of global taxation and redistribution, an alternative route to a more systematic global governance might need to be looked for in the concept of a strengthened regionalism with a social dimension (Deacon, 2001b; Room, 2004; Yeates, 2004). Within this scenario, the EU that anyway 'offers novel ways of thinking about governance beyond the state' (Held and McGrew, 2002b) would be joined by ASEAN for East Asia, the AU or SADC and other sub-regional groupings for Africa, SAARC for South Asia, some combination of MERCOSUR and the Andean Community in a Latin America Peoples Trade Agreement and other regions in a global federation of regions linked to, say, the Canadian-led L20 international governance mechanism within which regions rather than countries had a vote. In this case an international redistribution would be handled on an interregional basis and funds allocated on socio-economic criteria of need to some regions, which would then decide to allocate it to activities and projects within the region using similar mechanisms. As we saw in Chapter 7, regional social policies could then be devised that gave due recognition to diverse social and labour standards and reflected different cultural and religious approaches to social rights. Such a regional approach to a global social policy might, as we suggested, chime with the sentiments of many southern voices that react against a northern-driven global social democracy as strongly as they react against a northern-driven global neoliberalism (Bello, 2004).

This acknowledgement of the importance of protecting and respecting cultural pluralism and local diversity, notwithstanding the common political task that still faces us all, was expressed quite cogently by Cox in assessing the tasks facing Gramsci's organic intellectuals in today's world:

> Their task now is to bridge the differences among the variety of groups disadvantaged by globalisation so as to bring about a common understanding of the nature and consequences of globalisation, and to devise a common strategy towards subordinating the world economy to a regime of social equity. This means the building of a counter-hegemonic historic bloc that could confront the hegemonic forces of globalisation in a long term 'war of position' … Their task now is to be able to work simultaneously on local, regional and world levels. (1999: 26)

What is needed, I suggest, is more dialogue based on humility and mutual respect between social policy and social development intellectuals North and South, in the context of listening to the diverse voices of social movements informed as they are by a variety of cultural locations. This might facilitate the marriage of diversity in culture and experience with a common set of values concerning social justice and rights, as well as their conversion into a shared international political project to secure a socially just world. This would require, I still insist, some combination of equity-driven national social policies, strengthened regional social policies and a measure of global social redistribution, effective global social regulation, and the articulation and effective realisation of global social rights.

Further reading

For more on global social reform ideas: Held, D. (2004) *Global Covenant: The Social Democratic Alternative to the Washington Concensus.* Cambridge: Polity; and Patomaki, H. and Teivainen, T. (2004) *A Possible World: Democratic Transformation of Global Institutions.* London: Zed Press.
For more on global struggles from below: Munck, R. (2005) *Globalization and Social Exclusion.* Bloomfield, CT: Kumarian Press.

Related Websites

www.cgdev.org
www.helsinkiprocess.fi
www.dfid.gov.uk
www.sweden.se
www.forumsocialmundial.org.br

References

AFRODAD (2005) 'Tanzania and the Millennium Development Goals'. Zimbabwe: African Forum and Network on Debt and Development. www.afrodad.org

Ahde, M., Pentikainen, A. and Seppänen, J.-M. (2002) *Global Lottery*. Helsinki: Crisis Management Initiative.

Ahmad, S. and Schneider, J. (1993) *Alternative Social Security Systems in CIS Countries*. Washington, DC: IMF.

Alcock, P., Erskine, A. and May, M. (2003) *The Students' Companion to Social Policy*. Oxford: Blackwell.

Anderson, K. and Reiff, D. (2005) 'Global Civil Society: A Sceptical View' in Anheier, H., Glasius, M. and Kaldor, M. (eds.), *Global Civil Society 2004–5*. London: Sage.

Anheier, H., Glasius, M. and Kaldor, M. (2005) *Global Civil Society 2004–5*. London: Sage.

Armingeon, K. and Beyeler, M. (2004) *The OECD and European Welfare States*. Cheltenham: Edward Elgar.

Arrighi, G. (1993) 'The Three Hegemones of Historical Capitalism' in Gill, S. (ed.), *Gramsci, Historical Materialism and International Relations*. Cambridge: Cambridge University Press.

Asian Development Bank (1999) *Framework for Operations on Social Protection*. Manilla: Asian Development Bank.

Atkinson, A.B. (2005) *New Sources of Development Finance*. Oxford: Oxford University Press.

Aziz, S. (2005) 'International Taxation Alternatives and Global Governance', *Global Governance*, 11: 131–9.

Barr, N. (1994) *Labour Markets and Social Policy in Central and Eastern Europe*. Oxford: Oxford University Press.

Barrientos, A. (2004) 'Latin America: Towards a Liberal-Informal Welfare Regime' in Gough, I. and Woods, G. (eds.), *Insecurity and Welfare Regimes in Asia, Africa and Latin America*. Cambridge: Cambridge University Press.

Barrientos, A. (2006) 'Social Protection for the Poorest: Taking a Broader View', *Poverty in Focus*, 6–8.

Beattie, R. and McGillivray, W. (1995) 'A Risky Strategy: Reflections on the World Bank's Report Averting the Old Age Crisis', *International Social Security Review*, 48.

Bello, W. (1998) 'The Bretton Woods Institutions and the Demise of the UN Development System' in Paolini, A.J. and Jarvis, A.P. (eds.), *Between Sovereignty and Global Governance*. Basingstoke: Macmillan.

Bello, W. (2000) *Why Reform of the WTO Is the Wrong Agenda.* Bangkok: Focus on the Global South. www.focusweb.org

Bello, W. (2004) *Deglobalization: Ideas for a New World Economy.* London: Zed Press.

Bergesen, H.O. and Lundel, L. (1999) *Dinosaurs or Dynamos? The United Nations and the World Bank at the Turn of the Century.* London: Earthscan.

Bhagwati, J. (2003) 'Borders Beyond Control', *Foreign Affairs*, Jan.–Feb.

Bhagwati, J. and Hamada, K. (1982) 'Tax Policy in the Presence of Emigration', *Journal of Public Economics*, 18: 291–317.

Bhorat, H. (2006) 'An Income Grant to all South Africans?', *Poverty in Focus*, 9–10.

Biekhart, K. (1999) *The Politics of Civil Society Building: European Private Agencies and Democratic Transition in Central America.* Utrecht: International Books.

Birdsall, N. and Roodman, D. (2003) 'Global Development Index'. www.cgdev.org

Blair, T. (2001) Labour Party Conference Speech by the Leader of the Labour Party, Blackpool, October.

Boas, M. and McNeill, D. (2003) *Multilateral Institutions: A Critical Introduction.* London: Pluto.

Boas, M. and McNeill, D. (2004) *Global Institutions and Development.* Basingstoke: Palgrave.

Böhning, W. (2005) *Labour Rights in Crisis.* Basingstoke: Palgrave.

Borger, J. (2005) 'Roadmap for US Relations with the Rest of World', *Guardian*, 27 August.

Boutros-Ghali, B. (2006) *Reinventing UNCTAD.* Geneva: South Centre.

Braathan, E. (2000) 'New Social Corporatism: A Discursive-comparative Perspective on the World Development Report 2000/2001' in CROP (ed.), *A Critical Review of the World Bank Report: World Development Report 2000/2001: Attacking Poverty.* Bergen: Comparative Research Programme on Poverty (CROP).

Braithwaite, J. and Drahos, P. (2000) *Global Business Regulation.* Cambridge: Cambridge University Press.

Bretton Woods Project (2002) Bretton Woods Update 28. www.brettonwoodsproject.org

Bretton Woods Project (2004) Bretton Woods Update 41. www.brettonwoodsproject.org

Broad, R. (2006) 'Research, Knowledge and the Art of "Paradigm Maintenance"'. *Review of International Political Economy*, 13(3): 387–419.

Brown, G. (1999) 'Rediscovering Public Purpose in the Global Economy', *Social Development Review*, 3: 3–7.

Brown, G. (2001) *Tackling World Poverty: A Global New Deal, a Modern Marshall Plan for the Developing World.* London: Transport and General Workers Union.

Bruno, M. (1992) 'Stabilization and Reform in Eastern Europe'. Washington DC: IMF.

Bullard, F. (2005) 'Why UN Reform Is not a Priority'. www.focusweb.org

Buse, K., Drager, N., Fustukian, S. and Lee, K. (2002) 'Globalization and Health Policy: Trends and Possibilities' in Lee, K., Buse, K. and Fustukian, S. (eds.), *Health Policy in a Globalising World.* Cambridge: Cambridge University Press.

Callinicos, A. (2003) *An Anti-Capitalist Manifesto.* Cambridge: Polity.

Callinicos, A. and Nineham, C. (2005) 'Critical Reflections on the Fifth World Social Forum'. www.forumsocialmundial.org

Camilleri, J. and Falk, J. (1992) *The End of Sovereignty? The Politics of a Shrinking and Fragmenting World.* Aldershot: Elgar.

Campbell, D. (2004) 'Havens That Have Become a Tax on the World's Poor', *Guardian*, 21 April.

Cardenas, S. (2003) 'Emerging Global Actors: The United Nations and National Human Rights Institutions', *Global Governance*, 11: 23–42.

Casey, B., Oxley, H., Whitehouse, E., Antoln, P., Duval, R. and Leibfritz, W. (2003) 'Policy for Ageing: Recent Measures and Areas for Further Reforms', Economics Department Working Paper 309. Paris: OECD.

Castles, F. (2005) *The Future of the Welfare State: Crisis Myths and Crisis Realities*. Oxford: Oxford University Press.

Castles, S. and Davidson, A. (2000) *Citizenship and Migration*. Basingstoke: Macmillan.

Cerney, P. (1995) 'Globalization and the Changing Logic of Collective Action', *International Organisations*, 49: 595–625.

Chalmers, D. and Lodge, M. (2003) *The Open Method of Coordination and the European Welfare State*. London: ESRC Centre for Analysis of Risk and Regulation, LSE.

Chand, S. and Shome, P. (1995) *Poverty Alleviation in a Financial Programming Framework*. Washington, DC: IMF.

Chanda, R. (2001) *Trade in Health Services*. Working Paper WG 4:5 of the Commission on Macro-Economics and Health. Geneva: WHO.

Chau, A. (2004) *World on Fire: How Exporting Free-market Democracy Breeds Ethnic Hatred and Global Instability*. London: Heineman.

Chavez, D. (2006) 'Beyond the Market: The Future of Public Services', *Public Services Yearbook*. Amsterdam: Transnational Institute and Public Services International Research Unit.

Chen, L. and Desai, M. (1997) 'Paths to Social Development: Lessons from Case Studies' in Mehrotra, S. and Jolly, R. (eds), *Development with a Human Face*. Oxford: Clarendon.

Chen, L.C., Evans, T.G. and Cash, R.C. (1999) 'Health as a Global Public Good' in Kaul, K., Grunberg, I. and Stern, M. (eds), *Global Public Goods: International Cooperation in the 21st Century*. Oxford: Oxford University Press.

Cheru, F. and Bradford, C. (2005) *The Millennium Development Goals: Raising Resources to Tackle World Poverty*. London: Zed Books.

Christian Aid (2003a) *Struggling to be Heard: Democratizing the World Bank and IMF*. London: Christian Aid.

Christian Aid (2003b) *Taking Liberties: Poor People, Free Trade and Trade Justice*. London: Christian Aid.

Cichon, M. (2006) 'Social Protection at the ILO', Show and Tell Seminar on Social Protection, ILO. February 22nd.

Cichon, M., Pal, K., Leger, F. and Vergnaud, D. (2003) *A Global Social Trust Network: A New Tool to Combat Poverty Through Social Protection?* Geneva: ILO.

Clarke, J. (2004a) 'Changing Welfare, Changing States: The Shifting Conditions of the National in Comparative Studies', *International and Comparative Social Policy Seminar*, Bristol, 21–2 April.

Clarke, J. (2004b) *Changing Welfare, Changing States*. London: Sage.

Clarke, J. (2005) 'Welfare States as Nation States: Some Conceptual Reflections', *Social Policy and Society*, 4: 407–15.

Clunies-Ross, A. (2004) 'Resources for Development', *Global Social Policy*, 4: 197–214.

Cohen, S. (2004) *Searching for a Different Future: The Rise of a Global Middle Class*. Durham, NC: Duke University Press.

Commission of the European Community (2006a) *Communication: Financing for Development and Aid Effectiveness: The Challenge of Scaling Up, COM(2006) 85*. Brussels: European Commission.

Commission of the European Community (2006b) *Communication: Increasing the Impact of EU Aid, COM (2006) 88*. Brussels: European Commission.

Commission of the European Community (2006c) *Communication: Decent Work*. Brussels: European Commission.

Cooper, R. (1988) 'Towards a Real Global Warming Treaty (The Case for the Carbon Tax)', *Foreign Affairs*, 77(2): 66–79.

Cornia, G., Jolly, R. and Stewart, F. (1987) *Adjustment with a Human Face*. Oxford: Clarendon.

Cox, R. (1993) 'Structural Issues of Global Governance: Implications for Europe' in Gill, S. (ed.), *Gramsci, Historical Materialism and International Relations.* Cambridge: Cambridge University Press.

Cox, R. (1999) 'Civil Society at the Turn of the Millennium: Prospects for an Alternative World Order', *Review of International Studies*, 25(1): 3–28.

CROP (2000) *A Critical Review of the World Bank Report: World Development Report 2000/2001: Attacking Poverty.* Bergen: CROP.

Curtis, M. (2005) 'How the G8 Lied to the World on Aid', *Guardian*, 23 August.

Daly, M. and Rake, K. (2003) *Gender and the Welfare State.* Cambridge: Polity.

Dani, A. (2005) 'Policies for Social Development in a Globalizing World: New Frontiers for Social Policy', Discussion Paper for Technical Consultation on Social Policy at the meeting of the Social Development Advisors Network, Washington, DC, 14 February.

Davis, G. (2004) *A History of the Social Development Network in the World Bank 1973–2002.* Washington, DC: World Bank.

de la Porte, C. and Nanz, P. (2004) 'The OMC: A Deliberative-democratic Mode of Governance? The Case of Employment and Pensions', *Journal of European Public Policy*, 11: 267–88.

de la Porte, C. and Pochet, P. (2002) *Building Social Europe through the Open Method of Coordination.* Brussels: Presse Interuniversitaires Européennes.

Deacon, B. with Stubbs, P. and Hulse, M. (1997) *Global Social Policy: International Organisations and the Future of Welfare.* London: Sage.

Deacon, B. (1999) *Socially Responsible Globalization: A Challenge for the European Union.* Helsinki: Ministry for Social Affairs and Health.

Deacon, B. (2000a) 'Eastern European Welfare States: The Impact of The Politics of Globalization', *Journal of European Social Policy*, 10: 146–61.

Deacon, B. (2000b) 'The Future for Social Policy in a Global Context: Why the South Now Needs to Take the Lead', *Futura*, 2000: 65–70.

Deacon, B. (2000c) *Globalization and Social Policy.* Geneva: UNRISD.

Deacon, B. (2001a) *The Social Dimension of Regionalism: A Constructive Alternative to Neo-liberal Globalisation.* Helsinki: GASPP.

Deacon, B. (2001b) 'Northern Input for South–South Dialogue on Social Policy', *Cooperation South*, (2): 66–78.

Deacon, B. (2001c) 'A North–South Dialogue on the Prospects for a Socially Progressive Globalisation', *Global Social Policy*, 1(2): 147.

Deacon, B. (2003) 'Global Social Governance Reform' in Deacon, B., Ollila, E., Koivusalo, M. and Stubbs, P. (eds), *Global Social Governance: Themes and Prospects.* Helsinki: Ministry for Foreign Affairs of Finland.

Deacon, B. (2005) 'From "Safety Nets" Back to "Universal Social Provision": Is the Global Tide Turing?', *Global Social Policy*, 5(1): 19–28.

Deacon, B. (2006) 'Global Social Policy Reform' in Utting, P. (ed.), *Reclaiming Development Agendas.* Basingstoke: Palgrave.

Delanty, G. (2000) *Citizenship in a Global Age.* Buckingham: Open University Press.

Delmonica, E. and Mehrotra, S. (2006) *Eliminating World Poverty: Social and Macro-Economic Policy for the Millennium Goals.* London: Zed Press.

Dervis, K. (2005) *A Better Globalization: Legitimacy, Governance, and Reform.* Washington, DC: Centre for Global Development.

Desai, M. (2005) 'Social Democracy as World Panacea?' in Held, D. (ed.), *Debating Globalization.* Cambridge: Polity.

Desai, M., Holland, F. and Kaldor, M. (2006) 'The Movement of Labour and Global Civil Society' in Glasius, M., Kaldor, M. and Anheier, A.H. (eds.), *Global Civil Society 2005/6.* London: Sage.

Devetak, R. and Higgott, R. (1999) 'Justice Unbound? Globalization, States and The Transformation of the Social Bond', *International Affair*, 73: 483–98.

Dinello, N. (2004) 'Cairo Consensus: Reforms as a Path to Equitable Globalization', *Global Social Policy*, 4: 9–26.

Dinello, N. and Squire, L. (2005) *Globalisation and Equity: Perspectives from the Developing World*. Cheltenham: Edward Elgar.

Dodgson, D. (2000) 'Contesting Neo-liberal Globalisation at UN Global Conferences: The Women's Health Movement, United Nations and the International Conference on Population and Development', *Global Society*, 14: 443–63.

Dollar, D. and Kraay, A. (2001) *Trade, Growth and Poverty*. Washington, DC: World Bank Development Research Group.

Dolowitz, D. and Marsh, D. (1996) 'Who Learns What from Whom: A Review of the Policy Transfer Literature', *Political Studies*, 44: 343–57.

Drahos, P. and Braithwaite, J. (2002) *Information Feudalism: Who Owns the Knowledge Economy?* London: Earthscan.

Drahos, P. and Braithwaite, J. (2004) *Who Owns the Knowledge Economy? Political Organising Behind Trips*. Sturminster Newton: The Corner House.

Edelman, M. (2003) 'Transnational Peasant and Farmer Movements and Networks' in Kaldor, M., Anheier, A. and Glasius, M. (eds), *Global Civil Society*. Oxford: Oxford University Press.

Education International (2006) 'GATS: Education Is a Right Not a Commodity'. www.ei-ie.org

Ehrenreich, B. and Hoschschild, A.R. (2002) *Global Women: Nannies, Maids, and Sex Workers in the New Economy*. New York: Metropolitan Books.

Einhorn, J. (2006) 'Reforming the World Bank', *Foreign Affairs*, Jan-Feb.

Ellerman, D. (2005a) 'Can the World Bank Be Fixed', *Post-Autistic Economics Review*, 33: 2–16.

Ellerman, D. (2005b) *Helping People Help Themselves: From the World Bank to an Alternative Philosophy of Development Assistance*. Ann Arbor, MI: University of Michigan Press.

Elliott, L. (2005) 'Africa's Time Has Come and May Have Gone', *Guardian*.

Elson, D. (2002) 'Gender Justice, Human Rights, and Neo-liberal Economic Policies' in Molyneux, M. and Razavi, S. (eds), *Gender Justice, Development and Human Rights*. Oxford: Oxford University Press.

Emmerij, L., Jolly, R. and Weiss, T. (2001) *Ahead of the Curve: UN Ideas and Global Challenges*. Indianapolis, IN: Indiana University Press.

Emmerij, L., Jolly, R. and Weiss, T. (2006) 'Generating Knowledge in the United Nations' in Utting, P. (ed.), *Reclaiming Development Agendas*. Basingstoke: Palgrave.

Ervik, R. (2005) 'The Battle for Future Pensions: Global Accounting Tools, International Organisations and Pension Reform', *Global Social Policy* 5: 29–54.

Esping-Andersen, G. (1990) *The Three Worlds of Welfare*. Cambridge: Polity.

Esty, D.C. (1994) *Greening the Gatt: Trade, Environment and the Future*. Washington, DC: Institute for International Economics.

Eurodad (2006) 'EU Aid Effectiveness Package'. www.eurodad.org

Fabian Globalisation Group (2005) *Just World: A Fabian Manifesto*. London: Zed Books.

Falk, R. (1995) *On Humane Governance: Towards a New Global Polity*. Cambridge: Polity.

Falk, R. (2002) 'The United Nations System: Prospects for Renewal' in Nayyar, D. (ed.), *Governing Globalization*. Oxford: Oxford University Press.

Farnsworth, K. (2004) *Corporate Power and Social Policy in a Global Economy*. Bristol: Policy Press.

Farnsworth, K. (2005) 'International Class Conflict and Social Policy', *Social Policy and Society*, 4: 217–26.

Farrell, M. (2004) *The EU and Inter-regional Cooperation: In Search of Global Presence*. Bruges: United Nations University, Centre for Regional Integration Studies.

Farrell, M., Hettne, B. and van Langenhove, L. (2005) *Global Politics of Regionalism*. London: Pluto.

Felice, W. (1999) 'The Viability of the United Nations Approach to Economic and Social Human Rights in a Globalized Economy', *International Affairs*, 75: 563–98.

Ferguson, C. (1998a) *A Review of UK Company Codes of Conduct*. London: UKDFID.

Ferguson, C. (1998b) *Codes of Conduct for Business*. London: UKDFID.

Ferguson, C. (1999) *Global Social Policy Principles: Human Rights and Social Justice*. London: Department for International Development.

Focus on the Global South (2005) 'The Derailers' Guide to the WTO', Focusweb. www.focusweb.org

Foster, J.W. (2005) 'Governing Globalization–Globalizing Governance: New Approaches to Problem Solving', Report of the Helsinki Process on Globalization, Helsinki. www.helsinkiprocess.fi

Foster, J.W. (2006) *Report of Paris Ministerial Conference on Innovative Financing Mechanisms*. Geneva: North–South Institute.

Fues, T. (2006) 'The Prerequisite in Development: System-wide Coherence', World Economy and Development Brief 8. www.world-economy-and-development.org

Fumo, C., de Haan, A., Holland, J. and Kanji, N. (2000) *Social Funds: Effective Instruments to Support Local Action for Poverty Reduction*, Social Development Department Working Papers No.5. London: UKDFID.

GASPP (2005) 'Copenhagen Social Summit Ten Years On', *GASPP Policy Brief 6*. Helsinki: STAKES.

George, V. and Wilding, P. (2002) *Globalization and Human Welfare*. Basingstoke: Palgrave.

German Development Institute (2006) 'L20 and ECOSOC Reform', Briefing Paper 6/(2005). Bonn: German Development Institute.

German, T. and Randel, J. (2002) 'Reality of Aid 2002 Report', IBON Foundation. www.realityofaid.org

Ghigliani, D. (2003) *International Trade Unionism in a Globalising World: A Case Study*. The Hague: Institute of Social Studies.

Gilbert, C. and Vine, D. (2000) *World Bank: Structure and Policies*. Cambridge: Cambridge University Press.

Gillion, C., Turner, J. and Bailey, J. (2000) *Social Security, Pensions: Development and Reform*. Geneva: ILO.

Ginsburg, N. (1992) *Divisions of Welfare*. London: Sage.

Ginsburg, N. (2004) 'Structured Diversity: A Framework for Critically Comparing Welfare States?' in Kennet, P. (ed.), *A Handbook of Comparative Social Policy*. Cheltenham: Edward Elgar.

Girvan, N. (2006) 'The Search for Policy Autonomy in the Global South' in Utting, P. (ed.), *Reclaiming Development Agendas*. Basingstoke: Palgrave.

Glasius, M., Kaldor, M. and Anheier, H. (2006) *Global Civil Society 2005/6*. London: Sage.

Glatzer, M. and Rueschemeyer, D. (2005) *Globalization and the Future of the Welfare State*. Pittsburgh, PA: University of Pittsburgh Press.

Global Fund (2003) 'Guidlines for Proposals'. www.theglobalfund.org/en/apply/proposals

Global Fund (2005) www.theglobalfund.org (accessed 1 July 2005).

Global Health Watch (2005) *Global Health Watch 2005–2006*. London: Zed Books.

Global Policy Forum (2004) 'Global Compact Counter Summit'. www.globalpolicy.org

Goodin, R., Heady, B., Muffels, R. and Dirven, H. (1999) *The Real Worlds of Welfare*. Cambridge: Cambridge University Press.

Goodman, R., White, G. and Kwon, H. (1998) *The East Asian Welfare Model*. London: Routledge.

Gore, C. (2000) 'The Rise and Fall of the Washington Consensus as a Paradigm for Developing Countries'. *World Development*, 28: 789–804.

Gore, C. (2004) 'MDGs and PRSPs: Are Poor Countries Enmeshed in a Global-local Double Bind?', *Global Social Policy*, 4: 277–83.

Gottret, P. and Schieber, G. (2006) *Health Financing Revisited*. Washington, DC: World Bank.

Gough, I. (1979) *The Political Economy of the Welfare State*. Basingstoke: Macmillan.

Gough, I. and Woods, G. (2004) *Insecurity and Welfare Regimes in Asia, Africa and Latin America*. Cambridge: Cambridge University Press.

Gould, J. (2005) *The New Conditionality: The Politics of Poverty Reduction Strategies*. London: Zed Books.

Graham C. (1994) *Safety Nets, Politics and the Poor*. Washington, DC: Brookings Institute.

Grinspun, A. (2001) *Choices for the Poor*. New York: UNDP.

GSP Digest (2006a) 'GSP Digest', *Global Social Policy*, 6: 2.

GSP Digest (2006b) 'GSP Digest', *Global Social Policy*, 6: 1.

Haas, P. (1992) 'Introduction: Epistemic Communities and International Policy Coordination', *International Organisations*, 46: 1–35.

Hakkinen, U. (2000) 'Assessment of the Goal Attainment and Efficiency of Health Systems in the World Health Report 2000' in Hakkinen, U. and Ollila, E. (eds), *The World Health Report (2000): What Does It Tell Us about Health Systems?* Helsinki: STAKES.

Hakkinen, U. and Ollila, E. (2000) 'The World Health Report: What Does It Tell Us about Health Systems?', *Themes from Finland*. Helsinki: STAKES.

Hall, A. and Midgley, J. (2004) *Social Policy for Development*. London: Sage.

Hall, R. and Biersteker, T. (2002) *The Emergence of Private Authority in Global Governance*. Cambridge: Cambridge University Press.

Haq, M. (1998) 'The Case for an Economic Security Council' in Paolini, A.J. and Jarvis, A.P. (eds), *Between Sovereignty and Global Governance*. Basingstoke: Macmillan.

Hardt, M. (2002) 'Porto Alegre: Today's Bandung', *New Left Review*, 14: 112–18.

Hardt, M. and Negri, A. (2000) *Empire*. Cambridge, MA: Harvard University Press.

Hardy, D. (1991) *Soft Budget Constraints, Firm Commitments and the Social Safety Net*. Washington, DC: IMF.

Heidenheimer, H., Heclo, H. and Adams, C. (1991) *Comparative Public Policy*. New York: St Martin's.

Hein, W. and Kohlmorgan, L. (2005) 'Global Health Governance: Conflicts on Global Social Rights', German Overseas Development Institute. www.duei.de/workingpapers

Held, D. (2000) 'The Changing Contours of Political Community: Rethinking Democracy in the Context of Globalization' in Holden, B. (ed.), *Global Democracy Key Debates*. London: Routledge.

Held, D. (2004) *Global Covenant: The Social Democratic Alternative to the Washington Consensus*. Cambridge: Polity.

Held, D. (2005) *Debating Globalization*. Cambridge: Polity.

Held, D. and McGrew, A. (2002a) *Globalization/Anti-globalization*. Cambridge: Polity.

Held, D. and McGrew, A. (2002b) *Governing Globalization*. Cambridge: Polity.

Held, D., McGrew, A., Goldblatt, D. and Perrit, J. (1999) *Global Transformations*. Cambridge: Polity.

Helsinki Process on Globalisation and Democracy (2005) 'Mobilising Political Will'. www.helsinkiprocess.fi

Helton, A. (2003) 'People Movement: The Need for a World Migration Organisation', Open Democracy. www.opendemocracy.net

Henry, M., Lingard, B., Rizvi, F. and Taylor, S. (2001) *The OECD, Globalization and Education Policy*. London: Pergamon.

Hettne, B., Inotai, A. and Sunkel, O. (1999) *Globalism and the New Regionalism*. Basingstoke: Macmillan.

High-Level Advisory Group (2000) 'Report of the High-Level Advisory Group of Eminent Personalities and Intellectuals on Globalization and its Impact on Developing Countries'. Uruguay: Social Watch.

Hilary, J. (2005) 'DFID, UK and Public Services Privatization: Time for a Change', *Global Social Policy*, 5: 134–6.

Hines, C. (2000) *Localization: A Global Manifesto*. London: Earthscan.

Holden, C. (2002) 'The Internationalization of Long-term Care Provision: Economics and Strategy', *Global Social Policy*, 2(1), 47–67.

Holden, C. (2005a) 'Organizing Across Borders: Profit and Quality in Internationalized Providers', *International Social Work*, 48(5), 185–203.

Holden, C. (2005b) 'Global Social Policy and the Development of the Welfare State', Global Poverty and Global Justice Conference, 7–9 September, Newcastle.

Holden, C. (2006) 'Regulation, Accountability and Trade in Health Services', unpublished manuscript.

Holliday, I. (2000) 'Productivist Welfare Capitalism and Social Policy in East Asia', *Political Studies*, 48 (4): 706–23.

Holzmann, R. (1999) *The World Bank Approach to Pension Reform*. Washington, DC: World Bank, Social Protection Advisory Service.

Holzmann, R. and Jorgensen, B.N. (1999) *Social Protection as Risk Management*. Washington, DC: Human Development Net, World Bank.

Holzmann, R., Koettl, J. and Chernetsky, T. (2005) *Portability Regimes of Pension and Health Care Benefits for International Migrants: An Analysis of Good Practice*. Washington, DC: Human Development Network, World Bank.

Holzmann, R., Orenstein, M. and Rutowski, M. (2003) *Pension Reform in Europe: Process and Progress*. Washington, DC: World Bank.

Hurrell, A. and Woods, N. (1999) *Inequality, Globalization and World Politics*. Oxford: Oxford University Press.

ILO (1995) *Report of the Director General: Fifth European Regional Conference*. Geneva: ILO.

ILO (2001) *Social Security: Issues, Challenges, Prospects*. Geneva: ILO.

ILO (2004a) *Economic Security for a Better World*. Geneva: ILO.

ILO (2004b) *A Fair Globalization: The Role of the ILO*. Geneva: ILO.

ILO (2004c) *A Fair Globalization: Creating Opportunities for All*, Report of the World Commission on the Social Dimension of Globalization. Geneva: ILO.

IMF (1992) 'Statement by IMF on the Realization of Economic, Social and Cultural Rights', (E/CN.4/Sub.2/1992/57). Washington DC: International Monetary Fund.

IMF (1995) *Social Dimensions of Change: The IMF's Policy Dialogue*. Washington DC: International Monetary Fund.

IMF (1998) 'Equity and Economic Growth', Conference Background Paper. Washington, DC: International Monetary Fund.

IMF (2001a) 'Social Dimensions of the IMF's Policy Dialogue: Fact Sheet'. www.imf.org/external/np/exr/facts/social.htm

IMF (2001b) 'Social Impact Analysis of Economic Policies: Fact Sheet'.www.imf.org/external/np/exr/facts/sia.htm

Jacobs, M., Lent, A. and Watkins, K. (2003) *Progressive Globalisation: Towards an International Social Democracy*. London: Fabian Society.

James, E. (2005) 'How It's Done in Chile', *Washington Post*, 13 February.

Jobbins, D. (2005) 'Will GATS Be Good for Global Quality?', *Times Higher Education Supplement*, 11 November: 10.

Jolly, R. (1991) 'Adjustment with a Human Face: A UNICEF Record and Perspective on the 1980s'. *World Development*, 19: 1807–21.

Jolly, R., Emmerij, L. and Weiss, T. (2005) *The Power of UN Ideas: Lessons from the First Sixty Years*. Indianapolis, IN: Indiana University Press.

Jomo, K.S. (1998) *Tigers in Trouble: Financial Governance, Liberalisation and Crises in East Asia*. London: Zed Press.

Jordan, B. and Duvell, F. (2003) *Migration: The Boundaries of Equality and Justice*. Cheltenham: Edward Elgar.

Josselin, D. and Wallace, W. (2001) *Non-state Actors in World Politics*. Basingstoke: Palgrave.

Kaldor, M. (2003) *Global Civil Society*. Cambridge: Polity.

Kanbur, R. and Vine, D. (2000) 'The World Bank and Poverty Reduction: Past, Present and Future' in Gilbert, C. and Vine, D. (eds), *World Bank: Structure and Policies*. Cambridge: Cambridge University Press.

Kangas, O. and Palme, J. (2005) *Social Policy and Economic Development in the Nordic Countries*. Basingstoke: Palgrave.

Kaul, I., Grunberg, I. and Stern, M. (1999) *Global Public Goods: International Cooperation in the 21st Century*. Oxford: Oxford University Press.

Kaul, I., Conceicao, P., Goulven, K. and Mendoza, R. (2003) *Providing Global Public Goods*. Oxford: Oxford University Press.

Keet, D. and Bello, W. (2004) *Linking Alternative Regionalisms for Equitable and Sustainable Development*. Amsterdam: Transnational Institute.

Kell, G. and Levin, D. (2002) 'The Evolution of the Global Compact Network', Academy of Management Annual Conference, Building Effective Networks, Colorado, 11–14 August.

Kennet, P. (2001) *Comparative Social Policy: Theory and Practice*. Buckingham: Open University Press.

Kennet, P. (2004) *A Handbook of Comparative Social Policy*. Cheltenham: Edward Elgar.

Khor, M. (2000) *Globalization and the South: Some Critical Issues*. Penang: Third World Network.

Khor, M. (2001) *Rethinking Globalization: Critical Issues and Policy Choices*. London: Zed Press.

Khor, M. (2006) 'UN Reform Process Hotting Up', South–North Development Monitor. www.globalpolicy.org/reform

Killick, T. and Malik, M. (1991) 'Country Experiences with IMF Programmes in the 1980s, *ODI Working Paper 47*. London: ODI.

King, K. (2005) 'Knowledge-based Aid: A New Way of Networking or a New North–South divide?' in Stone, D. and Maxwell, S. (eds), *Global Knowledge Networks and International Development*. London: Routledge.

King, K. (2006) 'Knowledge Management and the Global Agenda for Education' in Utting, P. (ed.), *Reclaiming Development Agendas*. Basingstoke: Palgrave.

Koenig-Archbugi, M. (2002) 'Mapping Global Governance' in Held, D. and McGrew, A. (eds), *Governing Globalization*. Cambridge: Polity.

Koivusalo, M. and Ollila, E. (1997) *Making a Healthy World: Agencies, Actors and Policies in International Health*. London: Zed Press.

Kopits, G. (1993) 'Towards Cost-Effective Social Security Systems' in ISSA (ed.), *The Implications for Social Security Policies of Structural Adjustment*. Geneva: ISSA.

Kopits, G. (1994) 'Social Security in Economies in Transition', *Restructuring Social Security in Central and Eastern Europe*. Geneva: ISSA.

Korpi, W. (1983) *The Democratic Class Struggle*. London: Routledge and Kegan Paul.

Krajewski, M. (2003) 'Public Services and Trade Liberalisation: Mapping the Legal Framework', *Journal of International Economic Law*, 6: 341–67.

Kuptsch, C. (2006) *Merchants of Labour*. Geneva: ILO's International Institute for Labour Studies.

Kwon, H. (2001) 'Globalisation, Unemployment and Policy Responses in Korea: Repositioning the State', *Global Social Policy*, 1(1): 213–34.

Kwon, H. (2004) *Transforming the Developmental Welfare State in East Asia*. Basingstoke: Palgrave.

Langmore, J. (2001) 'The UN Commission for Social Development, February 2001: An Opportunity for International Political Evolution', *Global Social Policy*, 1(3): 277–80.

Lee, S. (2002) 'Global Monitor: The IMF', *New Political Economy*, 7(2): 283–98.

Lee, K. (2003) *Globalization and Health*. Basingstoke: Palgrave.

Lee, K., Buse, K. and Fustukian, S. (2002) *Health Policy in a Globalising World*. Cambridge: Cambridge University Press.

Lethbridge, J. (2002) 'Venture Capital and Private Equity Investments in Health Care', GASPP Seminar No.5, Dubrovnik, 26–28 September.

Lethbridge, J. (2004) 'Investment Strategies Underpinning Policy Promotion', GASPP Seminar No.7, Hamilton, 10–11 September.

Lethbridge, J. (2005) 'The Promotion of Investment Alliances by the World Bank: Implications for National Health Policy', *Global Social Policy*, 5: 203–226.

Linklater, A. (1999) 'The Evolving Sphere of International Justice', *International Affairs*, 75: 473–82.

Lotse, C. (2006) 'Brief Summary of Discussions at UNICEF ROSA/UNRISD/UNICEF IRC Workshop on Social Policy', Kathmandu, 24–25 May.

MacGregor, K. (2005) 'South Africa Claims Free Trade Will Undermine National Values', *Times Higher Education Supplement*, 11 November.

Mackintosh, M. and Koivusalo, M. (2005) *Commercialization of Health Care*. Basingstoke: Palgrave.

Marcussen, M. (2001) 'The OECD in Search of a Role: Playing the Ideas Game', Paper presented to the European Consortium for Political Research, Grenoble, April.

Marshall, K. and Butzbach, O. (2003) *New Social Policy Agendas for Europe and Asia*. Washington, DC: World Bank.

Martens, J. (2003) *The Future of Multilateralism after Monterrey and Johannesburg*. Berlin: Friedrich Ebert Stiftung Foundation.

Martens, J. (2005) *In Larger Freedom*. Berlin: Friedrich Ebert Stiftung Foundation.

Martin, P. (2006) 'Forming Clubs in Order to Enhance Efficiency: G20 and L20 as the main committee of world politics', Speech delivered at Multilateralism in Transition: Fragmentation, Informalisation and Networking Conference, Dresden, 8–9 June.

Martin, P., Abella, M. and Kuptsch, C. (2006) *Managing Labour Migration in the Twenty-first Century*. Geneva: ILO.

Maxwell, S. (2005) 'How to Help Reform Multilateral Institutions', *Global Governance*,11(4): 415–24.

Mayo, M. (2005) *Global Citizens: Social Movements and the Challenge of Globalization*. London: Zed Press.

Mehrotra, S. (2006) 'Job Law with Right to Information Can Cut Poverty in India', *Poverty in Focus*, June: 13–14.

Mehrotra, S. and Delmonica, E. (2005) 'The Private Sector and Privatization in Social Services: Is the Washington Consensus Dead?', *Global Social Policy*, 5: 141–74.

Mehrotra, S. and Jolly, R. (1997) *Development with a Human Face*. Oxford: Clarendon.

Mertus, J. (2005) *The United Nations and Human Rights: A Guide for a New Era*. London and New York: Routledge.

Meyer, J., Frank, D., Hironaka, A. and Tuma, N. (1997) 'The Structuring of a World Environmental Regime 1870–1970', *International Organisations*, 51(4): 623–51.

Milanovic, B. (2003) 'The Two Faces of Globalization: Against Globalization as We Know It', *World Development*, 31(4): 667–83.

Mishra, R. (1999) *Globalization and the Welfare State*. Cheltenham: Edward Elgar.

Mkandawire, T. (2004) *Social Policy in a Development Context*. Basingstoke: Palgrave.

Mkandawire, T. (2006) 'Targeting and Universalism in Poverty Reduction', *Poverty in Focus*, June: 3–5.

Monbiot, G. (2003) *The Age of Consent: A Manifesto for a New World Order*. London: Flamingo.

Munck, R. (2005) *Globalization and Social Exclusion*. Bloomfield, CT: Kumarian Press.

Nayak, S. (2003) *Monopolisation of Global Public Goods? Emigration of Medical Personnel from the South to the North*. Birmingham: Centre for Development Studies.

Nayyar, D. (2002) *Governing Globalization: Issues and Institutions*. Oxford: Oxford University Press.

Neill, S. (2005) 'G77 and China: Statement by HE Stafford Neill, Permanent Representative of Jamaica, to the United Nations and Chairman of the Group of 77'. www.globalforum.org

Newland, K. (2005) *The Governance of International Migration: Mechanisms, Processes And Institutions*, Global Commission on Migration background paper, www.gcim.org.

Norton, A., Conway, T. and Foster, M. (2000) 'Social Protection: Defining the Field of Action and Policy', *Development Policy Review*, 20: 541–67.

Nuthall, K. (2005) 'Secret Offer to Open Markets', *Times Higher Education Supplement*, 11 November.

O'Brien, R., Goetz, A.M., Scholte, J. and Williams, M. (2000) *Contesting Global Governance: Multilateral Economic Institutions and Global Social Movements*. Cambridge: Cambridge University Press.

O'Neill, O. (1991) 'Transnational Justice' in Held, D. (ed.), *Political Theory Today*. Cambridge: Polity.

Ocampo, J.A. (2006) 'Some Reflections on the Links between Social Knowledge and Social Affairs' in Utting, P. (ed.), *Reclaiming Development Agendas*. Basingstoke: Palgrave.

Ocampo, J.A. and Matin, J. (2003) *Globalization and Development: A Latin American and Caribbean Perspective*. Chile: Economic Commission for Latin America and the Carribean.

OECD (1981) *The Crisis of the Welfare State*. Paris: OECD.

OECD (1988) *Reforming Public Pensions*. Paris: OECD.

OECD (1990) *Health Care Systems in Transition*. Paris: OECD.

OECD (1991) *A Study of the Soviet Economy*. Paris: OECD with IMF, EBRD and World Bank.

OECD (1993) *Economic Integration, OECD Economies, Dynamic Asian Economies and Central and Eastern Europe*. Paris: OECD.

OECD (1994) *New Orientations for Social Policy*. Paris: OECD.

OECD (1997) *Shaping the 21st Century: The Contribution of Development Co-operation*. Paris: OECD Development Assistance Committee.

OECD (1998a) *Harmful Tax Competition: An Emerging Issue*. Paris: OECD.

OECD (1998b) *Pathways and Participation in Vocational and Technical Education*. Paris: OECD.

OECD (1999) *A Caring World: The New Social Policy Agenda*. Paris: OECD.

OECD (2000) *Towards Global Tax Co-operation: Progress in Identifying and Eliminating Harmful Tax Practices*. Paris: OECD.

OECD (2001a) *Report on the Operation of the OECD Guidelines for Multinational Enterprises*. Paris: OECD.

OECD (2001b) *Guidelines on Development Cooperation and Poverty Reduction*. Paris: OCED Development Assistance Committee.

OECD (2002a) *Ageing Societies and the Looming Pension Crisis*. Paris: OECD.

OECD (2002b) *Private Pensions Series No.4. Regulating Private Pension Schemes: Trends and Challenges*. Paris: OECD.

OECD (2004a) *Towards High-Performing Health Systems*. Paris: OECD.

OECD (2004b) *Private Health Insurance in OECD Countries*. Paris: OECD.

OECD (2004c) *The OECD's Project on Harmful Tax Practices: 2004 Progress Report*. Paris: OECD.

OECD (2005a) *Extending Opportunities: How Active Social Policy Can Benefit Us All*. Paris: OECD.

OECD (2005b) *Pensions at a Glance: Public Policies across OECD Countries*. Paris: OECD.

OECD (2005c) 'The UN Global Compact and the OCED Guidelines for Multi-national Enterprises: Complementarities and Distinctive Contributions'. www.oecd.org/investment

OECD (2005d) Sweden (2005) *DAC Peer Review: Main Findings and Recommendations*: Paris: OECD, Development Assistance Committee.

OECD (2005e) *Paris Declaration on Aid Effectiveness*. Paris: OECD:DAC.

OECD (2005f) 'The OECD's Project on Harmful Tax Practice'. www.oecd.org/ctp

OECD (2006a) 'Babies and Bosses: Balancing Work and Family Life', Briefing Paper. Paris: OECD.

OECD (2006b) *Promoting Pro-poor Growth-overarching*, Paper. Paris: OECD: DAC Network on Poverty Reduction (DCD/DAC/POVNET(2005)/REV1 27 January.

OECD (2006c) *Boosting Jobs and Incomes: Policy Lessons from Reassessing the Jobs Strategy*. Paris: OECD.

OECD 2002, 2003, 2004, 2005 (2006c) *Babies and Bosses: Reconciling Work and Family Life*, Volumes 1, 2, 3, 4 and Summary Conclusions. Paris: OECD.

Ollila, E. (2003) 'Health-related Public–Private Partnerships and the United Nations' in Deacon, B., Ollila, E., Koivusalo, M. and Stubbs, P. (eds), *Global Social Governance: Themes and Prospects*. Helsinki: Ministry for Foreign Affairs of Finland.

Open Society Institute (2005) *Restoring American Leadership: Cooperative Steps to Advance Global Progress*. Washington, DC: Open Society Institute.

Orenstein, M. (2003) 'Mapping the Diffussion of Pension Innovation' in Holzmann, R., Orenstein, M. and Rutowski, M. (eds), *Pension Reform in Europe*. Washington, DC: World Bank.

Orenstein, M. (2004) 'The New Pension Reform: Global Policy and Democratic Deliberation', *GASPP Seminar No.7 Hamilton, 9–11 September*.

Orenstein, M. (2005) 'The New Pension Reform as Global Policy', *Global Social Policy*, 5: 175–202.

Orszag, P. and J. Stiglitz. (1999) 'Rethinking Pension Reform: Ten Myths About Social Security Systems', Conference on New Ideas About Old Age Security. World Bank, Washington, DC 14–15 September.

Ortiz, I. (2006) *Social Policy Guidance Notes*. New York: UNDESA and UNDP. (June Draft.)

Oxfam (2005) 'Gleneagles: What Really Happened at the G8 Summit?' London: Oxfam Briefing Notes.

Page, S. (2000a) 'GDN Governance E-discussion'. www.worldbank.worldbank.org/hm/hmgdnet

Page, S. (2000b) *Regionalism among Developing Countries*. Basingstoke: Macmillan.

Pagrotsky, L. (2001) *A More Equitable Globalisation*. Stockholm: Ministry of Trade.

Pal, K., Behrendt, C., Leger, F., Cichon, M. and Hagemejer, K. (2005) *Can Low-income Countries Afford Basic Social Protection?* Geneva: ILO Social Security Department.

Parmar, I. (2002) 'American Foundations and the Development of International Knowledge Networks', *Global Networks*, 2: 13–30.

Patomaki, H. (1998) *Beyond Nordic Nostalgia: Envisaging a Social Democratic System of Global Governance*. Helsinki: Network Institute for Global Democracy.

Patomaki, H. (2001) *Democratising Globalisation: The Leverage of the Tobin Tax*. London: Zed Press.

Patomaki, H. and Denys, L. (2002) *Draft Treaty on Global Currency Transaction Tax*. Nottingham: Network Institute for Global Democratization.

Patomaki, H. and Teivainen, T. (2004) *A Possible World: Democratic Transformation of Global Institutions*. London: Zed Press.

Patomaki, H. and Teivainen, T. (2005) 'The Post-Porto Alegre World Social Forum: An Open Space or a Movement of Movements'. www.forumsocialmundial.org

Pearson, R. and Seyfang, G. (2001) 'New Hope or False Dawn: Voluntary Codes of Conduct, Labour Regulation and Social Policy in a Globalising World', *Global Social Policy*, 1(1): 49–78.

Pijl, K. van der (2003) 'Two Modes of Capitalist Incorporation', *Historical Materialism*, 11(3): 201–13.

Plant, R. (1994) 'Labour Standards and Structural Adjustment in Hungary', Occasional Paper 7, Project on Structural Adjustment. Geneva: ILO.

Pogge, T. (2002) *World Poverty and Human Rights*. Cambridge: Polity.

Pollock, A. and Price, D. (2000) 'Rewriting the Regulations', *Lancet*, 356.

Porta, D., Kriesi, H. and Rucht, D. (1999) *Social Movements in a Globalizing World*. Basingstoke: Macmillan.

Public Services International (1998) 'Transnationals in Public Services'. www.psi-int.org

Ramesh, M. and Asher, M. (2000) *Welfare Capitalism in South East Asia*. Basingstoke: Macmillan.

Rao, V. and Walton, M. (2004) *Culture and Public Action*. Stanford, CT: Stanford University Press.

Razavi, S. and Hassim, S. (2006) *Gender and Social Policy in a Global Context*. Basingstoke: Palgrave.

Reisen, M. van (1999) *EU 'Global Player': The North–South Policy of the European Union*. Utrecht: International Books.

Reynaud, E. (2002) *The Extension of Social Security Coverage: The Approach of the International Labour Office*. Geneva: ILO, Social Security Policy and Development Branch.

Richter, J. (2004a) *Public–Private Partnerships and International Health Policy*. Helsinki: Ministry for Foreign Affairs of Finland.

Richter, J. (2004b) *Building on Quicksand: The Global Compact, Democratic Governance and Nestlé*. Geneva and Zurich: CETIM, IBFAN/GIFA and Berne Declaration.

Rieger, E. (2005) 'The Wonderous Politics of Global Ideas', *Global Social Policy*, 5: 8–14.

Rieger, E. and Leibfried, S. (2003) *Limits to Globalization*. Cambridge: Polity.

Rimlinger, G. (1971) *Welfare Policy and Industrialisation in Europe, America and Russia*. New York: Wiley.

Rischard, J. (2002) *High Noon: Twenty Global Issues and Twenty Years to Solve Them*. Oxford: Perseus.

Roberts, M.J., Hsiao, W., Berman, P. and Reich, M.R. (2003) *Getting Health Reform Right: Guidelines for Improving Performance and Equity*. Oxford: Oxford University Press.

Roodman, D. (2005) 'The 2005 Commitments to Development: Components and Results', Centre for Global Development. www.cgdev.org

Room, G. (2004) 'Multi-tiered International Welfare Systems' in Gough, I. and Woods, G. (eds.), *Insecurity and Welfare Regimes in Asia, Africa and Latin America*. Cambridge: Cambridge University Press.

Rosenau, J. (1997) *Along the Domestic–Foreign Frontier*. Cambridge: Cambridge University Press.

Sachs, J. (2005) *The End of Poverty*. London: Penguin.

Sainsbury, D. (1994) *Gendering Welfare States*. London: Sage.

Saltman, R.B. and Buse, R. (2002) 'Balancing Regulation and Entrpreneurialism in Europe's Health Sector' in Saltman, R.B, Busse, R. and Mossialos, E. (eds.), *Regulating Entrepreneurial Behaviour in European Healthcare Systems*. Buckingham: Open University Press.

Sands, P. (2005) *Lawless World: America and the Making and Breaking of Global Rules*. London: Allen Lane.

Scharpf, F. and Schimdt, V. (2000) *Welfare and Work in the Open Economy*. Oxford: Oxford University Press.

Schechter, M. (2005) *United Nations Global Conferences*. London: Routledge.

Scherrer, C. (2002) 'The Globalization of Higher Education: The Trade Regime Dimension', GASPP Seminar Number 5: The Emerging Global Markets in Social Protection and Health, University Centre, Dubrovnik, 26–8 September.

Scholte, J. (2005) *Globalizations: A Critical Introduction*. Basingstoke: Palgrave.

Scholte, J. and Schnabel, A. (2002) *Civil Society and Global Finance*. London: Routledge.

Scholvinck, J. (2004) 'Global Governance: The World Commission on the Social Dimension of Globalisation', *Social Development Review*, 8: 8–11.

Schroeder, F. (2006) 'Innovative Sources of Finance After the Paris Conference': Friedrich Ebert Stiftung Dialogue on Globalization. Berlin: FES.

Sen, A. (1999) *Development as Freedom*. New York: Knopf.

Sen, G. (2004) 'The Relationship of Research and Activism in the Making of Policy: Lessons from Gender and Development', UNRISD Conference on Social Knowledge and International Policy Making, Geneva, 20–1 April.

Sen, G. (2006) 'The Quest for Gender Equality' in Utting, P. (ed.), *Reclaiming Development Agendas*. Basingstoke: Palgrave.

Sen, J., Arnand, A., Escobar, A. and Waterman, P. (2004) *World Social Forum: Challenging Empires*. New Delhi: Viveka Foundation.

Sexton, S. (2001) *Trading Health Care Away? GATS, Public Services and Privatisation*. Sturminster Newton: The Corner House.

Shakow, A. (2006) 'Global Fund–World Bank HIV/AIDS Programs: Comparative Advantage Study', Centre for Global Development. www.cgdev.org

Siarrof, A. (1994) 'Work, Welfare and Gender Equality: A New Typology' in Sainsbury, D. (ed.), *Gendering Welfare States*. London: Sage.

Siddiqui, J. (1995) *World Health and World Politics*. London: Hurst.

Sigg, R. and Behrendt, C. (2002) *Social Security in the Global Village*. New Brunswick, NJ: Transaction.

Silvey, R. (2004) 'Intervention Symposium: Geographies of Anti-sweatshop Activism', *Antipode*, 36: 191–7.

Singh, A. and Zammit, A. (2000) *The Global Labour Standards Controversy*. Geneva: South Centre.

Sklair, L. (2002) *Globalization: Capitalism and Its Alternatives*. Oxford: Oxford University Press.

Soederberg, S. (2006) *Global Governance in Question*. London: Pluto.

Solimano, A. (2001) 'International Migration and the Global Economic Order', World Bank Working Paper no 2720. Washington, DC: World Bank.

Soros, G. (2002) *On Globalization*. Oxford: Public Affairs.

St Clair, A. (2006) 'Global Poverty: The Co-production of Knowledge and Politics', *Global Social Policy*, 6: 57–78.

Standing, G. (2002) *Beyond the New Paternalism: Basic Security as Equality*. London: Verso.

Stean, J. (2005) 'The Potential and Problems of Human Rights and "Humane" Governance', ESRC Workshop on Alternatives to Neo-liberal Globalisation, University of Sheffield, February.

Stern, S. and Seligmann, E. (2004) *The Partnership Principle: New Forms of Governance in the 21st Century*. London: Archetype.

Stiglitz, J. (1998) 'More Instruments and Broader Goals: Moving Towards the Post-Washington Consensus', WIDER Annual Lecture, Helsinki, 7 January.

Stone, D. (2000) *Banking on Knowledge: The Genesis of the Global Development Network*. London: Routledge.

Stone, D. (2001) 'Think-Tanks , Global Lesson-drawing and Networking Social Policy Ideas', *Global Social Policy*, 1(3): 338–60.

Stone, D. (2004) 'Better Knowledge, Better Policy, Better World: The Grand Ambitions of a Global Research Institution', *Global Social Policy*, 4: 5–8.

Stone, D. (2005) 'Knowledge Networks and Global Policy' in Stone, D. and Maxwell, S. (eds), *Global Knowledge Networks and International Development*. London: Routledge.

Stone, D. and Maxwell, S. (2005) *Global Knowledge Networks and International Development*. London: Routledge.

Stone, D. and Wright, C. (eds) (forthcoming) *The World Bank's Decade of Reform and Reaction*. London: Routledge.

Strang, D. and Chang, P. (1993) 'The ILO and the Welfare State: Institutional Effects on National Welfare Spending', *International Organisation*, 47.

Streck, C. (2002) 'Global Public Policy Networks as Coalitions for Change' in Esty, D. and Ivanova, M. (eds), *Global Environmental Governance: Options and Opportunities*. Yale, NJ: Yale University Press.

Stubbs, P. (2003) 'International Non-state Actors and Social Development Policy', *Global Social Policy*, 3(3): 319–48.

Stubbs, P. (2005) 'Multi-level Governance and Policy Transfer in South Eastern Europe', SEERC Workshop, Zagreb, 4–5 February.

Stubbs, P. (2006) 'Towards an Ethnography of Welfare Reform', Baltics to Balkans seminar, Bristol, 8 February.

Subbarao, D. and Bonnerjee, A. (1997) *Safety Net Programs and Poverty Reduction: Lessons from Cross-Country Experiences*. Washington, DC: World Bank.

Sundaram, J.K. (2006) 'Current UN Reforms and Its Implications for Social Policy Work', UNICEF ROSA UNRISD UNICEF IRC Workshop on Social Policy: Towards Universal Coverage and Transformation for Achieving the MDGs, Kathmandu, 24–5 May.

Swank, D. (2002) *Global Capital, Political Institutions, and Policy Change*. Cambridge: Cambridge University Press.

Sykes, R., Palier, B. and Prior, P. (2001) *Globalization and European Welfare States: Challenges and Change*. Basingstoke: Macmillan.

Szalai, J. (2005) 'Poverty Traps of Post-Communist Welfare Reform in Hungary: A Fourth World of Welfare Capitalism on the Rise?', International Sociological Association RC19: Retheorising Welfare States, Chicago, 8–10 September.

Tanzi, V. (1992) *Fiscal Policies in Economies in Transition*. Washington, DC: IMF.

Tanzi, V. (1993) 'Transition to Market: Studies in Fiscal Reform', Washington, DC: IMF.

Taylor, L. (2000) *Liberalisation, Economic Development and Social Policy*. Oxford: Oxford University Press.

Tendler, J. (2004) 'Why Social Policy Is Condemned to a Residual Category of Safety Nets and What to Do About It' in T. Mkandawire (ed.), *Social Policy in a Development Context*. Basingstoke: Palgrave.

Therborn, G. (2000) 'Globalizations: Dimensions, Historical Waves, Regional Effects, Normative Govenance', *International Sociology*, 15: 151–79.

Thomas, M. (2005) 'Migrant Labour, Citizenship and Social Provision in Comtemporary Welfare States', ISA Research Committee 19, Annual Conference, Chicago: North West University. September.

Thomas, S. (2000) 'Taking Religious and Cultural Pluralism Seriously: The Global Resurgence of Religion and the Transformation of International Society', *Millennium: Journal of International Studies*, 29: 815–41.

Thompson, G. (2005) 'Alternative Globalizations', Presentation at ESRC Seminar on Alternative Globalizations, Sheffield, April.

Threlfall, M. (2002) 'The European Union's Social Policy: From Labour to Welfare and Constitutionalised Rights?' in Sykes, R., Bochel, C. and Ellison, N. (eds), *Social Policy Review 14*. Bristol: Policy.

Titmuss, R. (1974) *Social Policy*. London: Allen and Unwin.

Townsend, P. (2004) 'From Universalism to Safety Nets: The Rise and Fall of Kenynesian Influence on Social Development' in Mkandawire, T. (ed.), *Social Policy in a Development Context*. Basingstoke: Palgrave.

Townsend, P. and Gordon, D. (2002) *World Poverty: New Policies to Defeat an Old Enemy*. Bristol: Policy.

Toye, J. and Toye, R. (2006) 'The World Bank as a Knowledge Bank' in Utting, P. (ed.), *Reclaiming Development Agendas*. Basingstoke: Palgrave.

Transnational Institute (2004) 'Report of Alternative Regionalisms Programme'. www.tni.org

Trogemann, G. (2006) 'Conference Verbal Contribution', Mulilateralism in Transition, The Development and Peace Foundation's Summer Dialogue, Dresden, 8–9 June.

UKDFID (2000a) *Realising Human Rights for Poor People*. London: Department for International Development.

UKDFID (2000b) *Making Globalisation Work for the World's Poor*. London: UKDFID.

UKDFID (2006a) *Eliminating World Poverty: Making Governance Work for the Poor*. London: UK Government, DFID.

UKDFID (2006b) 'DFID and the G8 Presidency 2005: Gleneagles Implementation Plan for Africa'.

UN Millennium Project (2005a) *Towards Universal Primary Education: Investments, Incentives, and Institutions: Task Force on Education and Gender Equality*. London: EarthScan.

UN Millennium Project (2005b) 'Investing in Development: A Practical Plan to Achieve the Millennium Development Goals. Overview'. New York: UNDP.

UN Millennium Project (2005c) 'Who's Got the Power? Transforming Health Systems for Women and Children. Summary Report of the Task Force on Child Health and Maternal Health.' New York: UNDP.

UN Secretary-General (2000) *We the Peoples: The Role of the United Nations in the 21st Century*. New York: United Nations Department of Public Information.

UN Secretary-General (2001) *Enhancing Social Protection and Reducing Vulnerability in a Globalizing World*. Commission for Social Development E/CN.5/2001/2. New York: UN Economic and Social Council.

UN Secretary-General (2002) *Strengthening the United Nations: An Agenda for Further Change (A/57/387)*. New York: United Nations.

UN Secretary-General (2004) *Improving Public Service Effectiveness*. Commission for Social Development. E/CN.5/2004/(2005). New York: United Nations, Economic and Social Council.

UN Secretary-General (2005a) *Review of the Further Implementation of the World Summit for Social Development and the Outcome of the 24th Session of the General Assembly: E/CN.5.2005/2006*. New York: United Nations: Economic and Social Council, Commission for Social Development.

UN Secretary-General (2005b) 'In Larger Freedom: Towards Development Security and Rights for All, Report to the UN summit 2005'. UN Doc A/59/(2005). New York: United Nations.

UN Secretary-General (2006a) 'Coherence, Coordination and Cooperation in the Context of the Implementation of the Monterrey Consensus and the 2005 World Summit Outcome'. New York: Note by Sec. Gen. for Special High Level Meeting of ECOSOC with the Bretton Woods institutions, WTO, UNCTAD.

UN Secretary-General (2006b) 'Report of the Secretary-General on the Theme of the 2006 ECOSOC Coordination Segment'. New York: UN (Advanced unedited version).

UNCTAD (2006) *Doubling Aid: Making the 'Big Push' Work*. New York: UNCTAD.

UNDESA (2001) *World Public Sector Report: Globalization and the State*. New York: Division for Public Administration and Development Management.

UNDESA (2003) *Report on the World Social Situation (2003)*. New York: Division of Social Policy and Development.

UNDESA (2004) 'Agreed Conclusions on Public Sector Effectiveness', Commission for Social Development, 42nd Session, New York, 4–13 February.

UNDESA (2005a) *Report on the World Social Situation: The Inequality Predicament*. New York: Division for Social Policy and Development.

UNDESA (2005b) *Equity, Inequalities and Interdependence, Summary of the Debate at International Forum for Social Development, 4th Meeting, 5–6 October 2004*. New York: Division for Social Policy and Development.

UNDESA (2005c) Progress Towards the Millennium Development Goals. New York: UNDESA Statistical Division.

UNDESA (2006) *Social Justice in an Open World: The Role of the United Nations*. New York: The International Forum for Social Development, Division for Social Policy and Development.

UNDP (2003) *Human Development Report 2003: Millennium Development Goals: A Compact among Nations to End Human Poverty*. New York and Oxford: Oxford University Press.

UNDP (2005) *Human Development Report 2005: International Cooperation at a Cross Roads, Aid Trade and Security in an Unequal World*. Oxford: Oxford University Press.

UNESCO (1990) *World Declaration on Education for All: Adopted at the World Education Forum, Jomtien, Thailand*. Paris: UNESCO.

UNESCO (2000) *The Dakar Framework for Action: Adopted at the World Education Forum, Senegal, 26–28 April 2000*. Paris: UNESCO.

UNESCO (2002a) *Medium-term Strategy: Contributing to Peace and Human Development in an Era of Globalization through Education, the Sciences, Culture and Communication*. Paris: UNESCO.

UNESCO (2002b) *An International Strategy to Put the Dakar Framework for Action on Education for All into Operation, April (2002)*. Paris: UNESCO.

UNESCO (2004) *Education for All: The Quality Imperative. EFA Global Monitoring Report (2005)*. Paris: UNESCO.

UNESCO (2005) *Guidelines for Quality Provision in Cross-Border Higher Education*. Paris: OECD.

UNESCO (2006) 'Buenos Aires Declaration', *UNESCO Social and Human Sciences Newsletter*, 12(March–May): 16–17.

UNICEF (1993 et seq.) 'Economies in Transition Regional Monitoring Reports'. Florence: UNICEF International Child Development Centre.

UNICEF (1995) *The State of the World's Children*. New York: UNICEF.

UNICEF (2006a) 'UNICEF's Corporate Partnerships', New York. www.unicef.org

UNICEF (2006b) 'Convention on the Rights of the Child', New York. www.unicef.org

United Nations (1995) *Report of the World Summit for Social Development*. New York: United Nations.

United Nations (2001) 'Recommendations of the High-Level Panel on Financing for Development'. New York: United Nations.

United Nations (2005a) '2005 World Summit Outcome A/60/L.1'. www.un.org (accessed 17th September 2005)

United Nations (2005b) 'Revised Draft Outcome of the High-Level Plenary Meeting of the General Assembly of September 2005 (A/59/HLPM/CRP.1/Rev2), Annotated US Proposed Version'. New York: United Nations.

United Nations (2006a) 'Report of Global Commission on International Migration: Migration in an Interconnected World: New Directions for Action'. New York, CGIM. www.gcim.org

United Nations (2006b) 'Delivering as One: Report of the Secretary-General's High-Level Panel'. New York: United Nations.

United Nations Economic and Security Council (2005) *Achieving the Internationally Agreed Development Goals: Dialogues at the ECOSOC*. New York: United Nations.

United Nations Statistical Division (2005b) 'Millennium Development Goals Report 2005'. New York: United Nations.

United Nations System Chief Executive Board for Coordination (2002) 'High Level Committee on Management: Overview and Terms of Reference'. www.ceb.unsystem.org/hlcm/overview.htm

UNRISD (2005) *Gender Equality: Striving for Justice in an Unequal World*. Geneva: UNRISD.

Utting, P. (2000) *Business Responsibility for Sustainable Development*. Geneva: UNRISD.

Utting, P. (2006a) *Reclaiming Development Agendas*. Basingstoke: Palgrave.

Utting, P. (2006b) 'Introduction: Reclaiming Development Agendas' in Utting, P. (ed.), *Reclaiming Development Agendas*. Basingstoke: Palgrave.

Valdes, J. (1995) *Pinochet's Economists: The Chicago School in Chile*. Cambridge: Cambridge University Press.

Vasquez, E. and Mendizal, E. (2001) 'States and Challenges of Social Protection Policies in Latin America', *Cooperation South*, (2): 4–30.

Voipio, T. (2006) 'The Overarching Paper', personal correspondence.

Wade, R. (2001) 'Showdown at the World Bank', *New Left Review*, 7: 124–37.

Wade, R. (2002) 'Us Hegemony and the World Bank: The Fight over People and Ideas', *Review of International Political Economy*, 9: 215–43.

Wade, R. (2004) 'On the Causes of Widening World Income Inequality', *New Political Economy*, 9: 163–88.

Wagstaff, A., van Doorslaer, E., van der Burg, H., Calonge, S., Christiansen, T., Citoni, G., Gerdtham, M.G., Gross, L. and Hakinnen, U. (1999) 'Equity in the Financing of Healthcare: Some Further International Comparisons', *Journal of Health Economics*, 18: 263–90.

Wahl, P. (2006) *From Concept to Reality: On the Present State of the Debate on International Taxes*. Berlin: Friedrich-Ebert-Stiftung Foundation.

Wainwright, H. (2005a) 'Civil Society, Democracy and Power: Global Connections' in Anheier, H., Glasius, M. and Kaldor, M. (eds.), *Global Civil Society 2004–5*. London: Sage.

Wainwright, H. (2005b) 'WSF on Trial'. www.forumsocialmondial.org

Wallerstein, I. (2004) 'The Dilemmas of Open Space: The Future of the WSF', *International Social Science Review*, 56(4): 629–37.

Walt, G. (1993) 'WHO Under Stress: Implications for Health Policy', *Health Policy*, 24: 125–44.

War on Want (2004) *Tax Havens and Tax Competition*. London: War on Want.

War on Want (2005) *Profiting from Poverty: Privatisation Consultants, DFID and Public Services*. London: War on Want.

Waterman, P. and Timms, J. (2005) 'Trade Union Internationalism and Global Civil Society in the Making' in Anheir, H., Glasius, M. and Kaldor, M. (eds.), *Global Civil Society 2004–5*. London: Sage.

Watkins, F. (2000) *The Oxfam Education Report*. Oxford: Oxfam.

Wedel, J. (1998) *Collision and Collusion: The Strange Case of Western Aid to Eastern Europe*. New York: St Martin's.

Wedel, J. (2000) 'US Economic Aid to Russia: A Case Study in Subcontracting Governance' in Deacon, B. (ed.), *Civil Society, NGOs and Global Governance*, GASPP Occasional Paper 7, 33–44.

Wedel, J. (2004) '"Studying Through" a Globalizing World: Building Method Through Aidnographies' in Gould, J. and Secher Marcussen, H. (eds.), *Ethnographies of Aid: Exploring Development Texts Encounters*. Roskilde University IDS Occasional Paper 24, 149–74.

Weiss, L. (2003) *States in the Global Economy*. Cambridge: Cambridge University Press.

WHO (1978) *Alma Ata Declaration: Primary Health Care*. Geneva: WHO.

WHO (1981) *Global Strategy for Health for All by the Year 2000*. Geneva: WHO.

WHO (2000) *The World Health Report (2000): Health Systems, Improving Performance*. Geneva: WHO.

WHO (2001a) *Public Health and Trade: A Guide to the Multilateral Trade Agreement (January 2001 version)*. Geneva: WHO.

WHO (2001b) *Macroeconomics and Health: Investing in Health for Economic Development*. Geneva: WHO, Commission on Macroeconomics and Health.

WHO/ WTO (2002) *WTO Agreements and Public Health: A Joint Study by the WHO and WTO Secretariat*. Geneva: WTO/WHO.

Wilensky, H. and Lebeaux, C. (1958) *Industrial Society and Social Welfare*. New York: Russel Sage.

Wilkinson, R. (2002) 'Global Monitor: The WTO', *New Political Economy*, 7(1): 129–41.

Williams, F. (1989) *Social Policy: A Critical Introduction*. Cambridge: Polity.

Williams, F. (2001) 'Race/Ethnicity, Gender and Class in Welfare States: A Framework for Comparative Analysis', in Fink, J., Lewis, G. and Clarke, J. (eds.), *Rethinking European Welfare*. London: Sage.

Williams, F. (2005) 'Intersecting Issues of Gender, "Race" and Migration in The Changing Care Regimes of UK, Sweden and Spain', Annual Conference of the International Sociological Association's RC19, Chicago, 8–10 September.

Witte, J.M., Reinicke, W.H. and Bennet, T. (2000) Beyond Multilateralism: Global Public Policy Networks. *International Politics and Society*, 2.

Wolf, M. (2006) 'Modernizing the IMF', *Finance Times*, 21 February.

Woodward, D. (2005) 'The GATS and Trade in Health Services: Implications for Health Care in Developing Countries', *Review of International Political Economy*, 12: 511–34.

Woodward, R. (2004a) 'The Organisation for Economic Cooperation and Development', *New Political Economy*, 9: 113–27.

Woodward, R. (2004b) 'Global Monitor: The OECD', *New Political Economy*, 9(1): 113–27.

Woolcock, S. (1995) 'The Trade and Labour Standards Debate: Overburdening or Defending the Multilateral System', Paper for the CRUSA/RIIA Study Group, Oxford.

World Bank (1990) WDR2000: Poverty. Washington, DC: World Bank.

World Bank (1991) *Assistance Strategies to Reduce Poverty*. Washington, DC: World Bank.

World Bank (1992) *Poverty Reduction Handbook*. Washington, DC: World Bank.

World Bank (1992) *Education: Section Strategy*. Washington, DC: World Bank.

World Bank (1993) *WDR1993: Investing in Health*. Washington, DC: World Bank.

World Bank (1994a) *Higher Education: The Lessons of Experience*. Washington, DC: World Bank.

World Bank (1994b) *Averting the Old Age Crisis*. Washington, DC: World Bank.

World Bank (1996) *WDR1996: From Plan to Market*. Washington, DC: World Bank.

World Bank (1997) *Health, Nutrition and Population: Sector Strategy*. Washington, DC: Human Development Network, World Bank.

World Bank (1999a) *Education Sector Strategy Paper*. Washington DC: World Bank.

World Bank (1999b) 'Principles of Good Practice in Social Policy: A Draft Outline for Discussion and Guidance', paper for Executive Directors meeting as a committee of the whole, April 1st.

World Bank (1999c) 'Principles and Good Practice in Social Policy: An Outline for Discussion and Guidance', paper for joint development committee of World Bank and IMF, April 28th.

World Bank (1999d) 'Principles and Good Practice in Social Policy', communiqué of Development Committee, 28 April.

World Bank (2000) 'Global Public Goods', Paper for Joint Development Committee of World Bank and IMF. Washington, DC: World Bank.

World Bank (2001a) *WDR 2000/2001: Poverty*. Washington, DC: World Bank.

World Bank (2001b) 'ECOSOC–Bretton Woods Dialogue', Communiqué of Joint Development Committee of IMF and World Bank. Washington, DC: World Bank.

World Bank (2002a) *Policy Roots of Economic Crisis and Poverty*. Washington, DC: World Bank.

World Bank (2002b) *Private Sector Development Strategy*. Washington, DC: World Bank.

World Bank (2003a) *The Contribution of Social Protection to the Millennium Development Goals*. Washington, DC: World Bank: Social Protection Advisory Service.

World Bank (2003b) *Opening Doors: Education and the World Bank*. Washington, DC: World Bank Human Development Network.

World Bank (2003c) *WDR2004: Making Services Work for Poor People*. Washington, DC: World Bank.

World Bank (2004a) *Education for All-fast Track Initiative: Accelerating Progress Towards Quality Universal Primary Education*. Washington, DC: World Bank, Education Advisory Service.

World Bank (2004b) *The World Bank and the Copenhagen Declaration: Ten Years After*. Washington, DC: World Bank, Social Development Department.

World Bank (2004c) *Education Notes*. Washington, DC: World Bank.

World Bank (2005a) *World Development Report 2006: Equity and Development*. Washington, DC: World Bank.

World Bank (2005b) 'Flagship Global Course on Health Sector Reform and Sustainable Financing'. www.worldbank/WBSITE/EXTERNAL/TOPICS/EXHEALTHNUTRI-TIONANDPOPULATION

World Bank (2005d) *Empowering People by Transforming Institutions: Social Development in World Bank Operations*. Washington, DC: World Bank.

World Bank Institute (2006) Conference on Conditional Cash Transfers (CCTs), Istanbul, Turkey, June. www.worldbankinstitute.org

World Development Movement (2006) *Pipe Dreams: The Failure of the Private Sector to Invest in Water Services in Developing Countries*. London: World Development Movement.

World Economic Forum (2005) 'Finance for Development Initiative'. www.wef.org

World Trade Organisation (1996) *Guidelines for Arrangements on Relations with Non-Governmental Organisations*. Geneva: WTO.

Yeates, N. (2001) *Globalization and Social Policy*. London: Sage.

Yeates, N. (2004) 'Global Care Chains: Critical Reflections and Lines of Enquiry', *International Feminist Journal of Politics*, 6: 369–92.

Yeates, N. (2005a) 'The General Agreement on Trade in Services (GATS): What's in it for Social Security?', *International Social Security Review*, 58: 3–22.

Yeates, N. (2005b) *Globalization and Social Policy in a Development Context: Regional Responses*. Geneva: UNRISD.

Yeates, N. and Deacon, B. (2006) 'Globalism, Regionalism and Social Policy: Framing the Debate', UNESCO, High-Level Symposium on the Social Dimension of Regionalism, Montevideo, 21–3 February.

Zammit, A. (2003) *Development at Risk: Rethinking UN–Business Partnerships*. Geneva: South Centre-UNRISD.

Index